INTELLIGENT ACCOUNTABILITY

CREATING THE CONDITIONS FOR TEACHERS TO THRIVE

DAVID DIDAU

First Published 2020

by John Catt Educational Ltd,
15 Riduna Park, Station Road,
Melton, Woodbridge IP12 1QT

Tel: +44 (0) 1394 389850
Email: enquiries@johncatt.com
Website: www.johncatt.com

ISBN: 978 1 913622 27 5

Set and designed by John Catt Educational Limited

PRAISE FOR INTELLIGENT ACCOUNTABILITY

While there is widespread agreement that it is reasonable that teachers, schools and education authorities should be held accountable, what, exactly, accountability really means is rarely spelled out. As a result most accountability systems are either so loose as to be useless, or, at the other extreme, are so tight that they make it difficult, or even impossible to do what's needed to improve education, and can even produce perverse incentives that lead those working in the system to do things that are good for them, but counterproductive for their students. In this original and thought-provoking book, David Didau suggests that intelligent accountability has to start from an acceptance of the complexity of educational systems, which means that we will never know enough to design the perfect system. We can, however, by creating accountability systems that balance trust, accountability, and fairness, create schools with coherent approaches to improvement but that also honour the expertise of individual teachers. Highly recommended.

Dylan Wiliam, Emeritus professor of Educational Assessment at the UCL Institute of Education

It is often cited that good is the enemy of excellence but what is excellence? Can one person's definition of excellence be another person's satisfactory? David challenges us to think hard, to think deep and to think in an evidence informed manner about how to help teachers to flourish, how to keep the core job of teaching the core job. Didau really challenges the reader to consider carefully how leaders can create a climate and culture that allows teachers to thrive. This is an excellent book. Want to challenge your long held views? Read it!

Samuel Strickland, Principal of The Duston School

Didau is at it again – with his signature blend of incisive analysis and productive philosophising – this time treating us to a new lens with which to examine and improve leadership in schools.

Peps Mccrea, Dean of Ambition Institute and author of the High Impact Teaching series

This is a thoughtful book that will help school leaders to run better schools. It goes beyond the hero model of school leadership to get to the substance of school improvement. I recommend it to leaders at all stages in their careers.

Stuart Lock,
CEO, Advantage Schools

As with research informed practice in the classroom, when teachers move into roles of leadership, we need to understand what makes the best leaders effective. The influence we have on the lives, work and emotions of our staff is immense. As leaders, we need therefore to educate ourselves. In this excellent book David unpicks the components of what makes for really impactful and effective leadership in education. Starting from the compelling premise that our most important role as leaders to is make it as easy as possible for teachers just to teach; to remove the peripheral noise and let them, as professionals, get on with it; alongside support and challenge, guided by wisdom and love. He examines how we can motivate our staff, enabling them to become better practitioners, dispelling myths and drawing upon fascinating lessons, from educational research, motivational theory through to the aviation industry. A really valuable book for any school leader.

Clive Wright,
Head teacher, Saint Martin's Catholic Academy, Stoke Golding

What should we do if we find there's evidence that outcomes for pupils are higher – even if only marginally – if they are in schools where teachers experience high levels of collegiality? Well we don't dismiss the evidence: instead, we take a hard look at the constituents that make collegiality a reality. And this is what *Intelligent Accountability* sets out to do. It helps us to move beyond the pious, motherhood- and-apple-pie vagaries of some 'vision' statements and gets into the gritty detail of getting the work done. Didau gives us a compelling picture of what happens when clumsy accountability measures are exposed as crude proxies of compliance and when these are replaced with environments where professionals are likely to thrive. (Spoiler alert: they have nothing to do with spreadsheets.) The discussions arising from this thought-provoking book will help the sector move from the deficit model of school improvement to a surplus model. Highly recommended.

Mary Myatt,
Education writer and speaker

For years education needed someone to explain what accountability actually is and how it can be more than a horrible punishment. This book delivers on that need, and then some. A magisterial sweep of research from psychology, sociology, and economics all with the aim of helping school leaders support genuine improvements in teaching as opposed to simply generating feel-good moments. Not just about accountability, this book looks deeply at what it means to be a moral, good and intelligent leader – an extraordinary read, thoroughly recommended.

Laura McInerney,
Education journalist and co-founder of Teacher Tapp

David Didau writes with trademark rigour and insight to address one of the biggest challenges for our education system: how can leaders create the conditions where teachers and children flourish? *Intelligent Accountability* highlights the uncomfortable truths about the role of accountability in schools, the perverse incentives of many familiar school-based practices and the impact that these can have on teachers. Drawing on a wealth of evidence and insight, Didau asks school leaders to carefully consider the impact of school improvement, accountability and leadership approaches in their school. Challenging and informative, *Intelligent Accountability* is a timely reminder of the collective wisdom that lives within a school community and the importance of a culture that allows teachers to thrive.

Tom Rees,
Executive Director – School Leadership, Ambition Institute

What if everything you knew about leadership was wrong? David Didau challenges us as school leaders to think again about how we can best make a difference for our students and teachers. Not a book for the complacent leader – you will be challenged in every chapter, but a fresh and thought-provoking read that will make you think. Once again, David Didau does not disappoint.

Ruth Powley, Deputy Headteacher of Wilmslow High School
and author of Powerful Pedagogy

ACKNOWLEDGEMENTS

Full disclosure: I have never led a school and have spent comparatively little time in a position of school leadership.

What I do have is lots of experience of working for many different school leaders, and, through my work as a consultant, I have been privileged to see the inner workings of hundreds of different schools and have witnessed pretty much every approach to school improvement from the sublime to the ridiculous. Despite this, I'm painfully aware of what I know I don't know.

For that reason, I'm terrifically grateful to a fabulous selection of experienced school leaders who have contributed their advice, expertise and hard won wisdom. I am particularly grateful to Ruth Powley for her extensive insights on sufficiency and collective knowledge, and to Matthew Evans for his help in understanding intelligence in leadership.

Thanks also to Stuart Lock and Nick Rose, neither of whom are ever guilty of mincing their words, and to Matt Hood, Tom Sherrington and Dylan Wiliam for their erudition and generosity.

CONTENTS

For Maggie Mooney, the best head teacher I ever worked for.

INTRODUCTION

Why did you end up working in education? Was it to produce exquisite spreadsheets detailing students' performance in microscopic detail? Was it to break new ground in financial forecasting? Was it perhaps to find new ways to make teachers comply with ever more intricate demands on how their professional lives should be conducted? No, of course not: you became a teacher in order to make a difference to the lives of young people. All too often, the burdens and shackles of school leadership seem to make us forget why we wanted to teach in the first place. It's worth refocusing on the fact that being a school leader provides a unique and satisfying challenge as well as a weighty responsibility.

This book has two potential audiences: current and future school leaders. Of course, I'm hopeful that I may persuade current school leaders that the principles of intelligent accountability are worth pursuing, but, more importantly, I would like to convince those who are not sure whether they want to step into school leadership that if you want schools to be the sorts of places you would like to work in, then you'll probably need to take a hand in shaping them.

There are many endemic problems facing school leaders, but this book is focused on just one: how to help teachers flourish in order for students to flourish. This entails understanding how to be a responsive and responsible leader, how to lead sufficiently wisely and well in an uncertain world, what stands the most plausible chance of working, and which practices should be embraced and which can probably be safely jettisoned.

In the following chapters, I will discuss a set of principles designed to get the best out of teachers, thereby getting the best from your students. And when I say 'best', I categorically do not mean piling stress onto teachers in the hope of gaming exam results. In fact, as we'll see, the concept of 'best' may, in itself, be damaging. Sufficiently good is usually a safer bet than best. Instead, I will argue that by creating the conditions for teachers to thrive, we are likely to get much more of what we want: better exam outcomes; happy, rounded students; and teachers who are satisfied with their professional environment.

Making better bets

The principles of intelligent accountability should be thought of as 'good bets' rather than 'sure things'. While it may be true that "everything works somewhere but nothing works everywhere",[1] it's trivially true. Although pretty much any approach to teaching can be made to work – sort of – it's not whether an intervention works but *how well* it works in comparison to other interventions. Better to say, some things work in most contexts and other things rarely work anywhere. Some approaches to the curriculum and instruction have stood the test of time and are better suited to achieving the ends that most people value.

Too many decisions made in schools are bets made with little or no understanding of the odds or, to extend the metaphor, the 'form' of the runners and riders. This is gambling with children's futures. But why should we not bet everything on a brighter future? Sadly, too many decisions estimate the best case and ignore the worst. By all means imagine the best case, but this should always be tempered with a realistic awareness of the worst case. By thinking through worst case scenarios, we can make better bets. Steven Farr, executive director of Teach for All, says, "there is a widespread lack of understanding, clarity, alignment, and explicitness about how to train and develop expert teachers. The design choices or 'bets' teacher educators make are often implicit, unclear or even simply unconsidered."[2]

By not being clear about the bets we make – by not properly weighing up the stakes, thinking through the alternatives and consulting those most affected by our gamble – we end up hedging our bets or spreading them too widely across too broad a range of options. Instead of doing a few things well, we do a little bit of everything poorly.

Instead, we should be making 'educated bets' with a thorough knowledge of the evidence and weighed by a clear understanding of the problems we're trying to solve. If our bets are aligned with the purposes we've agreed, then by putting time and effort into the implementation and sustainability of our decisions, we avoid the unscrupulous optimism of best cases and address the possibility of the worst case coming to pass. As the economist Thomas Sowell warns us, "It is so easy to be wrong – and to persist in being wrong – when the costs of being wrong are paid by others."[3]

What is intelligent accountability?

In order for teachers to be 'good enough' we need to create environments where trust, accountability and fairness are held in balance. All are individually important, but each runs the risk of dominating the others. If any one of these matters overshadows the others, accountability is prone to being unintelligent; schools will not be led as effectively as they might be and teachers are less likely to thrive.

Human nature being what it is, if we're given too much trust – if no one checks what we're doing – we tend to become complacent and stop striving to be better. If accountability is overemphasised, then everyone becomes so concerned with trying to cover their backs and look good that they are inadvertently prevented from pursuing what might be a wiser course of action. Every teacher will need different levels of support in order to be as effective as possible. A school in which there is too much trust or too much accountability is likely to treat its staff unfairly. This is because equality – treating everyone in the same way – can be fundamentally unfair.

Intelligent accountability – the judicious balancing of trust, accountability and fairness – is more than simply trying to do the 'right thing'; it's about creating systems which make it harder to do foolish things. I know from experience that the vast majority of school leaders are well-intentioned individuals committed to making positive changes in the lives of students. Despite this, too many leaders end up acting in ways that turn out to be contrary to their values. All too often the reason behind this is fear.

The reality of how schools are currently held to account in many parts of the world stands in antipathy to the principles outlined above. School leaders are not trusted to lead effectively, high stakes, cliff-edge accountability pressures are piled on, and the very real threat of losing your livelihood is ever present for many school leaders working in the most challenging of contexts.

In an ideal world, we would wave a wand and correct the world's ills. Sadly, this is not the world we live in. While we're waiting for those who hold us to account to do the right thing, it is still incumbent on all of us to strive to be better. The good news, I hope, is that by adopting the principles of intelligent accountability and by creating the conditions for teachers to thrive, it becomes more probable that schools will improve performance on the measures by which they are held accountable.

But before we get into the details of how such a system might work, we need to prepare the ground.

A guide to reading

No one, no matter how expert they are, can avoid making mistakes. Uncertainty is a fact of life. You can never know enough to make perfect decisions, so it follows that your decisions will always be imperfect. Understanding that all decisions are inevitably flawed, and that to err is human, helps us to develop the all-important (but seldom evident) quality of humility. Certainty shuts down thinking – we are reluctant to think about what we're already sure about – whereas uncertainty prompts great self-awareness and promotes reflection and curiosity. Chapter 1 explores the power of accepting uncertainty and argues that we should temper our ignorance with collective knowledge. Balancing an awareness of the human tendency towards overconfidence with an acceptance of our own fallibility is a wiser, more sustainable approach to leadership.

All senior leaders work hard for their schools to improve, but not all schools seem to make the kind of improvements we would hope for. Why is it that teachers and students thrive in some schools but don't in others? In Chapter 2, we'll discuss two opposed models of school improvement: the deficit model (which assumes that problems are someone's fault) and the surplus model (which assumes that problems are unintended systemic flaws). By aligning ourselves to a surplus model we will, I argue, be more likely to create the conditions for teachers to thrive.

One of the consequences of only ever possessing incomplete information is that we have to place our trust in others. Although this sometimes feels uncomfortable, it's an inevitable part of life. Chapter 3 begins to consider the conditions in which teachers will thrive by looking at trust. We will consider why trust matters and how to get more of it. We will explore the links between trust and trustworthiness as mutually reinforcing concepts, and suggest that trusting teachers is probably less risky than the alternative.

Trust is all very well, but we know that people don't always do the right things. To trust blindly is foolish, so we need mechanisms for checking that others are performing with integrity. Chapter 4 examines when accountability works and when it doesn't. Research into people's behaviour when held to account offers a set of clear principles that we can use to improve what happens in schools. We will see how, by combining these principles with trust, we might go about making accountability systems more intelligent.

It is emblematic of our times that everyone should be treated equally. We strive for both equality of opportunity and equality of outcome in the knowledge that this is right and fair. But what if treating everyone in the same way is unfair? In Chapter 5, we'll explore the differences between fairness and equality and explain the research findings which show that, on the whole, people prefer fair inequality to unfair equality. Some teachers deserve more trust and require less scrutiny than others, but in order to satisfy the demands of equality we end up treating all teachers as equally untrustworthy. The more we trust teachers, the more autonomy they should be given; but if all teachers were treated equally autonomously, some would struggle and others may betray our trust. One of the most important tenets of fair inequality is that autonomy must be earned.

Counterintuitively, there is a body of research which seems to indicate that teachers don't just keep getting better with experience. While some teachers seem to improve throughout their careers, others plateau after the first three years. Perhaps the biggest factor underlying this finding is that schools make a crucial difference. Chapter 6 deals with the vexed issue of teacher (or teaching) quality, how hard it is to identify effective (or ineffective) individuals, why teachers need support in order to improve and how we might go about offering that support.

Intelligent leadership is the most vital ingredient in establishing a system of intelligent accountability and creating the conditions for teachers – and students – to thrive. Leaders are responsible for establishing the culture of their schools and, ultimately, make the most difference to the quality of teachers' professional lives. In the final chapter, I suggest some of the information school leaders need to know in order ensure teachers are thriving. I suggest that effective leadership cannot be summed up by generic traits and wishful thinking but must instead be rooted in domain specific knowledge. Of all the areas school leaders need to be knowledgeable about, the powers and pitfalls of metrics and data may be the one that has the most impact on teachers' well-being. I argue that the primary purpose of school leaders is to clear the ground in order that teachers can best teach their students. If school leaders stay focused on this purpose, then we are much more likely to create the conditions for teachers to thrive.

My hope is that you'll engage with the ideas in this book not as a list of prescriptions but as an invitation to think, reflect and reconsider some of your certainties. You may well experience moments of irritation, confusion or doubt; indeed, I hope you do. This is positive. It means you're thinking and not just nodding along. The greater your discomfort, the more probable it is that you have encountered something you need to reflect on more carefully. Try not to reject anything out of hand; there's gold in them thar hills. Of course, being irritated by an idea or assertion doesn't mean that I'm right and you're wrong, but it does indicate that you should try to keep an open mind for as long as possible.

CHAPTER 1

WHY WE NEED TO EMBRACE IGNORANCE AND LEARN TO LOVE UNCERTAINTY

One of the painful things about our time is that those who feel certainty are stupid, and those with any imagination and understanding are filled with doubt and indecision.

Bertrand Russell, *New Hopes for a Changing World* (1951)

We know less than we think

Recent efforts in education have been geared towards teachers being more research literate and decision making in schools being informed by evidence. Broadly, this is a welcome development, but as the statistician Nate Silver points out, "Even if the amount of knowledge in the world is increasing, the gap between what we know and what we think we know may be widening."[1] We can never know enough to make perfect decisions.

Imagine the sum total of human knowledge as a tiny island within a vast, black ocean of ignorance. The shoreline – where knowledge and ignorance overlap – is an area of uncertainty and risk. Most of the time, we occupy the centre ground of the island of knowledge where things are safe. Only rarely do we venture onto the shoreline to peer into the void. Acts of research and investigation are attempts to spin knowledge from the straw of ignorance so that we might sail cautiously out into the unknown.[2]

As former US Secretary of State Donald Rumsfeld tortuously put it: "there are known knowns; there are things we know we know. We also know there are known unknowns; that is to say we know there are some things we do not know. But there are also unknown unknowns – the ones we don't know we don't know."[3] Venturing too far into the 'unknown unknowns' is like trying to find a black cat in a darkened room. A task made especially difficult if there is no cat. Much easier to deal with, and concentrate on, what is already known. And when we're certain of what we know – when we occupy the centre of the island of knowledge – we feel safe and secure.

While the sum total of human knowledge is dwarfed by what is still to be discovered, our own individual islands of knowledge are microscopic; there is just too much knowledge out there for us to know it all. But, by building bridges and forming trade routes between the archipelagos made up of our collective knowledge – by acknowledging and seeking out the expertise within and beyond our schools – we can venture out into the void with greater security. However, there are still dangers with this approach. In Chapter 4, we'll examine how even pooling collective knowledge can lead to 'mimetic isomorphism', where school leaders imitate each other in the belief that someone else must know what they're doing.

However knowledgeable we are as individuals, we'll never know enough. Although, collectively, we stand a chance of knowing just enough to lead a school humanely as well as effectively, it's terribly easy to fall into the trap of justifying our actions by pointing out that everyone else is doing the same thing. School leaders have to be knowledgeable enough to know when not to follow the herd.

The power of the collective

There is no getting away from it: despite the limitations outlined above, as a school leader you are expected to know things. That being the case, one of following options is likely to be true:

- You *believe* you know everything you need to know.
- You *hope* you know everything you need to know.
- You *pretend* you know everything you need to know.
- You know you're *morally right* regardless of any evidence to the contrary.
- You admit you *don't know* everything you need to know.

Believing you know everything – even at some instinctive gut level – is deluded; hoping you know everything (or that someone else does) is foolish; pretending to know everything is dishonest. The worst of all options is to be so immune to facts, reason or criticism that you insulate yourself from reality. The only acceptable option is to admit that you don't know everything, but there are systemic pressures that make it hard for school leaders to admit their ignorance. "I don't know" tends to go down poorly with governors, teachers, parents and students alike.

If you're going to lead a school, you have to believe that you know enough to be of service, but the uncomfortable – and liberating – truth is that no one person can ever know enough to effectively run a school. The knowledge you need will be distributed among everyone who works within your school, and there will be pockets of expertise in every department and year team. If you restrict your collective knowledge to only those in senior leadership positions, your decisions will always be less intelligent than they could have been had you tapped the collective knowledge of the entire school community.

In *The Wisdom of Crowds*, James Surowiecki argues that we stand a much higher chance of making good decisions when we work collectively than when we operate in isolation.[4] However, he warns that there are conditions when even our collective intelligence is likely to misfire.

- **Homogeneity.** Unless there is genuine diversity in approaches and thought processes, senior leadership teams are more prone to conformity and become an echo chamber. As Matthew Syed says, "Homogenous groups don't just underperform; they do so in predictable ways. When you are surrounded by similar people, you are not just likely to share each other's blind spots, but to reinforce them … Encircled by people who reflect your picture of reality, and whose picture you reflect back to them, it is easy to become ever more confident of judgements that are incomplete or downright wrong. Certainty becomes inversely correlated with accuracy."[5]
- **Centralisation.** Management structures and hierarchies in schools tend to crowd out the expertise of classroom teachers. According to legend, the French king Louis XIV infamously declared, "L'etat c'est moi" (I am the state). It is all too easy for schools to become the personal fiefdoms of petty autocrats with subordinates mirroring back what they think the head teacher wants to hear.
- **Division.** The structure of schools increases the risk that knowledge and expertise will be divided into silos. To avoid this there need to be

systems in place to break down the walls between subjects and year teams, as well as those between middle and senior leaders.

- **Imitation**. Collective knowledge only works where viewpoints are independent. As soon as schools start blindly copying each other, the process falls flat.
- **Emotionality**. Collective wisdom can be easily undermined by peer pressure, herd instinct, social norms and even collective hysteria. It takes cool heads to avoid being subsumed by collective emotion and to tap into collective intelligence.

We can only access the collective intelligence within a school by encouraging others to express contrary opinions. Unless we access this source of socially distributed cognition we are not only likely to make disastrous decisions, we are also unlikely to recognise the extent of the disaster. To create the conditions for teachers to thrive you need to admit your individual ignorance and embrace the power of distributed cognition.

Certainty and its consequences

To think about the way we experience certainty, I want you to conjure up the spirit of one of your primitive ancestors. Picture yourself hunting for food on the savannah or in a primordial forest. Imagine, if you will, that you catch a glimpse of movement out of the corner of your eye. Is it a snake?

Although you can't be sure, the only sensible option is to act with certainty, assume that it is a snake and take immediate steps to avoid it. As a species, we're primed to act with certainty on minimal information. This incredibly useful survival instinct has served us well for countless millennia; if ever there was a tendency among some of our ancestors to thoroughly test out observations and have a good root around in the undergrowth to check for snakes, they did not survive to pass on their genetic material. We're descended from those who didn't check.

Acting decisively with minimal information may have served us well in the hostile environments of the past, but it is a less successful strategy in a relatively safe environment. A school is a relatively safe environment; the likelihood that anyone will die as a result of our decision-making is remote, which means it's much safer to really test our predictions and find out whether we're correct to believe as we do.* But, because we have an evolved preference for not checking, we continue to act as if we were in a hostile environment.

The metaphorical hunting ground represents potential sources of evidence, and the snake represents the possibility that we might unearth evidence that contradicts our cherished beliefs. Although finding contradictory evidence is unlikely to kill us, it may still be a threat to our pride (or even our employment!). *This*, we tell ourselves, is the correct way to run a school, to manage a class, to teach this subject, to interact with students. How do we know? We *just do*. We tend to have a lot invested in our beliefs – time, effort, credibility – and if we find evidence that we might be wrong, we run the risk of looking foolish. So, it makes sense not to check.

We are predisposed to seek out only that which confirms what we already believe and to ignore that which contradicts these beliefs. If we find evidence that confirms what we already believe – and we usually can – we will probably accept it as true. The philosopher Bertrand Russell observed:

> If a man is offered a fact which goes against his instincts, he will scrutinize closely, and unless the evidence is overwhelming, he will refuse to believe it. If, on the other hand, he is offered something which affords a reason for acting in accordance to his instincts, he will accept it even on the slightest evidence.[6]

The inclination not to test out anything that already makes sense to us is a useful mental shortcut that allows us to act decisively, but relying on these 'rules of thumb' leads to us making predictable mistakes.

The consequence of being certain about our beliefs is that when we feel sure we stop thinking. Why would we continue to think about something if we believe we already know the answer? If you think you already know how to drive up GCSE results in maths, how to improve the quality of work in Year 7 geography books, how to enrich Year 5 students' comprehension of non-fiction texts or how to boost the performance of Key Stage 1 children in the phonics screening check, then you're unlikely to consider alternatives. It's not that you're

---

* Admittedly, in the age of COVID-19 this might no longer be as true as we would wish. Even when schools are not contending with global pandemics, decisions can affect the lives of thousands of students and so will have real – and potentially negative – consequences.

necessarily wrong about any of these things, but it's improbable one person will have all the answers.

If we don't stop to test our beliefs, we're likely to overlook important sources of evidence and information. Ask yourself how much you want something to be true. The more we need something to be true, the more effort we're likely to invest in insulating ourselves from reality in order to make it seem true.

Although entertaining uncertainty is uncomfortable, it provokes curiosity and thought. When we're unsure we keep mulling things over; we put them on the back-burner; we sleep on them. We are rarely so open minded as when we feel certain.

That said, too much uncertainty may be as bad as too little. Most people hate seeing signs of uncertainty in leaders; just look at the way we treat politicians when they're asked a tricky question. We're desperate for them to respond with quick answers and easy certainty. If they were to admit they weren't sure, we'd be contemptuous. On the whole, we prefer our leaders to be wrong rather than unsure. We punish those who admit ignorance and are much happier when they're decisive, confident … and mistaken.

The same pressures are at work everywhere: if you're in a position of responsibility, people expect you to be decisive. They certainly don't want a period of prevarication while you agonise about what to do. Our intolerance for uncertainty means that there will always be a limited time for deliberation and, unless we accept that we're often wrong, we're likely not only to make poor decisions but also to hide the evidence of our mistakes from ourselves. However, the more knowledgeable we are about all aspects of education, the greater the likelihood of making better bets.

Helping teachers to improve is likely to be made easier if we embrace the uncomfortable truth that what we know is dwarfed by what we don't know. We may have some great ideas, but are they so great that they should be imposed on others who may know more than we do? Sometimes the answer might be yes, but knowing when to allow autonomy and when to impose constraints is inherently difficult. As we'll explore in later chapters, edicts imposed from above result in, at best, compliance. There are some areas of running a school where we might calculate that compliance is what we want, but there will also be aspects where we can expect it to backfire.

Learning to love uncertainty doesn't mean that we should endlessly prevaricate, instead it means accepting that decisions are always imperfect, made with incomplete understanding and should be subject to change when additional information comes along.

Why we're often wrong

Although we rarely appreciate anyone pointing out our mistakes, no one minds being fooled by an illusion. In fact, we tend to enjoy it. In this way, illusions are a gateway drug to humility. As the philosopher Simone Weil put it, "the virtue of humility is nothing more nor less than the power of attention".[7] If we are to learn from our mistakes, we must pay attention to them. True experts know when and what they don't know.

The images below are designed to open you up to the possibility that we are regularly wrong. Firstly, have a look at Figure 1.1.

Figure 1.1. Shepard's turning the tables illusion

If you were asked to select one of these tables to manoeuvre through a narrow doorway, you'd probably pick the one on the left. It looks narrower, right? Well, in fact, both tabletops have identical dimensions. The receding edges of the tables are seen as if stretched into depth; we see the two-dimensional images as if they have three dimensions. This causes us to perceive differently sized tables because of perspective foreshortening: the closer the object is in distance, the larger it is on our retina.

The only way we can see that the tabletops are identical is to rotate the images. Because seeing is believing, we're seldom inclined to test that what we perceive conforms to objective reality. Instead, we catch a glimpse and then act with certainty.

As well as failing to recognise what is in front of us, our minds are also primed to see patterns even where there are none. We see creatures in clouds, faces in wallpaper and patterns in data that just do not exist. Even when there are patterns, we fill in detail and jump to unsupported conclusions. Take a look at Figure 1.2.

Figure 1.2. Jastrow's duck/rabbit illusion

You can immediately see that the beak of the duck becomes the ears of a rabbit. But, although you can quickly and easily perceive both creatures, you have to make a choice as to which you will see at any given point. If you want to see the rabbit instead of the duck, you have to *decide* to do so.

It's often the case that when we argue about our perceptions, we are actually disagreeing about our interpretations. If we were both to observe the same lesson, I could be convinced that it was excellent, while you thought it was awful. Although we saw the same thing, we interpreted differently. Which of us is right? Well, maybe we both are. Or neither of us.

In the case of Figure 1.2, you might argue it's a duck while I swear blind it's a rabbit, but it doesn't take an enormous amount of critical thinking to accept that ducks and rabbits don't really look like this. Ducks have feathers and rabbits have fur; this is just a dot and a squiggle. Our minds are quickly and easily fooled into seeing what we want to be true. Once we've decided what it is we are seeing, we struggle to let go of mistaken ideas. If we applied the same level of analysis where it's less obvious that two things might simultaneously be true, we might make fewer avoidable errors.

Now take a look a Figure 1.3.

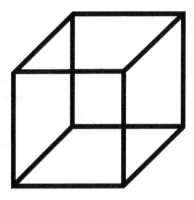

Figure 1.3: The Necker cube

If you've not encountered the Necker cube before, your first thought is probably to dismiss it as uninteresting. After all, you've seen hundreds of three-dimensional representations of cubes, right? But stare at it intently for about five seconds and see if you notice anything unusual happen.

The back wall suddenly pops and becomes the front! If you continue looking it will eventually pop back. The slightly clunky analogy I'm making here is that if we look with an open mind and an attitude that there may be more out there than we already know, then sometimes we'll see things we didn't expect. But, if we look at anything with a sense of certainty and familiarity, then we'll probably see exactly what we expect and become increasingly confident in our flawed judgement.[8] Maybe we judged that lesson as poor because we didn't understand what the teacher was doing? Or maybe we thought it was great because it contained a superficial feature we really liked and therefore missed its lack of substance?

Whenever a problem occurs, we 'pattern match' and automatically compare it to other, similar seeming problems we've encountered before. The more certain we are that *this* problem is the same as *that* problem, the more likely we are to dismiss incongruent details as irrelevant and focus on the bits we recognise. But, although two problems might share superficial similarities, sometimes they could be quite different on a deeper level.

Naturally, classrooms and schools are infinitely more complex than two-dimensional images, but that just means there is infinitely more scope for making mistakes and failing to see reality as it actually is, rather than as we might wish it to be. The more complex a system is, the greater our capacity for error.

When observing teachers, we see what we expect. If we approve of them and expect them to be effective, we'll interpret whatever occurs in a positive light; if we disapprove of them or expect to see poor performance, we will tend to interpret events more negatively. The more we can view people and events with an open mind and a sense that we have something to learn, the more likely we are to see things we weren't anticipating. And the more convinced we are that every problem is familiar, the more likely we are to be convinced by our own expertise.

Why experience doesn't always lead to expertise

There are many professional domains where experience doesn't automatically lead to expertise. Take the example of radiologists. A 2004 analysis of 500,000 mammograms and 124 radiologists was unable to find any evidence that years of experience leads to increased skill in diagnosis, resulting in many thousands of unnecessary biopsies and hundreds of cases where malignant tumours were missed.[9] What typically happens is that a radiologist will be sent a mammogram of a patient she will never meet, make a diagnosis and return it, never to find out whether it was correct. Although her ability to correctly diagnose tumours may or may not be increasing, her confidence in her own expertise certainly is.

Similarly, in *House of Cards*, Robin Dawes details how clinical psychologists with over 10 years' experience are no better at diagnosing and treating mental illnesses than those fresh out of medical school.[10] But all experienced clinical psychologists believe they are genuine experts. This pattern has been repeated in many different domains; so much so that Robin Hogarth has identified what he calls 'wicked domains' in which experience routinely fails to lead to expertise.[11]

A wicked domain is a learning environment where feedback on performance is absent or biased.[12] This is equivalent to playing golf in the dark: you never find out where the ball went so you never get better at hitting the ball. But it's worse than that. Because feedback in wicked domains is biased, it leads us to believe that we're becoming experts even when we're not. We become ever more confident and certain that we're right: a dangerous combination.

Hogarth also identified so-called 'kind domains' which provide accurate and reliable feedback. He cites meteorology as a good example:

> The meteorologist is well-placed to develop accurate intuitions. She has much knowledge about how weather systems develop as well as access to much current information on which she can base her forecasts; she also receives accurate and timely feedback on the accuracy of her forecasts.[13]

The crucial difference is that when a meteorologist makes a prediction it has no bearing on whether it rains, but when clinicians – or teachers – make a diagnosis or decision, they act on it, thus altering reality to conform to their expectations and warping any feedback they get.

Gary Klein has led research into these kind domains and shown that when we get solid feedback, we become genuinely intuitive.[14] His studies into firefighters, neonatal nurses, military commanders and other professions have shown that in these fields, experienced practitioners just know the right course of action to take in seconds.[15] According to Klein, "reliably skilled intuitions are likely to develop when the individual operates in a high-validity environment and has an opportunity to learn the rules of that environment".[16]

High validity environments – kind domains – are predictable. This allows expertise to develop as people learn to recognise patterns. The reason a chess grandmaster can make incredibly rapid, highly intuitive decisions is because chess is fairly predictable. Teaching is not. There is probably little we can do to reduce this complexity and chaos, but despite this, teachers can become highly skilled at recognising patterns within classrooms, which allow them to predict how students will behave and can make their judgement sometimes seem almost magical.

Hogarth shows that even where a domain may have some 'kind' aspects, it can also have a 'wicked' effect on the genuine development of expert intuition:

> The physician in the emergency room … must make speedy decisions and will not always receive adequate feedback. Indeed, *the typical feedback he receives is short term: how the patient responds to his immediate actions.* It is rare that the physician ever really finds out what happened to the patients he treated within a longer, and perhaps more relevant time frame. Some patients simply go home after treatment and never return to the hospital; others are cared for in different departments of the hospital, and so on.[17]

Although surgeons' short-term survival rates dramatically improve with years on the job, long-term survival rates and other complications don't.

Teaching may be similar to surgery. Although teachers get better at certain aspects of the job, they may not improve in others. For instance, teachers improve rapidly at managing classrooms. Students provide immediate feedback on the effectiveness of their teachers' decisions; they either behave or they don't. Teachers get daily opportunities to learn from their mistakes and can see their practice improve as they hone in on the best way to interact with different classes. But the feedback teachers get on 'instructional support' tends to be 'low validity', which helps to explain why teachers are less likely to improve in this area.[18]

Instructional support includes things like promoting higher order thinking, giving formative feedback and using language to promote thinking. Why don't we get better at these things? Possibly because we get very little feedback on whether the instructional support we offer is any good. One of the most useful and important concepts for teachers to understand is the distinction between learning and performance. Performance is what students can do in the moment. It is all that we can ever observe. Learning takes place inside a student's mind and as such cannot be observed directly. We can make inferences about learning based on the performances we see, but performances at the point of instruction are a particularly poor predictor of learning. What students can do in a lesson – or in response to feedback – tells us very little about what they might be able to do at another time and in another context.

In fact, the existence of 'desirable difficulties' in effective learning make it even more difficult for our students to provide effective feedback even if they wish to. For example, practising the same procedures again and again over a short period tends to lead to better performance in the short term, and usually feels intuitively right to students. But this feedback provides unhelpful evidence for teachers on what we can expect to be effective over the longer term. Contrary to our intuitions, there is a compelling body of research which shows that reducing current performance – and allowing students time to forget in-between practice sessions – is more likely to lead to more durable expertise being acquired.[19]

Unlike behaviour management, where we get instant and highly effective feedback on our mistakes (students either do or don't comply with our expectations), we rarely, if ever, discover the effects of our teaching on learning. This is because the feedback we get is biased. The domain of behaviour management is high validity whereas the domains of assessing students, giving feedback and teaching difficult concepts are low validity. And school leadership – at one more step removed – has even lower validity, with school leaders unable to see the effects of their decisions.

School leaders regularly have to deal with situations and tasks that they have not had an opportunity to master. As we become more familiar with our environment, we become more confident. The danger is that in a low validity environment, experience does not automatically lead to expertise. The more confident we become in our abilities, the harder it can be for us to learn. We tend to believe that because we are expert in some areas of our jobs, we must be expert in all areas. This leads inexorably to overconfidence in dealing with problems in which we have little or no skill.

Avoiding overconfidence

We are motivated to think well of ourselves; we all tend to selectively remember our successes and forget our failures. This means we're prone to mistaking luck for judgement. Those who believe themselves to be successful leaders tend to have one thing in common: they trust their judgement. And why not? Their intuitions must have proved their worth otherwise they wouldn't be successful, right?

Well, maybe not. Psychologists Daniel Kahneman and Gary Klein argue that overconfidence is at the root of most poor decisions, with Kahneman suggesting that "the amount of success it takes for leaders to become overconfident isn't terribly large".[20]

We construct narratives to account for our success and these stories help us to rationalise our actions. Although we may not actively seek to deceive anyone, it's ridiculously easy to fool ourselves.[21] Our stories become exaggerated over time and we are rarely, if ever, held to account. No one checks 'the facts' even if it were possible to do so, and it becomes impossible for us to tell the difference between the uncomfortable reality that we're lucky and the comforting myth that we're born leaders.

According to Kahneman, "Overconfidence is a powerful source of illusions, primarily determined by the quality and coherence of the story that you can construct, not by its validity."[22] The stories we tell ourselves are often post-hoc rationalisations constructed after the fact: *exam results went up because of the excellent decisions I made*. There may be a whole host of alternative explanations, but the most compelling narrative wins out.

But why are we so seduced by the narrative of overconfidence? We like leaders who make others feel confident in their judgements, even if there's no strong basis for the judgement. Very often leaders achieve a reputation for success when all they have done is take chances that reasonable people would avoid. If your gambles pay off, you're hailed as a super head; if they don't, you disappear into obscurity (or consultancy!).

Let that sink in for a moment. Many successful school leaders seem to possess two important qualities:

1. They are lucky risk-takers.
2. They make the rest of us feel good about sharing in their risks.

Our desire for certainty overrules our need to make rational, informed decisions, even when the stakes are high. And here's the kicker: lucky risk-takers use hindsight to reinforce the feeling that their gut is very wise. Hindsight creates a powerful illusion that the situation was clearer than it really was and that the outcome was always certain. We are relieved to have a strong leader to cut though uncertainty and make bold decisions. After all, the risks have paid off, right? Well, yes, but for how long? Unless you believe in the supernatural, luck is just a matter of probability. You only have to be lucky once to get a reputation for being a successful school leader, but sooner or later even the luckiest guesser is going to be wrong.

But the same qualities are also possessed by unlucky leaders who took risks which didn't pay off. Our attribution of these qualities as those of strong leaders is survivorship bias. This occurs when we draw conclusions only from examples which have passed some sort of selection criteria and systematically discount those which have not.

Figure 1.4. Survivorship bias
Randall Munroe: https://xkcd.com/1827

Survivorship bias is hard to spot (see Figure 1.4). When we consider the reasons for our successes we take an inventory of our actions and understandably conclude that it must be what we did that made a difference. It's exactly this sort of faulty logic that leads to self-made millionaires telling school students not to worry about exams; after all, they left school with nothing but a pocketful of pencil shavings and look at them now![23] The trouble is, these people are successful despite their lack of formal qualifications, not because of it. The overwhelming majority of people who do badly at school do not become millionaires.

Just because you have been successful does not mean that others will benefit from imitating you; often, we can learn more from examining failures and thinking about what didn't work. Where there's compelling evidence that an approach might have merit, don't discount it because it's different from your current practice.

The psychologist Daniel Kahneman advocates the use of 'premortems', where decision-makers are asked to imagine they are one year down the line from introducing a new policy or project and it has gone spectacularly and horribly wrong. They then detail all the things that contributed to the project's failure. Kahneman says, "in general, doing a premortem on a plan that is about to be adopted won't cause it to be abandoned. But it will probably be tweaked in ways that everybody will recognize as beneficial."[24]

Our intolerance of uncertainty favours the overconfident. Certainty seems to indicate a lack of nuance and sophistication in our thinking. The Dunning–Kruger effect is the finding that almost everyone overestimates their own competence, and the poorest performers are the least aware of their own incompetence. This is because we have no way to account for what we don't know we don't know.

After comparing participants' tests results with their self-assessment of their performance in such diverse fields as sense of humour, grammar and logic, David Dunning and Justin Kruger proposed that, for a given skill, the incompetent not only fail to recognise their own lack of skill but also fail to recognise genuine skill in others. Encouragingly, they also found that if incompetents are given training in an area at which they are identified as being unskilled, they are able to recognise and acknowledge their own previous lack of skill.[25] As Dunning observes, "If you're incompetent, you can't know you're incompetent … the skills you need to produce a right answer are exactly the skills you need to recognize what a right answer is."[26]

Of course, this is not to say that school leaders are foolish – the Dunning–Kruger effect applies to everyone – but it does suggest that leaders will have a tendency towards overconfidence, not because they're leaders but because they're human. Additionally, the more narcissistic you are, the greater your capacity for self-deception appears to be.

The need for professional scepticism

School leaders need to be aware that there are strong biases in human reasoning, but being aware of such biases will not prevent them and may, in fact, normalise them. The scientific method is the most successful framework humans have developed (to date) to minimise the influence of bias in observations and conclusions, so effective school leadership must use the scientific method to test and falsify claims about education. Part of that method is exercising scepticism. This means we should be open to new, potentially better ideas, but subject them to rigorous scrutiny.

The uncritical acceptance of pseudoscience has flourished in education. In 2008, for example, Ben Goldacre excoriated Brain Gym as a "vast empire of nonsense ... being peddled, for hard cash, in state schools up and down the country".[28] Many other fads and gimmicks have been uncritically accepted and, despite their lack of empirical support, continue to find adherents. While some claims are more plausible sounding than others, it's silly to suppose that even the most reasonable approaches to school improvement are likely to be successful when they are imposed from above, with teachers expected to willingly enact school leaders' whims with no opportunity to question or critique.

This is what it means to be professionally sceptical. Every teacher and school leader owes it to the children they teach to resist poorly thought-out claims and pseudo-scientific mumbo jumbo and to raise reasonable challenges whenever it seems a mistake is about to be made, while remaining open to professional learning and enquiry. If we're presented with claims that seem too good to be true, we should ask what would show the claim to be false. Is the claim structured in such a way that it can never be tested? We owe it to ourselves to find out whether the claim has been tested.

In *What Every Teacher Needs to Know About Psychology*, Nick Rose and I made this suggestion:

> Whenever we are tempted to pursue a particular course of action and hunt for evidence to support our ideas we should be wary of cherry picking. A common strategy of charlatans is to only present narrow evidence that appears to support their claim – whilst ignoring any body of work which refutes it. Is the evidence being provided only from a single study or just one researcher? Check online to see what the counter-arguments are for a claim before you decide. If anyone says, "Well, you can't prove it *doesn't* work," remember that the burden of proof falls on the person making a scientific claim, it is not the sceptic who has to provide evidence that the claim is wrong.[29]

Imposing change is rarely as effective as we would like it to be. It's a commonly held belief that teachers hate change. This is patently untrue: see how they react to being given lighter teaching loads! What teachers hate is negative change. A lot of change in schools adds to teachers' workload and is often unnecessary. When improvements aren't immediately forthcoming, school leaders start looking at what other schools are doing – growth mindset interventions, knowledge-rich curriculums, restorative justice – and start thinking about how to implement whatever seems most exciting, whether or not it's aligned with their school community's values.

Teachers become exhausted and demoralised by constant switches in direction. Instead of changing direction in the belief that a new policy or strategy might provide miraculous results, it's a better bet to focus on improving the implementation of what you've previously committed to. After all, if focusing on vocabulary development or retrieval practice seemed like a good idea last year, why is it not worth persevering with this year? If such decisions are consensual, then staying on track is so much easier. Fair enough if we decide that a previous decision was mistaken, but we should have the courage to say and tell teachers explicitly they should stop doing *this* in order to focus on *that*. Instead, the expectation is often that more and more is piled onto teachers' plates.

When we decide that change really *is* necessary, the evidence should sell the benefits. The following questions provide a useful starting point for planning, implementing and evaluating new initiatives:[30]

Questions to ask before implementing new policies

- Can we define the problem we are trying to solve? What is supposed to improve? If the problem is too vague (e.g. well-being) how will we know whether our intervention is having any effect?
- What evidence is there to suggest the intervention will work as expected? Where does the research come from? How secure are the findings? Is it classroom based research, laboratory findings or just theorising? Can the intervention be implemented so that it has fidelity to that evidence?
- How will we know if things are working sufficiently well? It's important to announce in advance how improvement will be measured and what kind of improvement will constitute a success. If we want introduce a new intervention to improve students' reading, how confident can we be that there is a meaningful way to measure whether the new intervention is better than what is already in place? We are notoriously biased in favour of novelty, so we need to be sure that the answer is a lot better than, "This feels right."
- When should we expect the improvement to occur? We shouldn't have to wait forever; a commitment to trying something can't

be open-ended. It seems reasonable to know in advance when progress will be evaluated.
- What will happen if our goals are not met? If the strategy doesn't seem to be going as planned, at what point will we admit defeat? Will we adjust what we're doing? Is there any kind of contingency?
- Will this cause extra work? If so, what should teachers do less of?
- Are we acknowledging teachers' experience and expertise? If teachers are asked to try something that sounds implausible, it's not good enough to dismiss concerns with, "All the research supports it." The fact that it sounds too good to be true doesn't mean an intervention won't work, but teachers need to be given compelling reasons for ignoring the evidence of their experience.

By considering these questions and providing a forum for teachers to express professional scepticism, we not only improve our decision-making, but we are also contributing to creating the conditions for teachers – and students – to thrive.

Every decision – even not making a decision at all – contains an element of risk. The best we can do is to minimise the risks and attempt to honestly evaluate the effects of our decisions.

A framework for sensible decision-making

- Involve as wide a diversity of opinions as possible in establishing a clearly agreed set of purposes (e.g. better academic outcomes for students). If there is a consensus around these agreed purposes, all staff will be aligned in the same direction.
- Be equally clear about red lines (not adding to teachers' already unsustainable workload is an important consideration).
- Identify sources of evidence that will help you to test whether you are achieving your agreed purposes.
- Implement decisions carefully, tweaking and adapting as necessary.
- Build in opportunities to extract evidence from the system in order to check how well your decisions are being implemented.
- Avoid testing leadership decisions in a binary way (success vs. failure). Instead, find out what side effects are emerging. Is

the intervention working in some ways but having a negative influence on other goals you've agreed?
- Revisit and refine approaches in order to stay focused on achieving agreed purposes.

School leadership always entails making judgements under uncertainty. You are unlikely to ever know unequivocally that you've made the best decision and will almost certainly make many suboptimal decisions. Evaluating the effectiveness of your decisions is fraught with difficulty, but the steps outlined in the next section might help to improve the process.

Evaluating decisions

It is important to position the point of evaluation as close as possible to the intervention in question. If, for instance, you have trialled a new approach to increase students' reading fluency, then you should measure their fluency both before and after your invention. If students' scores improve, then you can be reasonably sure that the increase is caused by the intervention.

The danger of using national examination data as evidence is that it's both too distant from the point of intervention and will be affected by too many variables to plausibly attribute to one intervention (see pages 119–121 for more details).

There are various levels of impact that you can evaluate:

Awareness

The most basic level of evaluation is to ascertain the extent of teachers' awareness of whatever you have trained them in. This can be achieved simply by asking, "What do you know about X?"

Attitudes, beliefs and confidence

Beyond simple awareness, the next level of evaluation is to find out whether thinking has altered. If teachers believe that your approach is sensible, they are much more likely to have a positive approach to implementing it. Similarly, if staff are made to feel more confident about how to implement a new strategy, you can expect it to work better. Self-reports that give teachers a questionnaire which allows them to respond to statements with a five-point Likert scale (with answers ranging from strongly agree to strongly disagree) are the easiest way to evaluate changes in attitudes, beliefs and confidence. Despite the well-known unreliability of self-report, there is evidence that teachers can be encouraged to provide reliable data if steps are taken to anonymise surveys and encourage honest, divergent responses.

Systems

One of the most straightforward ways of evaluating decisions is to check the extent that systems have changed. However, just because a system has been put in place doesn't mean that it's being used or that it's not producing perverse incentives (see pages 74–76). Careful evaluation of systems requires school leaders to consider how systems are being used. For instance, if a school implements a system for centralising detentions, does this result in more students being referred for centralised detentions? If the answer is no, the temptation is to assume that, since the system is in place, it's providing an effective deterrent and students' behaviour has improved. But has it? Schools leaders need to compare their evaluation of a metric with the evidence of their own eyes: what is the state of behaviour in classrooms and corridors?

Staff practice

If behaviour continues to be poor, it could be that the system is too onerous for teachers to be bothered to use it or that teachers feel they might be penalised if they do use it. This means we have to monitor what teachers actually do. The most common way of evaluating staff practice is through lesson observations or 'learning walks'. We'll discuss the problems with classroom observation in detail in Chapter 6, but school leaders should be aware that the act of observation changes behaviour. If teachers feel you are 'looking for' something, they will often do their best to make sure you see it. In Chapters 3, 4 and 5 we'll discuss how to circumvent this difficulty.

Student outcomes

In order to really see whether a decision is being successfully implemented, you have to be able to evaluate its effects on students' outcomes. If teachers have changed their practice but it's having no measurable impact on student performance, then it may be that the intervention is ineffective. As the economist Bryan Caplan says, "When someone insists their product has big, hard-to-see benefits, you should be dubious by default – especially when the easy-to-see benefits are small."[32]

For this reason, you should be clear about how you will evaluate students' outcomes before you decide on a new intervention: decide what you want to improve, work out how to measure the improvement, obtain a baseline measure before the intervention is implemented, and then decide on the interval between baseline and evaluation in *advance*.

By taking these steps we won't insulate ourselves from making mistakes, but we will reduce the likelihood that we fool ourselves.

Accepting the complexity of what we can't know for sure

The world is far more complex than our limited perceptions of it allow us to see. We are all regularly and often wrong. The preference for certainty can get in the way of good decision-making. The better we are at admitting we're not sure, that evidence is always contingent, that the world is greater than we can grasp, the less likely we are to get entrenched in our inevitable errors.

Teaching is a particularly complex domain. And the more we learn, the more complex it becomes. Complexity is ever at odds with certainty. Professor Lee Shulman encapsulates this perfectly:

> I have concluded that classroom teaching ... is perhaps the most complex, most challenging, and most demanding, subtle, nuanced, and frightening activity that our species has ever invented ... The only time a physician could possibly encounter a situation of comparable complexity would be in the emergency room of a hospital during or after a natural disaster.[33]

What teachers do in classrooms contains so many imponderables that to reduce it to a set of certainties or formulas, while tempting, is often foolish. When a situation is not complex, issuing instructions is straightforward. If you have insisted that teachers must greet students at the door or enforce the school's rule on uniform, and they are not doing it, then it's perfectly acceptable to say that they should. But the more complex the situation, the harder it becomes to tell teachers what they *should* do. When it comes to a teacher's pedagogical choice we can say, "These are the sorts of things good teachers seem to do." We might even reasonably say, "Try doing this." But, unless we are witnessing a disaster unfold, we ought to avoid saying, "You *must* do this." (See pages 110–114 on non-negotiables.)

As we'll see in Chapter 6, all this is made more problematic by our utter inability to reliably identify good teachers. While statistical studies reveal that some teachers must be better than others, we're hopeless at being able to pick out good teachers at an individual level. All the tools we have (observation, student outcomes, student surveys) are flawed in different ways. But this doesn't stop us from feeling certain, from feeling as if we can intuitively *just know* who is a good teacher and who isn't. Obviously enough, these hunches are more likely to be wrong than cautious use of observation, value-added measures and student surveys.

As a school leader, you have a responsibility to improve teaching, but judging the quality of teaching is a good example of making high stakes decisions in a complex domain. Part of the reason for this complexity is that learning is invisible. We cannot see in the here and now what students will be able to do elsewhere and later; all we can observe is current performance.

What we are able to observe in the here and now can be influenced by predictable mental shortcuts. For instance, if we already believe a teacher is good or bad we will look for evidence to confirm our beliefs; if a teacher's approach to teaching is similar to our own we will be predisposed to approve of it. Because of this, it's much more difficult than we believe to tell if a teacher is above or below average, and therefore we should be less confident in our judgements and attach much lower stakes to observations.

Acknowledging uncertainty and seeking out collective knowledge can lead to better decision-making. As you read on, try to consider what you don't know as much as what you do, and remind yourself that you might be wrong. The more you find yourself feeling irked by a suggestion, the greater your capacity to rationalise disconfirming evidence away. If you read on with a sense of openness and a willingness to consider new ideas, you may learn something you weren't expecting.

All this is a foundation to the principles of intelligent accountability outlined in the following chapters.

Summary of Chapter 1

- We always make decisions with incomplete knowledge; no amount of data or information will allow us to make perfect decisions.
- We are all prone to predictable cognitive biases; decisions made quickly or in isolation are more likely to be suboptimal.
- Certainty makes us incurious and close-minded. We are likely to make better decisions if we can maintain uncertainty.
- Experience often leads to overconfidence. but success is as likely to be due to luck as expertise.
- Seeking collective knowledge and striving to align decision-making to a collective purpose can reduce some sources of uncertainty.
- Sufficiency is more desirable than unrealistic perfectionism.
- Overconfidence can lead to the best case and 'this works' fallacies; make sure you have planned for the worst case scenario and have a plan for checking your biases.
- Being honest about our mistakes is likely to build humility and help us to avoid overconfidence.
- Professional scepticism – being open to ideas but scrutinising them – is an important part of decision-making.
- Teaching is a complex domain and therefore top-down decisions made about teaching should be made with particular caution.

CHAPTER 2

THE SURPLUS MODEL OF SCHOOL IMPROVEMENT

It is easier to discover a deficiency in individuals, in states, and in Providence, than to see their real import and value.

Georg W. F. Hegel, *Lectures on the Philosophy of History* (1837)

How should we go about improving a school?

It's become an axiomatic truth that "the quality of an education system cannot exceed the quality of its teachers".[1] To what extent this is actually true is arguable, but it's fair to say that the quality of teaching in a school is both important and something that can be improved. If we believe that bad teachers are dragging down our education system, this might make us keen to identify which teachers are good and which are bad, and justify campaigns to rid the system of the bad. Of course, this is overly simplistic. More charitably, if we could reliably identify good teachers, then we might also be clearer about what it is they do and make better efforts to train less effective to teachers to do what the most effective do well.

This is important because, as Rob Coe and colleagues put it, "what teachers do, know and believe matters more to the achievement of students than anything else we can influence".[2] So, when thinking about how to go about improving a school, two questions are important:

1. Do you believe all teachers can improve?
2. Do you know how to get the best out of all teachers?

The answer to the first question feels straightforward: either you do or you don't. But what about *that* teacher? What about the one you'd really rather wash your hands of and shunt off on to someone else? Are some teachers lost causes or can every teacher improve? In typically provocative style, Dylan Wiliam has said, "The most important question we should ask teachers is, 'Do you think you need to improve?' If they say, 'Yes,' work with them. If they say, 'No,' fire them."[3] While this may feel unduly harsh, it contains an important element of truth. If teachers don't believe they need to improve they may be a lost cause. Teachers who don't believe they *can* improve are a different kettle of fish. Sometimes we have to believe for them.

Surprisingly, perhaps, teachers don't necessarily get better with experience. Various studies have demonstrated that when we compare students' outcomes to teachers' years of experience, we tend to see sharp rises in the first few years but these flatten off and even decline over time.[4] Other studies have produced similar findings.[5]

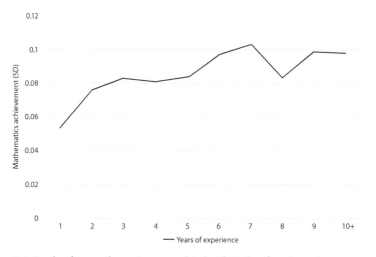

Figure 2.1. Teachers' years of experience correlated with students' mathematics test scores
Source: M. A. Kraft and J. P. Papay, Can professional environments in schools promote teacher development? Explaining heterogeneity in returns to teaching experience. *Educational Evaluation and Policy Analysis*, 36(4) (2014), 476–500.

That said, the type of school you work in matters. When schools are ranked on how supportive they are, we can see that teachers working in more supportive professional environments tend to become more effective over time than colleagues working in less supportive environments. Over a five-year period, teachers working in the top 25% of schools improve, on average, 20% more (in terms of student outcomes) than teachers working in the least supportive quartile.[6]

This shouldn't be surprising. We know from research into a variety of domains that three facts consistently predict the working environments in which workers are most likely to thrive: supportive learning environments, concrete learning processes and leadership that reinforces learning.[7] Additionally, teachers who work in schools where they are encouraged to collaborate frequently, receive meaningful feedback about their teaching and are recognised for their efforts will on average improve at faster rates.[8]

Good bets for improving teaching	What this looks like in practice
Supportive learning environment	• Instructional coaching (see Chapter 6) which focuses on long-term retention and transfer of knowledge rather than short-term performance in the classroom. • Teachers negotiate performance targets that align with long-term learning goals and are within their power to attain. • Failures are treated as an opportunity to learn from mistakes rather than causes for distrust. • Teachers earn the autonomy to decide how they should teach.
Concrete learning processes	• Professional development that focuses on sustained implementation of a few 'high yield' strategies (e.g. providing formative feedback). • Coaching is based on the practice of discrete elements rather than broad principles (see the list on pages 34–36). • Teachers earn the autonomy to focus on their own training goals.
Leadership that reinforces learning	• Accountability processes are aligned with long-term learning goals. • Teachers are held to account for the trust they are given. • Leaders provide opportunities for teachers to engage in reciprocal observation of colleagues. • Leaders 'look at' what teachers are doing and ask probing questions rather than 'looking for' lists of approved activities. • Leaders support teachers in using well-constructed systems for managing students' behaviour.
Teacher collaboration	• Teachers are given scheduled opportunities to discuss and share successful instructional practices. • Teachers are given scheduled time to plan and evaluate the curriculum together.
Meaningful feedback	• Feedback is focused on long-term learning goals (i.e. whether students have retained and can apply information taught in previous lessons). • Feedback is negotiated; if teachers request feedback they are more likely to act on it. • Feedback is given on aspects of teaching that are within teachers' ability to control.
Recognition of effort	• Leaders acknowledge that teachers are working hard and seek to reduce unnecessary workload. • Teachers' efforts are shared among staff and treated as a collective source of pride.

Table 2.1. Good bets for improving teaching

No matter how talented an individual may be, whether teachers continue to improve depends, to a large extent, on the culture of the school in which they work. As you can see from Table 2.1, few of these items are within a teacher's control. If school leaders do not actively put these things in place and guard them as sacrosanct, teachers – and therefore students – are less likely to improve.

Let's recast Wiliam's question to one aimed at senior leaders: *do you think all teachers can improve?* Think carefully. If you say 'yes', there's hope for you. If you say 'no', maybe it's you who needs firing!*

This second question is an invitation to consider what was covered in Chapter 1. By now, you should be ready to accept that individualistic certainty tends to be harmful, whereas collective approaches to knowledge will tend to pay off. Although you may have all sorts of great ideas for how to help teachers improve – some of them may have an impressive track record of success – you can't know how best to reach *all* teachers in *every* circumstance. Some approaches show greater promise than others. For instance, the instructional coaching model has a strong evidence base and is probably a good bet (see Chapter 6), but it still might not work with all teachers in all situations. Admitting your lack of certainty creates the possibility that you may have the humility and realism to seek advice and support from others, and it makes it more likely that you'll approach the work of helping teachers to improve with patience and tentativity.

The deficit model

Schools often seem to be run on a 'deficit model' whereby any deficiencies or failings are attributed to a lack of understanding, information, effort or good will.[9] The efforts of 'experts' (school leaders, inspectors, consultants, senior teachers, etc.) who understand what needs to be done are stymied by the actions (or inaction) of non-experts (classroom teachers) who do not. In a deficit model, failings are attributed to the inability of non-experts to understand or enact "realistic budgets, plans and targets". Instead, following the logic of 'deliverology', these must be determined by experts and "fully owned by management".[10]

---

* Obviously, firing teachers is rarely simple and not something most school leaders ever find comfortable. The ins and outs of formal disciplinary and capability procedures and employment rights lie far beyond the scope of this book. There are standard protocols that schools should follow which you can find out more about in: Teaching Regulation Agency, *Teacher Misconduct: Disciplinary Procedures for the Teaching Profession* (May 2020). Available at: https://www.gov.uk/government/publications/teacher-misconduct-disciplinary-procedures.

The deficit model assumes all would be well if only teachers and leaders were more motivated, worked harder or were somehow 'better' in some undetermined way. Undesirable outcomes are due to someone's bad faith, incompetence or lack of skill. The kind of appraisal meetings where teachers or middle leaders are held to account for the failure of their students to have achieved higher grades are absurd. To act in this way, school leaders have to believe that teachers know how to teach better but, for some reason, are choosing not to do so.

According to this way of thinking, problems will be solved if these deficits can be addressed in some way. Deficits are dealt with by supplying more information and imposing stricter parameters, tighter deadlines and clearer consequences. If only we could establish responsibility, apportion blame and force everyone into line, success would be guaranteed. This is the logic behind the way much of the education system manages the accountability process: schools and teachers cannot be trusted to do the right thing and take responsibility for their own development, so they need to be coerced with the cudgel of accountability until they fall into line.

This edifice depends on the notion that there are experts and that these experts know best. Department for Education officials, Ofsted inspectors, education consultants and senior leaders are the experts, and so it falls to them to ensure that deficits are made up and troublesome classroom teachers are brought into line. Of course, sometimes senior leaders are the experts in matters of safeguarding, finance, timetabling and other areas beyond the ken of classroom teachers. But when it comes to the question of creating the conditions for teachers to thrive, we should acknowledge that expertise is likely to be distributed across the full range of staff members, many of whom will not be senior leaders.

The bird's eye view afforded by senior leadership tends to be prized above the more grassroots expertise of the classroom. There is an inherent and usually unexamined assumption that if you're a leader, it's because you are in some way better than 'ordinary' teachers. What if it were agreed that school leaders achieve their positions not because they 'know best', but because their ambitions and inclinations are different? If we were to begin by assuming that teachers *and* leaders were basically trustworthy, hard-working and knew what they were doing, then it might be easier to accept that great school leadership is often about getting out of the way of those experts who are not leaders and allowing them to improve.

Teachers are frequently advised by experts on how they should teach. Sometimes this advice may be useful and welcome, but when teachers are told to teach in ways they disagree with, the very best we can expect is compliance. One of three outcomes is probable. Teachers will either:

1. Comply in the belief that they are unfit to have their own professional opinions.
2. Play the game but do so resentfully and without real engagement.
3. Struggle to comply with impossible demands, be perceived as failures and 'supported' out of the profession.

In each scenario, students – and particularly the most disadvantaged students who most need effective teaching˙ – suffer.

Ultimately, the rationale of the deficit model is to get rid of ineffective teachers and replace them with effective ones. But where will these effective teachers come from? It's not as if schools are inundated with wonderful prospective teachers clamouring to get into the profession. If anything, we're experiencing a recruitment and retention crisis. There is a "double leaching effect" in education as both early career entrants and more experienced teachers leave the profession.[11] An analysis of the Organisation for Economic Co-operation and Development's 2013 Teaching and Learning International Survey (TALIS) found that England's teachers were the fifth youngest internationally and therefore the least collectively experienced.[12]

Teachers are an increasingly precious commodity, but the deficit model treats them as a resource to churn through and spit out. Rebecca Allen and Sam Sims call schools that burn through teachers in this way 'sausage factories' and estimate that there are around 122 schools in the UK with extremely high turnover rates of newly qualified teachers.[13] The upshot is that teachers who have had the misfortune to work in one of these schools are overwhelmingly likely to leave the profession. Currently, there are no consequences for treating such a precious resource in such a criminally wasteful manner.

A Department for Education research report into factors affecting teacher retention in 2018 suggested the following solutions:

---

* A rule of thumb: the most advantaged students will, on average, succeed academically despite the decisions taken in a school, whereas the success of the most disadvantaged students is likely to depend on the quality of education afforded by their school.

- Greater levels of support and understanding from SLT – "for example, in terms of the management of pupil behaviour, and the ability to have open and honest conversations".
- Greater focus on progression opportunities.
- Reducing workload at a school level.
- Improved working conditions.
- Professional recognition, with senior leaders trusting teachers and giving them "freedom and autonomy to mark and plan".[14]

All of these would be welcome, but they are perhaps too vague to reverse the trends and retain disgruntled teachers.

Allen and Sims suggest that one solution might be to make information on staff retention available to prospective employees, so they have a better chance of making an informed decision about what they might be getting into. Another potential solution would be to hold schools to account for the retention of early career teachers as part of inspections. Of course, such ideas would have to be implemented with caution. If we assume that schools must be the reason for poor staff retention, then we too would be guilty of deficit thinking. A more generous assumption would be that certain school contexts are more challenging to work in than others and this can result in higher rates of staff burnout. Just as schools should believe the best of teachers, inspection regimes ought to treat schools with the same principle of charity until there is hard evidence for assuming the contrary.

Either way, the deficit model – especially when pushed to extremes – has a lot to answer for.

Caveat: It's important to acknowledge that just as the overwhelming majority of teachers are well intentioned, so are the overwhelming majority of school leaders. Those leading schools in challenging circumstances are as much a victim of poor accountability systems as teachers.

The surplus model

But what if we ran our schools on a surplus model? What if we assumed that teachers were basically trustworthy, hard-working and knew what they were doing? Even if we assumed that all teachers have the best of intentions, we know that the road to hell is paved with good intentions. Although good intentions

45

are not enough, an institutional belief that teachers are essentially out to do their best changes institutional culture. Instead of seeking out responsibility and apportioning blame for any perceived failure, in a surplus model the working assumption would be that there must be an impediment preventing teachers from doing the right thing, and if we can only find and smooth out the obstacles, people will naturally do what is in the children's best interests.

This might sound naive. Every senior leader has worked with teachers who are, for one reason or another, struggling. While such teachers can mostly be supported to improve, there may be a small minority who are too lazy or nefarious to do so. A surplus model doesn't just ignore this possibility, but it does assume – until proven otherwise – that teachers are well intentioned and responsible.

This doesn't mean leaders should never fire incompetent employees, and it doesn't mean that senior leaders shouldn't make tough decisions, but it does mean that we should begin by assuming that everyone has current and developing expertise. If our analysis ends when we identify guilt for making mistakes (or being incompetent), we are less likely to recognise the systemic factors which made these errors possible. Individuals must be accountable for their actions, but systemic failures are the responsibility of school leaders. Understandably, some leaders find it inconvenient to look beyond human error.

A sensible surplus model insists that trust is reciprocal and that autonomy is earned. (We'll consider this further in Chapter 5.) Instead of resulting in ever tighter accountability, such a model produces greater trust. And, when teachers are trusted to be their best, when they are acknowledged as knowing more about teaching their subjects to their students in their classrooms, then they are allowed to select solutions that may be far better than those chosen by less knowledgeable leaders. The more trust and responsibility teachers are given, the more they are empowered to find out what might be more effective, and the more likely they are to achieve mastery. Table 2.2 suggests other differences between the surplus and deficit models.

	The deficit model	The surplus model
Guiding assumption	Things would be better if teachers …	Things would be better if leaders …
Views about workload	Teachers could work harder.	Teachers already work as hard as possible.
Questions posed	Whose fault is it?	What is preventing this?
Where expertise is located	With leaders.	With all staff members.
School response	Tighter accountability systems.	Greater trust and responsibility.
Guiding principle	Manipulation and coercion.	Cooperation and dialogue.
Outcome for teachers	Compliance.	Mastery and autonomy.
Mindset	Problem finding.	Problem solving.
Leadership style	Directive.	Responsive.

Table 2.2. Surplus and deficit model assumptions

One of the most bitter ironies is that schools who most need to operate a surplus model – schools considered to be failing – are also those where the risk of doing so may seem untenable. This creates a vicious cycle in which accountability without trust leads to teachers being too fearful to exercise their professional judgement. On the other hand, schools considered successful feel able to risk trusting their staff and, consequently, teachers at these schools are more likely to thrive, leading to further success.

Sufficiency leads to surplus
In contrast to the built-in insufficiency of a deficit model, the surplus model is premised on sufficiency. The constant urge for schools to be better than 'good enough' encourages a lack of realism.

The point is that everything comes at a cost. When considering our expectations of ourselves, what is the cost of striving to meet nebulous notions of what it means to be outstanding versus the benefit of trying to be good enough to provide students with an academic education and keep them safe? The price in education is calculated primarily in time and effort. Yes, of course, money is hugely important – especially if you haven't got much – but our time is strictly finite; we can only spend it once. This is the opportunity cost.

Aristotle saw any form of extremism as unhealthy and held up the golden mean – the desirable middle between excess and deficiency – as chief among virtues. You can have two much of a good thing: too much courage results in

47

recklessness and an excess of accountability erodes trust. How many school leaders have fallen foul of the desire to be judged outstanding and lost sight of the greater good contained in simply turning up and teaching students?

Vilfredo Pareto, an Italian engineer and sociologist, noted that 80% of most tasks can be completed in 20% of the available time. Conversely, completing the last 20% of a task takes 80% of the effort. While getting an outstanding judgement is certainly possible, the effort involved may result in diminishing marginal returns. Increasingly frantic urgings to work ever harder become increasingly inefficient. Pareto's 'law of the valuable few' suggests that in most fields of endeavour, we spend most of our time on those activities that produce the least impact. This sounds like a counsel of despair until we reverse the formulation: what takes the least time probably accounts for most of the impact you aim to achieve.

Sufficiency might best be represented by a 'Pareto improvement': a change that can make at least one person (e.g. a student) better off without making anyone else (e.g. a teacher) worse off. There is little point in asking teachers to enact change which will have a significantly negative effect on their well-being.

Caveat: The danger is that because there is no commonly agreed purpose of education, the 'reality' of leadership decisions has nothing meaningful to be measured against. For instance, if school leaders believe that 'reality' involves preparing students for jobs which haven't been invented yet, then 'sufficiency' might involve getting rid of school subjects and teaching generic skills. In the absence of genuine expertise, it's possible to justify anything, even when the results are disastrous.

Voltaire's maxim, "the best is the enemy of the good",[15] suggests that by striving for unrealistic goals we're more likely to miss being good enough. In fact, the effort put into satisfying an external agency's ever shifting definition of 'outstanding' is exactly the kind of deficit thinking that prevents schools from being sufficiently good at providing students with a broad, rich education and keeping them safe.

That said, some things – like the development of curriculum – are never 'done'. Although thinking in terms of a perfect curriculum is probably a category error, that doesn't mean we shouldn't take both a long-term, iterative view while also keeping an eye on the sufficiency of what needs to happen now. A curriculum needs to be in place; students need to be taught *something*. While we're striving towards improving what the curriculum offers, we also have to ensure what we have is good enough for next lesson.

If we were to agree that schools need to be 'sufficiently good,' then leaders might be more willing to take a surplus view of their most important resource: teachers.

Why schools don't improve

Because the deficit model of school leadership is focused on blame and accountability, rather than responsibility and autonomy, teachers are incentivised to pass the buck and cover their backs while leaders are cast in the role of paternalistic guardians of standards. Not only does this lead to a divisive 'us and them' culture, but everyone is so preoccupied with the fear of being blamed that they are less likely to learn from their mistakes.

In a surplus model, because no one is 'to blame', the psychological safety exists to focus on identifying and eliminating the reasons for problems so they don't reoccur. For instance, a surplus model will assume that student behaviour problems are more probably a cause of ineffective teaching than a consequence. Leaders in a surplus model will take responsibility for imposing an orderly, mutually respectful school culture so that teachers can teach and students can learn. By contrast, a deficit model will assume that poor student behaviour is the result of poor teaching. If teachers are more accountable for taking individual responsibility for students' behaviour, they will either improve or quit. Or so the reasoning goes.

A deficit model designs policy with the expectation that teachers can – or should – work harder. Such an approach is doomed to fail because, for the most part, teachers are at capacity. Their fingers are worked to bloody stumps, so expecting them to pile something else onto their already teetering workloads is not just unreasonable – it's stupid.

In a surplus model, there is an understanding of the effects of workload and stress. Time is spent working out what kinds of expectations are reasonable and then stripping out competing demands to ensure that those things deemed most essential can be prioritised. New initiatives will tend to focus on doing less better rather than doing more.

Where a deficit model results in an ever greater burden produced by the need for monitoring and 'quality assurance', a surplus model assumes that teachers will want to do the right thing and design systems that harness the power of trust, thus allowing teachers greater autonomy and the freedom to be their best.

It's easy to stop blaming others for failure when we're not worried about being blamed in turn, but the best courses of action are rarely the easiest. The greatest risk is in continuing to operate a model in which teachers are sacrificed on the altar of 'school improvement'. School systems can become blunt instruments that bind rather than support teachers. This is self-defeating: whatever gains are made will only be shallow and short term. If we want teachers to thrive they must be free to learn from their mistakes, and that's only likely in a surplus model.

Better systems

All schools need systems; great schools have great systems. Without systems, schools condemn their communities to a war of all against all. Without great systems, successful teachers are like warlords in a failed state: through force of personality they maintain order in their classroom or department but are forced to tolerate chaotic corridors and dysfunctional behaviour elsewhere. The key is to design systems that do not provide perverse incentives for teachers to do the wrong things.

A system which fails to value the contribution of all teachers is a long way from great. The deficit model recognises that some teachers 'get it'. They comply, they're able to juggle impossible demands and somehow perform on cue. They're rewarded, and everyone one else is under threat. Not because they're not working hard, but because they're not meeting the expectations of 'experts'. This is formalised in the language we use to grade schools: some are 'good' or 'outstanding' and everyone else 'requires improvement'.

But if schools are going to be truly great, *everyone* requires improvement. We all need to be better because we can be. As we've seen, many teachers plateau in terms of improving students' attainment after three years of teaching. The factor that seems to most affect whether teachers continue to improve beyond the first three years is the quality of the school. Schools which operate under a surplus model are more likely to both implement systems for supporting teachers' development and monitor those systems to make sure they are not producing perverse incentives.

Schools differ from other organisations in that they need systems to ensure three specific purposes: (1) maintaining high standards of student behaviour, (2) focusing on learning rather than performance and (3) planning, implementing and evaluating a broad curriculum.

1. Maintaining high standards of student behaviour

School culture must be conducive to students learning hard to master curriculum materials. If individual teachers are expected to manage students' behaviour without support, they will be incentivised to ignore low level disruption. A good behaviour system will provide clear consequences for misdemeanours and encourage teachers to have extremely high expectations of students' behaviour by removing as much administration time and effort as possible. (See pages 164–168 for more on this.)

2. Focusing on learning rather than performance

Teachers need to receive feedback on students' learning rather than on their current performance. Systemic approaches to providing feedback on the quality of teachers' instruction is focused on what Robert Coe has called "poor proxies for learning".[16] These incentives encourage teachers to concentrate on short-term, visible goals. To focus on learning (defined as creating "relatively permanent changes in comprehension, understanding, and skills of the types that will support long-term retention and transfer"[17]) requires systems to consider not what's happening in the here and now, but how to evaluate what students can do elsewhere and later.

3. Planning, implementing and evaluating a broad curriculum

An effective school curriculum must contain the material students most need to learn in order to be academically successful and ensure that it is carefully sequenced to support these long-term aims. Matthew Evans argues that "The challenge of school leadership is the challenge of achieving 'curriculum authenticity'" – that is, moving away from a focus on the grades students get and more towards a breadth of education that is "empowering, equitable and true, constructed with integrity and intellectual honesty".[18] The possibility that such a curriculum becomes a reality is remote unless subject leaders are supported by systems aligned to this aim.

Implementing systems in line with these ends allows both teachers and school leaders to make better decisions and focus on what is most important. Without systems designed in this way, schools are more likely to be buffeted by shifting priorities and passing fancies.

What can we learn from aviation?

Flying is a dangerous business. All sorts of things can go wrong and any one of them could result in disaster. That said, it has become a cliché that flying is the safest way to travel. No other form of transportation is as scrutinised, investigated and monitored as commercial aviation. According to research into flight safety, over the 19 years between 1975 and 1994, the death risk per flight was one in seven million. It doesn't matter whether you fly once every three years or every day of the year. In fact, based on this incredible safety record, if you did fly every day of your life, probability indicates that it would take 19,000 years before you would succumb to a fatal accident. That's pretty good going. In comparison, the risk of being involved in a fatal train accident is one in a million. Driving, something generally considered so safe that most adults find it relatively easy to get a license, results in 3,700 deaths every day worldwide and 1.3 million per year. [19] You are, on average, many more times less likely to die on a plane than in your car.

The stakes are so high in aviation that mistakes cannot be tolerated. Whenever a plane crashes, immense efforts are made to learn the causes of the crash and to introduce systems to ensure the same conditions never reoccur. This has meant avoiding the instinct to find culprits and to instead focus on finding solutions. One of the many hard lessons learned by the aviation industry is that distributing responsibility and challenging hierarchical authority saves lives. From examining flight recorders and listening to cockpit recordings, crash investigators know that otherwise avoidable accidents have been caused by dysfunctional relationships between airline crew. The traditional model was that the captain was in absolute authority and questioning his actions was unthinkable. This led to co-pilots and cabin crew keeping silent when they noticed the captain making a mistake.

There are clear dangers in leaving people to organise themselves because our natural inclination is to defer to those in authority and pass the buck to others down the line. The airline industry's response was a system they called crew resource management (CRM). The idea "was to transform a culture in which error was defined as 'weakness' – which, in turn, led to shame, blame, and punishment – into a culture of learning and teamwork". [20]

Human errors would be addressed but also studied to find out what they could reveal about how to prevent and mitigate their effects. Crucially, captains were given the explicit responsibility of effectively managing the rest of the crew, not just the functioning of the cockpit. In turn, crew members were trained not to blindly follow instructions but instead to question, contribute and, if necessary, intervene to ensure the safety of the aircraft and its passengers.

Responsibility is shared among the crew with all crew members expected to contribute to decisions and be in full possession of all information. Much thought has been given to training individuals to frame their input constructively and to negotiate and resolve disagreements calmly and efficiently, so that any conflict leads to a stronger collective understanding of potential problems. Under this system, team members are not considered irritants or obstacles but as crucial resources for making flights safer and the captain's job easier.

Although the captain still issues instructions, team members are expected to monitor and support each other and are given a voice in decision-making. Everyone, regardless of rank or seniority, is held to account for pointing out potential mistakes, asking for clarification and explanations and resolving problems.

What about education?

Mistakes in aviation are potentially catastrophic; when we get things wrong in education no one dies. But the same pressures that cause pilots to make mistakes are also at work to prevent teachers and school leaders from acting in the best interests of their students. What if we sought to balance the 'orders' teachers are given with the instruction to monitor others and point out if head teachers or senior leaders are making mistakes? There will always be sources of knowledge and expertise within a school not possessed by the senior leaders. Unless leaders seek this out, decision-making will be suboptimal. For instance, has the expertise of modern foreign language teachers been harnessed when designing a literacy policy? Unless senior leaders know everything that special educational needs and disability teachers know, then the new teaching and learning policy might end up adversely affecting the most vulnerable students. How can we find out what 'mastery' means when teaching phonics in an early years foundation stage classroom? By asking the teachers responsible for teaching it.

These sources of knowledge tend to be either overlooked or ignored. If we want to create the conditions for teachers to thrive, then we need a systematic overhaul of the way schools are organised and led. Systems in schools operating under a surplus model are designed to seek out all sources of expertise and incentivise teachers to contribute their critique of new ideas. If teachers feel their voices are not valued – or, worse, if they think they may be punished for offering a contrary opinion – then decision-making will suffer.

As in aviation, one of the greatest barriers to improvement is the hierarchical structure of schools. The philosopher Jeffrey Nielsen observes that open and honest dialogue only takes place between those who consider themselves equals.[21] Where there are power imbalances, we tell those above us only what we think they want to hear and those beneath us only what we think they need to know. Because communication is at best partial and at worst dishonest, not only does this erode trust but it also creates a gap between what we *think* is true and what is *actually* happening.

The principles underpinning CRM are those of distributed cognition. This means that everyone in a team needs to know how to perform their individual tasks, but also to be aware of how their roles affect the activities of everyone else, even if those people are working out of sight at any given moment.

Getting rid of power imbalances doesn't mean getting rid of school leaders. Just as a captain is required to pilot a plane and take ultimate responsibility for the safety of everyone on board, so a school needs a single point of accountability to be responsible both for its day-to-day running and its longer term direction. If enacted in schools, a model of socially distributed cognition would require teachers to be empowered to be thoughtful, flexible, responsible and professionally sceptical. It would also mean that school leaders are accountable for the treatment of the teachers they are responsible for leading. Intimidation and coercion are always abuses of power.

Under current management systems, although teachers are often given significant autonomy within their classrooms, they are usually expected to dutifully follow instructions. We tend to say that we want teachers to act like professionals, but do we really mean it?

A formative approach to school improvement

Blanket assumptions that school improvement is either straightforward or hopelessly convoluted are equally flawed. Although school improvement is possible, it is complex and nuanced. As we'll explore in the chapters that follow, there are sufficiently knowledgeable and realistic approaches that represent good bets.

To the uninitiated, anything new or surprising can seem impossible. To the first people to see the Wright brothers in action, a machine flying through the sky must have appeared miraculous. To these onlookers, flying their own plane would have been unimaginable. And, yet, the Wright Flyer wasn't a miracle;

it was merely the product of sufficient knowledge and realistic engineering. Schools, like planes, don't just take off. School improvement may be harder to quantify than aerodynamics, but it has a better chance of working when it is approached with sufficient knowledge and realism.

The problem with 'outstanding leadership' as a frame of reference is its vagueness. It could mean almost anything to anyone. Perhaps more helpful is the concept of 'formative leadership' – that is, leadership which responds to its context. If we criticise teaching that is one-size-fits-all and lacks any formative assessment or evaluation, surely a one-size-fits-all approach to school leadership is equally likely to be ineffective?

A more formative approach to school leadership builds in learning through error and acknowledges that although mistakes are inevitable, repeating the same mistakes is inexcusable. It embraces the need to learn the nuts and bolts of school improvement through the experience of leading a curriculum or pastoral team. Within a formative approach there are no shortcuts to expertise. Leaders understand the need to serve their apprenticeship on the back row of the staffroom and continue to make the time to listen to as many views as possible within the school. You may not always like what you hear, but these views represent the cognitive diversity of a school; these are the people that you need to win over. When school leadership is approached formatively and iteratively, school improvement aligns to represent the opinions of the majority and is less likely to feel imposed and resented.

Operating under the deficit model, education is as hierarchical as it gets. Head teachers cower beneath the fiery eye of school inspectors and government officials; senior leadership teams are compliant echo chambers mirroring the head teacher's perspective; teachers fear censure and criticism; students are trained to pass exams rather than experiencing the breadth and beauty offered by subject disciplines. Although it doesn't have to be this way, change is hard because there is so much vested interest in the status quo. Adopting a surplus model offers some hope. If schools were serious about creating the conditions for teachers to thrive, then CRM, distributed cognition and the principles of intelligent accountability might provide a way forward.

Summary of Chapter 2

- The quality of teaching is one of the few factors within our control that is a good bet for improving the quality of a school.
- Teachers are a scarce and valuable resource that needs to be nurtured and protected.
- Teachers are more likely to increase their effectiveness in schools with supportive learning environments, concrete learning processes and leadership that reinforces learning.
- School leaders need to believe that all teachers can improve, despite the fact that they may not know how best to work with certain individuals.
- The deficit model of school improvement assumes that problems are due to lack of effort or expertise and seeks to apportion blame.
- The surplus model of school improvement assumes that all teachers are well intentioned and working at capacity, and seeks to uncover reasons for problems.
- The deficit model will tend to result in tighter accountability, whereas the surplus model is more likely to result in greater trust.
- Deficit models create a culture of suspicion and offer incentives for people to behave perversely.
- Schools can learn the value of distributed cognition from aviation.

CHAPTER 3

TRUST

It is impossible to go through life without trust: that is to be imprisoned in the worst cell of all, oneself.

Graham Greene, *The Ministry of Fear* (1943)

We're crippled without trust. Every decision – no matter how great or small – relies on trust. We trust that the sun will rise in the morning, that our consignment of board pens will be delivered, that the school Wi-Fi will work when we need it to, that the milk in the staffroom fridge hasn't gone sour. We trust our parents when they tell us the date of our birthdays, we trust our doctor when they tell us that the lump we've found is nothing to worry about, we trust our teachers when the tell us the date of the Battle of Hastings. But more than this, we need to trust that others will do as they say and, in turn, we need to be trusted by others.

Sometimes we learn that our trust was misplaced. This can be disorientating and damaging. Trust is based on reliability. As we learn through repeated experience that we can rely on things being as we expect, then we begin to place our trust in them and stop worrying. If we can't rely on our car starting in the morning or we know that the Wi-Fi is prone to going on the fritz at exactly the wrong moment, then we stop trusting. We plan for contingencies and look for alternatives in which to place our trust.

Interpersonal trust is different from the mechanical trust that we place in inanimate objects. If our chair collapses we tend not to take it personally.

Although we have been 'let down' in a literal sense, we haven't been betrayed in quite the same way as when another person turns out to be faithless or unreliable. When we trust other people, we have an expectation that they will act in certain ways, make certain choices and meet their obligations. When people let us down it hurts; we feel betrayed and we're likely to hold a grudge.

The way we understand trust depends on our standpoint. Economists see trust as a self-interested transaction: we trust people when we can see that it's in their own best interest to cooperate with us. In evolutionary terms, trust is viewed as reciprocal altruism: you scratch my back and I'll scratch yours. But in our everyday experience, trust is based on reputation and experience.

Confucius believed that three things were needed for a ruler to govern: weapons, food and trust. If a ruler is unable to hold on to all of these he should give up the weapons first, followed by the food. Trust, he thought, should be guarded to the last.¹ This is true for everyone and every institution. It may be difficult to govern without a standing army to enforce your will or when people are hungry, but if there's no trust, there's no hope at all. In the context of schools, weapons and food are analogous to the sticks and carrots used to motivate teachers, but trust is still trust.

Schools – like all organisations – run on trust. If we cannot trust others to act within agreed parameters then everything breaks down. The larger the school, the less likely it is that we possess the personal knowledge of every individual staff member required to make a sound judgement, so the source for our trust – or lack of it – becomes reputational. When an individual is perceived to have a trustworthy reputation, we tend to let disconfirming evidence slide. If a teacher has a less enviable reputation, leaders will tend to judge even minor issues with undue harshness.

As we'll see, trust comes from trustworthiness. If schools show themselves to be trustworthy then it's easier to trust that they're doing a good job. The same applies to teachers. But someone has to make the first move – trust has to go both ways. But just as schools can't decide to be trusted by society, teachers can't choose to be trusted by school leaders. This stand-off is akin to the prisoner's dilemma.

The prisoner's dilemma

What is the best way to succeed in the world? Are we better off cooperating or being selfish? Consider the prisoner's dilemma. Imagine that you are a member of a criminal gang and that you and a confederate have been arrested and are awaiting interrogation. You are both locked in solitary confinement with no means to get your stories straight. Lacking sufficient evidence to convict the two of you on the principal charge, the police have enough to convict you both on a lesser charge. The police offer you both the same deal: if you betray your confederate and testify that they committed the crime, you'll be released. If you both turn on each other, you'll both serve time for the lesser charge. Can you trust your confederate to stay silent or will you drop them in it and make a bid for freedom? What would you do?

This scenario, first outlined in the 1950s, is a standard example of a game analysed by game theory. There are four possible outcomes:

1. If A and B each betray the other, each of them serves two years in prison.
2. If A betrays B but B remains silent, A will be set free and B will serve three years in prison.
3. If A remains silent but B betrays A, A will serve three years in prison and B will be set free.
4. If A and B both remain silent, both of them will serve only one year in prison (on the lesser charge).[2]

The best outcome for each individually is that they defect and betray their partner while benefitting from the other's trust. The best bet for both is for each to cooperate and stay schtum, but the crucial element in deciding who will do what is trust. Are we better off cooperating with others or fending for ourselves?

Of course, we might not have particularly high expectations for criminals' codes of ethics, but the same principle holds true in every walk of life. As Onara O'Neill put it, "Trust is not a matter of blind deference, but of placing – or refusing trust with good judgement."[3] We have to constantly make choices between what is most expedient for ourselves and what will most benefit everyone else. If we're too trusting, we fear being taken advantage of by free-riders (selfish individuals who betray the trust of the group and grab all they can get). But if we don't trust, then we're thrust into a Hobbesian "war of all against all".[4]

To investigate the premise of whether it is better to trust (cooperate) or backstab (defect), the political scientist Robert Axelrod ran a tournament to pit strategies of defection and cooperation against each other to see which would be the most successful. He invited a number of well-known game theorists to submit strategies to be run by computers. In the tournament, programs played games against each other and themselves repeatedly. Each strategy specified whether to cooperate or defect based on the previous moves of both the strategy and the opponent. Strategies included programs such as 'always defect', 'always cooperate' and many more complex variations. The tournament was won by Anatol Rapoport's strategy named Tit-for-Tat.[5]

The rules for Tit-for-Tat are beguilingly simple: start by cooperating and then copy your opponent's moves. If your opponent always cooperates, so do you; if your opponent defects, you do too. Successive cooperative moves build trust, but crucially Tit-for-Tat was also forgiving. If after defecting and then suffering the consequences of retaliation you decided to play fair, Tit-for-Tat wouldn't hold a grudge.

The consequences of distrust

Prisoner's dilemmas are not just abstract, logical problems, they play out in schools on a regular basis. The beauty of the Tit-for-Tat strategy is that it didn't take much for the algorithm to begin trusting other algorithms to cooperate. In the real world we're not so forgiving; once bitten, twice shy. Distrust is a moral judgement. If we perceive someone as untrustworthy, we think less of them; we think of them as having done – or likely to do – something wrong.

The majority of teachers believe they're doing a reasonable job. If a teacher runs afoul of a work scrutiny or is 'learning walked' by a critical senior colleague who feels students are not performing as expected while they were present, they might find themselves on the receiving end of some 'support'.

Many teachers thus supported resign. This might be because they and everyone else recognise that they're not up the job and that young people's precious life chances are in jeopardy. Perhaps. But there also exists the possibility that scrutiny and criticism can have an undermining effect on teachers' ability to teach well. There is a plethora of observer biases which suggest that our behaviour changes when we're observed.[6] If we feel our judgement isn't trusted and that someone is breathing down our necks, just waiting to point out every little error or failing, we probably won't perform at our peak. Likewise, if others believe us to be trustworthy, it seems reasonable that we're likely to feel more confidence in our abilities and turn out a bravura performance.

Making teachers more fearful is unlikely to improve results, but why is it that some school leaders don't trust teachers? In some cases, it will be because the teacher is not trustworthy, in others it may be because the leader is not sufficiently knowledgeable to understand what she is observing. Trust is built on knowledge. The more leaders know about what teachers should be teaching and what constitutes effective long-term learning in the subject they're observing, the easier it is both for the teacher to trust that the leader is sufficiently knowledgeable to recognise what they're doing and for the leader to trust that the teacher is teaching effectively.

But this doesn't resolve the stand-off. School leaders might be advised to adopt a tit-for-tat approach to trusting teachers: trust first until teachers prove themselves untrustworthy. This may feel scary but the alternative is a vicious downward spiral.

We need to remember that problems are more often concerned with teaching than teachers. By forgetting this we make problems personal. If a teacher really is underperforming, the objective should be that they improve and become a better teacher. If 'support' is coloured with distrust, there is a good chance that it will have the opposite effect.

Trust and well-being

According to Onara O'Neill, a lack of trust in the workplace has led to 'a culture of suspicion' which has generated ever greater demands for accountability, undermined professional responsibility and trust, and led to adverse effects on health and well-being.[7] Teaching is now one of the three professions with the highest reports of stress: 53% of education professionals have considered leaving education over the past two years.[8] It could be that teaching is an inherently stressful job but other sources reveal a bleaker picture.

In 2001, the then Education Secretary Estelle Morris acknowledged that, "many teachers say they feel themselves stretched almost to breaking point".[9] The following year, the Department for Education and Skills published a report which estimated that teachers spent 20% of their time on non-teaching tasks such as photocopying, processing forms for school trips or other administrative activities. Morris promised "a concerted attack on any bureaucracy" that might get in the way of teaching.[10] Despite teachers no longer expected to take on admin tasks, put up classroom displays or cover lessons for absent colleagues, workload seems to have increased in the intervening years.

When the UK government issued its Workload Challenge report in 2015, an unprecedented number of teachers got in touch to complain about the burdensome, bureaucratic requirements of 'unnecessary and unproductive' data managements, planning and marking.[11]

The 2019 annual survey from the teaching union, the NASUWT, found that:

- 73% of teachers would not recommend teaching as a career.
- 77% reported feel stressed in the last year.
- 85% reported excessive workload as a concern.
- 66% said that were unable to spend enough time with family and friends.
- 56% felt they were not empowered as teachers.
- 86% said teaching impacted negatively on their well-being; 70% reported that their mental health had been affected and 57% that their physical health had suffered.
- 65% felt that their well-being was not taken seriously by managers and 59% that their opinions were not valued by school leaders.

In 2018, Ofsted's interim findings on teachers' well-being and workload reported similar findings:

- 28% of respondents reported low well-being at work, 26% medium, 35% high and 11% reported very high.
- 31% of teachers reported low well-being at work compared with 18% for senior leaders.
- 25% of all respondents had been absent from work due to health problems caused or made worse by work, excluding accidents.
- 76% of teachers reported that their job impacted negatively on their mental health and 60% reported that it impacted negatively on their physical health.
- 62% of all respondents believed that teaching was not valued by society.[13]

All of this is strongly suggestive that very many teachers do not feel trusted or valued. If teachers' mental and physical health is suffering, what effect might this have on their students?

The solution is not, perhaps, as obvious as some might think. For instance, trying to increase employees' well-being directly by offering programmes designed to increase productivity and well-being doesn't work.[14] We are more likely to increase well-being by making those we work with feel more trusted.[15] Trust – and distrust – can easily become self-fulfilling prophesies. There is reason to think that people become more (or less) trustworthy because we either trust or distrust them. As the economists Lars Feld and Bruno Fray put it, "trust breeds trust".[16]

The need for trust in schools

In their study, *Trust in Schools*, Anthony Bryk and Barbara Schneider found that those schools with the highest achievement levels also had the highest levels of trust within their school communities.[17] Although it seems clear that trust is the cornerstone on which great teaching is built, it is in such desperately short supply. There can be little doubt of the toxic and pernicious effects of teachers' workload. In a sane and rational universe, something would be done about the dreadful toll this takes. Never mind the appalling waste of talent, the time and money we needlessly fritter away should be argument enough.

A few years ago, I took part in a cost/benefit analysis in a primary school. I first discussed with senior leaders what they thought teachers spent their time doing and then observed some lessons and talked to teachers and pupils about what really happened. Practices varied from teacher to teacher, but one observation jumped out at me: older, more experienced staff knew how to play the game and interpret the rules; younger, less experienced teachers tended to follow the rules closely.

Older, cannier teachers do what they need to do to survive: when the classroom door is closed, they get on with the business of teaching children as they've always done – sensibly, compassionately and effectively. Younger teachers struggle valiantly to be the teachers they want and need to be, but are often adrift in a sea of accountability processes and compliance measures which mean they're too busy filling in pointless paperwork to teach effectively. In one teacher's class, I estimated that she spent about 70% of her day on activities designed to prove to senior leaders that she was doing her job. In order to keep her head above water, she then took home vast piles of work night after night. I warned senior leaders that without help she was in danger of self-destructing within the year. In the end she took matters into her own hands and quit.

What can we learn from this? Maybe she wasn't up to the job. Maybe it's right and proper that she recognised her unfitness to handle the responsibility of educating the next generation. Maybe this process of culling is simply the survival of the fittest. Or maybe it's an unpardonable and brutalising lack of regard for the basic right of teachers to both do a job and have a life outside of that job. Ultimately, I think the message is that teachers need a certain amount of cynicism to survive the first five years.

In some quarters, it seems to have become a default assumption that teachers are feckless layabouts who, left to their own devices, would slop cheap coffee over the students' books and do the barest minimum in lessons. Certainly, when I was a student in the 1980s there were some teachers like that. My history teacher 'taught' the wrong GCSE syllabus and the entire class failed. He shrugged his shoulders and nothing happened. I had an English teacher whose classroom was next door to the staffroom. After he'd set some work he'd slope off to smoke his pipe. If we got too rowdy, he'd pound on the wall for us to shut up.

Although there were some incredible excesses back in the 'bad old days' before Ofsted was a gleam in Chris Woodhead's eye. But there was also space for some wonderful eccentrics. Many, perhaps most, of them are long gone. I worked with a fabulous old boy who had taught at the school for over 30 years. He could recite vast tracts of Shakespeare, Keats and Donne and had a quotation for every occasion. He'd taught the students' parents, sometimes grandparents, and was a much loved member of the community. When the school went into special measures he was put under intolerable pressure to change the way he taught, despite his excellent results. He went from confident pomp to incompetence in less than a year and gratefully accepted the offer of early retirement.

The argument usually goes that although the accountability measures we take for granted in schools take their toll, they are necessary. Without the lists of 'non-negotiables' there would be a free-for-all. But few teachers are in it for the money or the social standing. Almost all decide to teach because they want to make a difference. They're passionate. They care. There may be a few bad apples, but why should we allow them to spoil the whole barrel through lack of trust?

There are many schools where teachers *are* trusted. It's not naive to believe that there might be a better way. While it may be true that the quality of an education system cannot exceed the quality of its teachers, it's almost impossible for the quality of teaching to exceed the quality of school leadership. It's ludicrously easy for poor leadership to destroy good teachers.

An insidious culture of fear and suspicion has become endemic, and it's doing much more harm than good. Why should teachers be expected to give up so much of their home and family lives to fulfil the requirements of their job? Teachers work ever longer hours, but is this really desirable or even necessary? International comparisons show that teachers in other countries don't have anything like the same weight of workload expectations.[18] It's past time that we risked making a better wager.

Pascal's wager

Famously, the French mathematician and philosopher Blaise Pascal proposed that, on balance, it was a good bet to gamble of the existence of God. If God exists the consequences of not believing in him were too awful to consider – perpetual torment – but that if there is no God the only consequence of our misplaced faith is that we might feel disappointed or a bit silly. When weighing up the costs of a lack of faith, Pascal concluded that doing one's best to act as if God existed was the only sensible gambit.

Whatever your religious views, maybe we should take a similarly pragmatic approach to weighing up the costs and benefits of how we treat teachers. What are the consequences of taking the surplus model approach and choosing to believe teachers are basically trustworthy? If our default position is to distrust, then although a few might find a way to shine, we are likely to undermine a great many teachers. If, on the other hand, we trust that teachers will, when happy and supported, do the right thing, there's a good chance we'll be proved right much of the time. If an individual betrays our trust they can be dealt with on a case-by-case basis. Even if some teachers turn out to be untrustworthy, the risk of trusting teachers is likely to be a good bet. If leaders take the time to get to know what teachers know (to the extent that is possible), trust can be placed judiciously. In the absence of good information and mutually trusting relationships all we have is blind faith, which is probably unsustainable.

If, for instance, teachers are struggling to mark their books, consider what could be done to help them. The unspoken expectation that they take ever more work home is untenable. Be clear: if they have too much marking to cope with, then this is in part the school's fault and responsibility. Similarly, if teachers are struggling to maintain acceptable standards of behaviour, make sure supportive systems are in place and don't make staff feel guilty for using them.

Trusting teachers is risky. If you trust them to be honest they may tell you things you don't want to hear. If you trust them to be autonomous they may do things you don't want them to do. If you allow teachers the space to be professionally sceptical they may come to conclusions that don't align with yours. But not trusting teachers may be an even greater risk.

Distrusting teachers and placing them under the microscope of accountability processes might improve outcomes over the short term, but it is not a sustainable or efficient way to run a school over the longer term. For schools to improve sustainably they need to make use of the collective intelligence of everyone who works within them. If it's true that improving teaching is one of the best routes to long-term success, then trusting teachers might be the best way to get there.

Trustworthiness, honesty and expertise

To be trusted we must be trustworthy. As well as being common sense, there is good evidence that trusting employees is the wisest course of action when they are considered trustworthy.[19] Similarly, as we shall explore in the next chapter, accountability only works when those being held to account trust those making the judgement. Trust and trustworthiness are reciprocal. In a culture of mistrust, someone has to break the cycle to establish this virtuous reciprocity. This responsibility must fall to school leaders.

High trust environments seem a good bet for helping teachers to improve. Arguably, the two most important factors in making ourselves more trustworthy and creating a high trust environment are honesty and expertise. Without these two qualities in our schools, an insufficiency or deficit is built in, preventing us from acting with sufficient knowledge and realism and thereby undermining our decision-making as leaders.

1. Honesty

The truth is a commodity in short supply. The world around us is objectively real and packed with immutable facts, but it is also a never-ending conveyor belt of spin, fake news, advertising, self-promotion and bullshit. It can often seem hard to distinguish between the two. In a world where so much of our information is second – or third – hand, how can we work out what's true and what's not? We can start by not telling deliberate untruths.

But even this is fraught with difficulty. Some things are straightforward: it's obviously wrong to smear the reputation of others and commit fraud, but is it also wrong to make yourself look a bit better than you are by varnishing the unflattering truth? Surely, it can't be wrong to spare the feelings of those who would feel devastated if they knew what we really thought? And wouldn't it be social suicide – an act of self-harm – not to conceal our deepest, darkest secrets?

Lying is knowingly giving false information with the intention to deceive or mislead. The philosopher Sissela Bok defines a lie as "an intentionally deceptive message in the form of a statement".[20] Lying diminishes trust. If people didn't generally tell the truth then no one could be trusted. The irony here is that for lying to be effective, we have to trust that most people tell the truth most of the time. Even liars suffer if there is no trust. This is an instance of the prisoner's dilemma: everyone is best off if we all tell the truth.

The act of lying displays a disregard for other people. The liar treats those who are lied to as a means to achieve her purpose, rather than as inherently worthwhile and deserving of our trust. Our lies lead others to base their decisions on false information, and thereby curtail their freedoms and choices. We might decide it's in another's best interest for the truth to be withheld, but who are we to make such a decision? Also, as language is essential to cooperation and survival, we have an obligation to use it truthfully. Whenever we use language we effectively make a 'contract' to use it in a particular way – and one of the clauses of this contract is not to use language deceitfully.

While those we lie to no doubt suffer because of the lies we tell, perhaps most importantly, lying corrupts the liar. When we practise to deceive we force ourselves into weaving an increasingly tangled web. We have to remember all our revisions of reality and this makes us wary of those we have lied to in the past. We put our credibility at risk and, no matter how powerful our lies can make us feel, no one wants to end up as the boy who cried wolf. Consequently, our sense of our own integrity is damaged. Telling lies becomes a habit; if we regularly tell small lies to impress others, we're more likely to become inured against the consequences of telling bigger, more malicious lies to gain advantage over others.

But what of the white lie? What of those occasions when our intentions are good? And what of the kinds of lie that might protect us from harm? These are obviously more complex. Bok proposes what she calls the publicity test: which lies, if any, would survive the appeal for justification to reasonable persons?[21] Applying this test as a thought experiment would require us to bring together everyone affected by a particular lie – the liar, those lied to and anyone else who might be affected – and then ask this jury to judge our arguments to determine if the lie was justified. In practice, of course, this is impossible, and so Bok proposes that we first inspect our conscience, then ask friends and then finally reputable and respected independent persons. This is still an impossibly high bar in most situations and the best most of us can accomplish is to consult our conscience. The problem here is that we are invariably biased in our own favour and will go to great lengths to convince ourselves that our actions are righteous and justified.

What consolations are offered to the liar by philosophy? Well, a utilitarian would assess a lie on its consequences: if telling a lie did more good than telling the truth, than the lie was not only justified, it was right. But, as Bok's thought experiment makes clear, reasonably assessing the consequences of a lie is fiendishly hard. St Augustine thought lying was always wrong but that some lies were more forgivable than others. Thomas Aquinas agreed and divided lies into three types: malicious (those intended to harm), jocose (those told for fun) and officious (those intended to be helpful). Immanuel Kant, on the other hand, decided that lies are always wrong and the end never justifies the means.

Before embarking on a lie, Bok suggests that we should first ask whether there are truthful alternatives to dealing with the particular problem. Then we should consider what moral justifications we might have and what counter-arguments can be raised against those justifications. Finally, we can imagine what a public jury of reasonable persons might say about our lie. Sounds like an awful lot of trouble, doesn't it? Much simpler to tell the truth.

The big problem with all the moral justifications for lying is that they depend on two beliefs: that what we currently know is enough to predict the future (that what we know is all that needs to be known) and that reality could not be borne without trying to manipulate it into the shape we arrogantly believe it should be.

Kierkegaard saw the need to lie as leading us into a state where it is increasingly easy to ignore error and pretend that the negative consequences we experience don't exist or aren't our fault. This way of living is inauthentic. If we are inauthentic we continue to act in ways that our own experience has demonstrated to be false. By making excuses for those around us, by tolerating things we find irritating, by wishing for a quiet life, by allowing ourselves to live a lie, we erode the possibility of happiness. Truth, on the other hand, "is the ultimate, inexhaustible natural resource. It's the light in the darkness."[22]

The truth can set us free. If we accept all this, it might make running a school and a classroom freer and easier. If those responsible for directing the accountability machine of education told the truth – that they don't actually have the right answers, or even know if there are right answers, or know that they could do any better themselves – we could all stop pretending that there are 'magic bullets' for school improvement and have more authentic conversations about challenges and solutions. If school leaders were to tell the truth, they would stop doing things that they have been told Ofsted or the government 'want' or that might help them to game results so they look better.

When teachers aren't trusted, they won't be honest. When asked to provide student progress data for mid-year data collection, a colleague once said, "I'd rather not get bollocked twice," and proceeded to make up the data he knew the school leaders wanted to see. If teachers are prevented from being honest, you won't be able to accurately evaluate the effectiveness of your initiatives. If teachers told the truth, it would make it easier for leaders to have reliable collective knowledge on which to base their decision-making.

In both cases, teachers and leaders could make it clear when government or school policies drain the joy and vitality from their job and refuse to let it pass unchallenged. But honesty requires bravery. School leaders and teachers could stop finding ways to justify their results and cover their backs, and instead take responsibility for mistakes and commit to doing better in the future. If teachers told the truth to their students, then their students would respect them for it. And if students told the truth, their teachers would respect them in turn. If the truth was common currency in schools, where would bullying hide? Would the quiet, determined and hard-working be able to thrive? With truth would come trust. And if students trust their teachers, then justice becomes possible. This probably feels like a risk. It is, but what is the alternative? Who wants to work in a system run on lies?

Honesty stands the best chance of working because if we believe that knowledge and realism are necessary to effective decision-making, then lack of honesty is not just a moral deficiency, but it also militates against effective school improvement. Without honesty, our collective knowledge is fatally compromised and therefore insufficient. This leads to overconfidence, error and a mismatch between what school leaders 'know' and what teachers 'know'.

2. Expertise

Honesty and good intentions are not enough. Building trust is often cited as a generic leadership skill, but trust exists between individuals who possess some knowledge of each other; without this knowledge trust is blind and foolish. To be worthy of trust you have to know what you're talking about. We can't always trust experts – especially if they're not always honest (especially with themselves) – but we will more readily take the word of someone who is genuinely knowledgeable than that of a random chancer. This doesn't mean we should never venture an opinion about something we're not an expert in, but it does mean we should know our limits, provide sources for our assertions and admit the possibility that we may be wrong.

Like all organisations, schools need specialists, but these specialists should only be trusted on matters pertaining to their expertise. Some teachers will see themselves as experts on their own students. As such, even though they may not always possess the big picture, they're likely to know better than anyone else how to teach their classes and, therefore, they should be considered trustworthy within these parameters. If they were to start offering advice to other teachers teaching different subjects to children of different age groups, then they would be seen as less worthy of trust.

Much more harm can be done when senior leaders have an unrealistic view of their expertise. These leaders will often believe themselves to be experts on aspects of running a school and be under the impression that there might be some benefit to micromanaging subject specialists. This is probably not true. Improbable, but not impossible. Maybe this kind of senior leader really does know best, but in order for teachers to trust such an individual they need to see evidence. Honesty within schools, including self-honesty, allows senior leaders to judge more knowledgeably and realistically what they know and what they don't know, and to avoid the dangers of overconfidence and the best case fallacy.[23]

Evidence is the watermark of expertise. Although evidence can be flawed, incomplete and abused, it is essential in generating trust and trustworthiness, as opposed to credulity. As you've been reading this book, you'll have noticed that I reference my bolder claims with notes linking to a range of different sources. Some of these sources are academic research papers and some are references to knowledgeable experts. You may not be interested in chasing down any of these references, but they're there if you want to test the trustworthiness and credibility of my statements. Alternatively, you might decide to trust my word based on your opinion of me – opinions based on our experiences are also an important source of evidence.

Either way, senior leaders should seek to demonstrate their expertise – thus bolstering their trustworthiness – by showing they are knowledgeable, aware of counter-arguments, realistic and nuanced in their assertions, but also by demonstrating their abilities through direct lived experience. Lesson observation is a case in point: if you want a teacher to stop doing what they think is worthwhile, be prepared to model why your way is better. Expertise includes both 'knowing what' and 'knowing how'. Expert school leaders will possess mental models of how to apply their expertise in a range of school based situations, but most importantly for our purposes, they will have acquired through practice the habit of defaulting to a position of trusting teachers. Also important is the ability to separate our preferences from genuine expertise. Saying, "I wouldn't have done it that way," is to state a subjective personal preference rather than an objective statement of expertise.

By the same token, teachers have a responsibility to be experts in their subjects, to be as knowledgeable as possible about their students and to develop informed professional scepticism. We all have the right to be trusted – at least until we're shown to have betrayed that trust – but rights are only meaningful when placed alongside corresponding responsibilities. Trust and trustworthiness may be mutually reinforcing but they come with obligations and duties.

The relationship of mutually reinforcing rights and responsibilities is much more complex and tangled than is sketched out in Table 3.1, but seeing how both teachers and leaders contribute to trust and trustworthiness might help you to reflect on what other rights and responsibilities you might have.

	Teachers	Leaders
Rights	• To be treated with respect. • To be trusted as acting in the best interests of students.	• To be treated with respect. • To be trusted as acting in the best interests of the school.
Responsibilities	• To cooperate with all reasonable expectations. • To commit to continual improvement.	• To remove all demands that get in the way of teachers teaching effectively. • To avoid coercion and intimidation.

Table 3.1. Teachers' and leaders' rights and responsibilities

Arguably, there has been too much compliance and learned helplessness in education, leading teachers and school leaders into the trap of credulity in the face of implausible improvement strategies. Dylan Wiliam makes the following suggestion:

First, all teachers agree that they need to improve their practice, not because they are not good enough, but because they can be even better. Second, teachers agree to focus on things that are likely to have benefits for their students, so no more time on Brain Gym, learning styles, lesson study, or neuroscience because it's frankly self-indulgent to spend time on things that may or may not help students when there is solid evidence about what does help students.[24]

Trust also relies on being willing to let others in on your thinking and expose your practice. This works both ways: teachers welcoming senior leaders into their classrooms and senior leaders taking the time to explain the evidence base and rationale for decisions. If both parties know more about how the other thinks and what they believe, both will have greater confidence in each other's honesty, integrity and expertise. One of the most egregious displays of distrust is when leaders conduct staff surveys but then don't publish the results.

Although accountability alone will not improve teaching, as we will see in the next chapter, it is a necessary but poorly understood part of the equation.

Summary of Chapter 3

- Trust is an essential component for the efficient working of schools. The less teachers are trusted, the greater the need for monitoring and accountability.
- A policy of tit-for-tat – assume other people are trustworthy and willing to cooperate until they prove otherwise – is not only the most successful evolutionary adaptation for the smooth running of social groups, it's also a sensible way to treat teachers.
- Teachers thrive when they feel trusted; when we distrust others, their performance is more likely to decline than improve.
- Trust is a crucial factor in teachers' well-being.
- Pascal's wager suggests that the benefits of assuming teachers are untrustworthy outweighs the costs of assuming they are not.
- If we want to be trusted we must also be trustworthy; the two most important factors indicating our trustworthiness are honesty and expertise.
- Honesty requires more than simply avoiding lies. Not only does dishonesty erode trust, it also enables us to ignore our mistakes and pretend that the negative consequences we experience don't exist or aren't our fault.
- To be worthy of trust we must prove that we are knowledgeable and interested in evidence.

CHAPTER 4
ACCOUNTABILITY

A body of men, holding themselves accountable to nobody, ought not to be trusted by anybody.

Thomas Paine, *Rights of Man* (1791)

What stops us from taking the risk and trusting teachers is, in part, the very real fear that some will cut corners, take shortcuts and slack off. But it is also a product of the deficit model: misguided approaches to enforcing 'best practice' and the perceived need to hold teachers and schools to account for meeting key performance indicators. To mediate against these pressures, we put accountability systems in place. The point of accountability is to increase trust: the more information we have on what teachers are doing, the more we should be able to trust that they are teaching effectively, or if they're not, to intervene and make sure they either improve or quit. But does it work?

On some measures, maybe it does. Possibly, in the past, teachers (and schools) were extended too much trust. Possibly we didn't do a good enough job, especially with the most disadvantaged students. For instance, when I moved to Bristol in the early 2000s it was the lowest performing local authority in England. It was normal for schools to report A*–C grade GCSE pass rates of below 20%. Over the last 20 years, tighter accountability processes have ensured that this has become a thing of the past. But although we probably needed tighter accountability systems, we've arguably overcorrected.

Even hard-working teachers with the best of intentions can still be ineffective, so we need to know more, gather more information, compile more spreadsheets. The irony is, making teachers and schools more accountable results in placing ever greater trust in systems of audit and control. This leads us to judge quality with key performance indicators rather than through informed and independent evaluation. We use these systems to support trust, but all too often they end up distorting the proper aims of education: that children receive a broad and balanced education that equips them to participate fully in society. We need to think carefully about whether we might do better to take my version of Pascal's wager and trust either that teachers are well intentioned or that education is best served by placing ever greater trust in systems of control.

Many teachers I meet are afraid to make nuanced professional judgements, even when they are experienced and are relative experts in their specialism. When I make suggestions on how they could manage workload, organise the classroom, speak to students, select curriculum content or plan lessons, I'm very often confronted with, "That sounds like a great idea but I wouldn't be allowed to do it."

Too many school systems have become blunt instruments used to bind rather than support teachers: rewarding compliance, penalising professional judgement and independent thought and creating perverse incentives.

Perverse incentives

There is a common assumption that to get people to do what you want, all they need is the appropriate spur. The deficit model assumes that unless teachers are sufficiently motivated with carrots and sticks they will do the wrong thing. The problem is that, although incentives work, they often work in unexpected and undesirable ways.

Former Soviet premier Nikita Khrushchev is reported to have said, "Call it what you will, incentives are what get people to work harder." Following this logic, the Soviet system incentivised glass plant managers according to the tonnage of sheet glass they produced. Inevitably, factories churned out sheet glass so thick as to be useless. In an effort to sort out bourgeois shirkers, apparatchiks changed the rules so that the square metreage of glass produced was rewarded instead. They responded by producing glass so thin and fragile it would shatter as soon as you looked at it.

Teachers' behaviour is similarly affected by school accountability systems. Because schools are held to account for students' exam results, if there's a perception that one examination board is offering an easier syllabus, school leaders will be motivated to select that course even if they believe it is educationally inferior. This way of thinking trickles down into classrooms: if students are misbehaving and not working hard enough, we might try to offer them incentives with online 'solutions' that offer tangible rewards in exchange for house points or the like.

Performance related pay is intended to reward the most effective teachers by getting them to prove how effective they are, but most teachers are already motivated to do the right thing. Although teachers want to be adequately remunerated for their efforts, they teach because they want to. There aren't many teachers holding on to exciting new methods for teaching spelling or oxbow lakes until somebody offers to pay them extra.

If we don't have the sticks and carrots of accountability to incentivise teachers, then we're in the terrifying position of simply trusting that they will do the right thing. But if people are properly incentivised, so the reasoning goes, they will act with motivation, determination and efficiency.

Inevitably, schools always want to take a little bit more from those who work in them. Teachers are exhorted to ever mightier works by sharing values and vision, but nothing beats the simplicity of carrot and stick. But as soon as an incentive is offered, people change. We tend, unerringly, to respond to incentives by doing what is in our best interests. We respond to the letter of the initiative rather than the spirit; we ignore the intention and focus solely on the incentive.

The culture of suspicion produced by the deficit model incentivises the profession to engage in what Onara O'Neill has referred to as 'defensive teaching'.[1] We are motivated to cover our backs and do what is most expedient, not what is best.

Consider also how schools have been encouraged to increase the performance of students in receipt of the pupil premium. Of course, it's a wonderful thing that we should seek to narrow the attainment gap between the most disadvantaged and the most privileged, and it makes complete sense to scrutinise what all this public money is being spent on. Therefore, for a number of years schools were held to account for the gap between the achievement of their pupil premium students and everyone else. It wasn't considered good enough for students in receipt of the pupil premium to be doing better than the national average or even better than everyone else's. Schools were compelled to ensure there was no gap between different cohorts of students *within* their own school. Schools that failed this seemingly impossible hurdle failed inspections. Cynically, it's far easier to achieve this aim by reducing the performance of the rest of your cohort than it is to increase the performance of the most disadvantaged.

Good incentive systems consider both intent and reward. When managing change we tend to focus on problems. We look at what is preventing people from behaving in the ways we want them to behave rather than focusing on those instances of success. Most people willingly tread the path of least resistance, so if we offer incentives that make it easy to replicate these successes, we might be more likely to see the changes we want.

Is accountability creating perverse incentives?

- What do you want teachers to change? Be specific about exactly what you want them to do differently.
- To what extent might teachers' behaviour be caused by systemic rather than individual failures? How can systems be improved?
- Incentives work best when they affect how we feel. Find out how teachers feel now and articulate clearly how you would like them to feel.
- What can you take away to ensure that teachers are not too exhausted to make the desired change? Consciously opt out of old initiatives and prioritise the need to reduce unnecessary workload.
- Which teachers are already doing the things you want others to do? Make sure you recognise teachers' efforts and share examples of the practice you want to encourage.
- Teachers will be motivated to avoid being blamed for mistakes and to take credit for successes. What unexpected changes could occur? How will you prevent them from occurring?

How on earth have we managed to get to this point?

Institutional isomorphism

Over time, all organisations – and all schools – come to resemble each other more and more. The sociologists Paul DiMaggio and Walter Powell called this process 'institutional isomorphism'.[2] They identified three distinct types of isomorphic pressure: coercive, mimetic and normative.

Coercive pressures stem from external scrutiny. Where there are preannounced criteria of what is 'good', auditors and inspectors look for these things and those they audit and inspect are under pressure to show them what they want to see. The checklist culture that pervades some schools ensures that teachers conform or are rooted out. Christine Gilbert's tenure as head of Ofsted between October 2006 and June 2011 has been caricatured as 'the child-centred inquisition'. Group work, active and self-directed learning were held up as unquestioned good things. Schools scrambled to make sure they were seen to be doing what the inspectorate approved of, and teachers were either pressured to conform or 'supported' into leaving the profession. Any dissent was crushed.

In evolutionary terms, mimetic isomorphism accounts for the greater part of human culture: we look to each other to see what works, copying any good new tricks. Within education, school leaders scrutinise Ofsted reports to find out what approaches are currently fashionable and successful. Teachers often describe themselves as 'magpies', helping themselves to new gimmicks and shiny resources. It would be nice to think that there was some sort of iterative quality control process, with the worst ideas being weeded out as they prove themselves unsuccessful, but sadly this is not how things work. Bad ideas are amazingly resilient because mimicking what others are doing is a safer bet than taking a risk on something new or distinctive.

The third reason all schools are alike is because that is what we've come to believe schools *should* be like. As a general rule, we approve of what we think is normal. We are social animals and benefit enormously from shared resources, protection and the ability to engage in acts of reciprocal altruism with reduced risks of exploitation within social groups. Conversely, exclusion from a group tends to have a highly detrimental effect on an individual's capacity to survive and reproduce. Therefore, we've evolved a complex range of strategies for maintaining our membership and status within social groups. The social group that is 'school leaders' is, in part, defined by conforming to a widely understood set of values and beliefs.

What we *say* is important exerts far less influence than what we're seen to *do*. What we accept becomes acceptable. If teachers are expected to behave in particular ways – spending hours marking books or differentiating lessons with engaging activities – then there will be normative pressures on new teachers to fit in. If school leaders are supposed to be tough, uncompromising and obsessed by metrics, it's hard for new leaders to stand apart and do something different.

The need for accountability

It's not good enough to blame individuals: school leaders are products of the same system, the same culture of fear and compliance as are teachers. If we're ever to sculpt a system in which teachers are supported, it needs to be one in which head teachers enjoy the same benefits. Within the current system, if school leaders allow teachers take risks, accountability falls, with a leaden clang, on the head teacher. We have created a system in which there are inexorable institutional pressures to blame, seek excuses, conceal mistakes and pass the buck. No one can thrive in a system like this.

Although these pressures appear to originate with increasingly draconian governmental oversight, ultimately they are what we have collectively decided is the best way to hold each other to account. Education possibly suffers more than other areas of public service because everyone has been to school, everyone has met a few feckless teachers in their time and a fair few have been to rubbish schools. We know there are crap schools and teachers out there, and it's frustrating to think these worst case examples get away with it. Education also suffers from the fallacy of 'common sense'. More people are inclined to think that they could teach, or could be prime minister, than are inclined to think that they could land a jumbo jet or undertake brain surgery.

So, rather than trusting schools and teachers, we regularly check and measure their performance in the hope that this continual disruption and distraction – the equivalent of pulling up a plant by the roots to check it's growing – will somehow help matters.

One argument is to do away with accountability measures altogether and simply trust teachers to do their jobs well. After all, no one goes into teaching for self-serving, greedy motives. Teachers are, almost by definition, a well-intentioned, caring bunch who are motivated to make a positive difference in the lives of young people. Sadly, this is the best case fallacy. Those who wax lyrical on the boundless possibilities offered by an exciting, unfettered future and urge change, progress and the uncritical veneration of the new, ignore both the lessons of the past, the realities of the present and the full range of possibilities offered by the future. The checks and balances offered by accountability systems are necessary.

Deficit and surplus models of accountability

A major barrier to teacher improvement is the way we are held to account. We are asked to justify and explain why students failed to make the grade, and we are under pressure to make excuses and conceal mistakes to avoid being blamed. Instead of admitting that what we're doing doesn't appear to be effective, we shrug and say, "These things happen" and "What can you expect with kids like these?" Sometimes we blame specification changes or marking protocols: it must be the fault of the exam board, Ofqual, the Department for Education. I've heard failure blamed on timetabling, sports fixtures, room temperature and a litany of equally implausible excuses.

Once in an exam analysis meeting I attended, a school leader who taught in a particular department said that the reason the exam results in that department were so poor was because of their outstanding teaching. They concentrated on independent learning and refused to spoon-feed. This obviously meant kids did less well in tests.

We also have a distorted accountability relationship with data in schools that is not always honest or expert. Where mid-year data is used to tell leaders what they want to hear, and to show them what they want to see, it is not being used honestly or expertly as a meaningful and sufficient diagnostic and improvement tool. This in turn prevents the acquisition of sufficiently realistic knowledge to inform effective action.

If we want to improve as teachers, we have to acknowledge where we could be better. In a deficit model, poor performance is seen as an error or malfunction, as something requiring blame and correction. Precisely because most teachers work so hard and invest so much into their working lives, they are arguably more likely, not less likely, to respond poorly or avoidantly in a culture that trashes their best efforts and makes the examination of performance so high stakes. Perhaps the difference in education is not that it has particularly harsh accountability structures compared to a business model, but that those within education are so personally invested in their jobs and motivated by their purpose. For this reason, clumsy accountability mechanisms can easily cut to the heart of a self-critical teacher's self-concept.

Anybody who has worked for any length of time with teachers will realise that they are generally pretty responsible and self-critical human beings. It makes sense, if you think about it, that people who choose to spend their days educating young people within the framework of a school timetable are likely to be generally responsible and dependable; in the same way it makes sense that mountaineers are likely to enjoy fresh air, risk and adventure. What if teachers therefore avoid accountability, not because they are feckless and irresponsible but because they are intrinsically responsible and self-critical? For this reason, the imposition of a careless extrinsic accountability system can cause overload, anxiety and avoidance.

Therefore, teachers (and school leaders, come to that) do not need the imposition of a confessional or inquisitorial environment in which to 'acknowledge their errors', but an enquiring, responsive and realistic environment in which to reflect on questions such as:

- What worked sufficiently well?
- What didn't work sufficiently well?
- What could have worked even better?
- Why did this work here and not there?

To return to the concept of the truth creating freedom: where teachers are safe from blame they are more likely to be honest, to stop making excuses to you (and themselves) and to take responsibility for exploring what they might do differently and better. Arguably, it is only the power of the desire to avoid the sunk cost fallacy* and high stakes recrimination that can outweigh and distort the inherent motivation for improved mastery.

One positive change to school culture would be to replace the norm for using evidence to confirm our prejudices to using it to explore how we might think and act differently. This type of intelligent accountability benefits school leaders by allowing them to acquire sufficient realistic knowledge about what is working and not working, thereby improving their decision-making.

Morality and accountability

Unless we believe ourselves to be socially accountable, we are likely to put more effort into looking good than being good: what others think of us is more important than what we think of ourselves.

---

* A sunk cost is one that has already been incurred and cannot be recovered. The fallacy comes from investing more and more resources in a project in the hope that eventually it will be able to repay the investment, instead of cutting your losses and walking away.

You might think that having high self-esteem could insulate you from being overly concerned about the opinions of others, but you'd be mistaken. People who identify as having high self-esteem actually believe they stand high in the esteem of others – they think well of themselves *because* others think well of them. In an experiment, participants who identified themselves as possessing high self-esteem saw that sense of self deteriorate when they saw the unflattering rankings of a hidden audience as they spoke about themselves to camera.[3] As Jonathan Haidt puts it, "They might indeed have steered by their own compass, but they didn't realise that their compass tracked public opinion, not true north."[4]

We're only likely to display the right kind of character traits when we're held accountable for our behaviour by, as Adam Smith put it, an "impartial spectator". In *The Theory of Moral Sentiments*, Smith argued that morality emerges through a human desire to get on with others. When they're born, children know nothing of morality but discover, through trial and error, which behaviours are considered acceptable and which aren't, resulting in "a mutual sympathy of sentiments".[5] Most of us conform to social norms, and what is accepted quickly become acceptable. The rather uncomfortable truth is that morality stems from accountability.

Not all accountability is equal

Jennifer Lerner and Phil Tetlock define accountability as the "explicit expectation that one will be called on to justify one's beliefs, feelings, or actions to others … and implies that positive or negative consequences hinge on the acceptability of one's justification".[6] Without some kind of accountability we are more inclined to cheat or slacken. This is human nature. If no one is watching or interested, then we are much more likely to be selfish and lazy, and more likely to rely on snap judgements rather than carefully thinking things through.[7]

But, as we've seen, there are predictable problems with holding people accountable, especially in a deficit model system. Poor accountability is liable to result in compliance, resentment, powerlessness and self-justification. As Lerner and Tetlock put it, "accountability is not a cognitive cure-all for lazy or unresponsive workers" and "only highly specialized subtypes of accountability lead to increased effort".[8]

When accountability pressures are askew, 'looking good' is preferred to 'being good' (see Table 4.1).

Looking good	Being good
Getting high results.	Providing a rich and rounded education.
Being popular with students.	Trying to meet students' needs.
Performing well in observations.	Teaching what needs to be taught.
Being seen to plan elaborate lessons or policies.	Planning only what is required to teach effectively.
Keeping up to date with marking.	Keeping up to date with the quality of students' work.

Table 4.1. The differences between looking good and being good
Adapted from M. Evans, *Leaders with Substance: An Antidote to Leadership Genericism in Schools* (Woodbridge: John Catt Educational, 2019), p. 89.

How can we get accountability right? Research has focused on holding people to account for their decisions and actions under the following conditions:

- Whether the audience's preferences were known or unknown.[9]
- Whether the audience was interested in accuracy or expediency.[10]
- Whether the audience was well informed or naive.[11]
- Whether the subject was aware of being held accountable before or after a judgement was made.[12]
- Whether the subject was aware of being held accountable before or after committing to a course of action.[13]

By comparing the results of each these conditions, accountability is most likely to lead to positive behaviours and improved performance when:

1. We know we will be accountable to an audience before we are judged or commit to a course of action.
2. The audience's views are unknown.
3. We believe the audience is well informed and interested in accuracy.

When these conditions are met, people tend to do the right thing.[14] This is intelligent accountability.

We need both trust *and* accountability to bring out the best in teachers. The question we need to be asking is: how can we trust teachers to be good, instead of forcing them into looking good? Let's examine each of the three conditions above to see why they might be necessary and how to make them work in practice.

1. We must know we will be accountable before we are judged

The knowledge that someone – anyone – is aware of what we're doing changes what we deem to be acceptable. When we know we'll have to explain or justify our actions, we are much more likely to reflect self-critically, consider multiple perspectives, anticipate objections made by 'reasonable others' and revise our beliefs in response to evidence.

But, if we only find out we were accountable after the fact, trust is eroded. For accountability to feel fair, it must be preannounced; suddenly pitching up in someone's classroom with a clipboard and a stern glare only makes them feel like you're out to persecute them. The gotcha culture of unannounced learning walks can have a toxic effect on the trust necessary for teachers to thrive.

2. The audience's views must be unknown

In a hierarchical system, if everyone knows what the boss likes, she'll only be shown what she wants to see. If we look for evidence of our preferences, the best outcome is that we'll find what we were looking for. If those in authority predefine what good looks like and hold us to account for meeting a set of standards, we will give the appearance of meeting those standards. This results in equally undesirable outcomes:

- **Compliance.** Some people will just do whatever they are told to do. Some will do it well, some will give the impression of doing it well and others will struggle. They will assume managers know best and try hard to please them.
- **Pretence.** Some people will feel they know better and assume managers are foolish or corrupt. They will sometimes give the appearance of playing the game but will, as far as possible, ignore the accountability process.
- **Conflict.** If teachers are particularly contrarian, they may even deliberately emphasise lack of compliance to highlight their independence from 'management'.

Some of those who are successfully compliant will feel pretty good about being able to meet managers' demands, but everyone else will experience a combination of failure, guilt, fear and resentment. None of these emotions are particularly useful for helping individuals to grow and progress. The bitterest irony, though, is that even when these accountability systems appear to be successful, they promote a lack of curiosity and blind adherence to a set of partially understood principles and a mentality of being forced to jump through hoops. We lose the ability to make considered professional judgements and embark on 'cargo cult' teaching – following the forms and structures of teaching but without understanding the underpinning theory or science.[15] Managers who prefer uncritical staff reveal their own insecurities and weaknesses; you might not like teachers asking awkward questions, but this shows both that they care and are independent thinkers, something that we profess to believe is important in learning.

This model has a built-in insufficiency and goal displacement effect because it privileges compliance over expertise. Therefore, the collective of the organisation is diminished; decisions are not grounded in honesty and lack expertise and realism. Collective knowledge and responsibility are weakened and the weight of decisional capital rests on the narrow cliff edge of the leader's preferences. Instead of looking for our preferences to be met, if we look at what teachers are doing, sometimes we'll learn things we would never have expected.

3. We must believe the audience is well informed and interested in accuracy

Accountability needs to be seen as fair. Most teachers understand the need to be accountable for the performance of the students in their classes. They are, understandably, more reluctant to be held accountable for the student who never attends their lessons. Effective accountability needs to be reasonable and honest.

Unless we believe those holding us to account are interested in accuracy, rather than simply having their preferences met, we tend to become fearful, cynical and risk-averse. If those in authority are not considered trustworthy, the system starts to break down. This is exactly what happens when school leaders believe they're dealing with a 'rogue' inspector; accountability becomes a game where school leaders are forced into the role of recalcitrant children, hiding their perceived shortcomings, made to feel ashamed of failure, and desperately trying to prove their worth in a system that appears to lack honesty and therefore validity. This means that all our cognitive bandwidth is taken up with persuading others that we've made the right choice instead of trying to be our best.

Similarly, if teachers don't trust that school leaders are knowledgeable and genuinely interested in improving outcomes over the long term, they will be forced into the same game of cat and mouse. When we decide we know better than classroom teachers how they ought to teach their classes, we inevitably end up doing something foolish and ignoring the collective knowledge of the organisation. Instead, we should always ask teachers to talk about the reasons for the decisions they've made, and then listen. Often, teachers' explanations reveal things we might not have guessed. If explanations are plausible then teachers should be trusted; if they don't they may need additional support. School leaders should ask teachers what they think needs to be done, what support they need to make these things happen and then hold them to account for doing whatever they've said they should do.

A false dichotomy?

Human nature tends to create dichotomies; right or wrong, traditional or progressive, child centred or teacher led. Some dichotomies can be useful ways to frame a debate, but others close down the possibilities offered by alternative ways of thinking.

A false dichotomy is a logical fallacy committed when we present only two options when in fact there are others. Typically, we would then go on to construct an argument which demonstrates that anyone holding the 'only other option' is clearly delusional.

Here are some patently false dichotomies:

- Either you're for wearing school uniform or you're not.
- Either you have a fixed mindset or you have a growth mindset.
- If you don't believe that teachers perform best when they're trusted, you're part of the problem.

Each of these propositions presents what appears to be a rational choice but excludes other possible alternatives. Sometimes these are easy to spot, but this is not always the case. In the last example, we may be dazzled by the simplicity and utility of this finding and not stop to consider whether there are other possibilities worthy of examination.

But lazily brushing aside someone's considered opinion as being a false dichotomy allows us to ignore potentially important issues. The fact that there is a dichotomy, false or not, alerts us to something which requires further examination in order that we make the most informed choices possible. In one sense, all dichotomies are false in that they are just ways of viewing the world.

The problem comes when we try to compromise. In the spirit of taking the best of both, many people are committing what I've come to think of as the 'and fallacy': you can't always eat your cake and have it.* Some positions might really be mutually exclusive: Christianity and atheism, say. You could attempt to argue that there is a possible compromise between these positions but you would probably be wasting your breath. Or what about science and astrology? Science depends on testing theories with well-designed tests, while astrology requires no such proof to be considered efficacious – we just have to believe in it. It's no good just to dismiss this dichotomy by saying there's a time and place for both. There might well be a time and place for both, but these times and places exclude each other. They do not overlap.

Although you can always choose to do a bit of both A *and* Z, they will either be diluted or incompatible.

Figure 4.1. A false dichotomy?

The answer is rarely in the middle, but it can come from integration.

Maybe we could hold competing ideas in tension by viewing their development in three stages: thesis, antithesis and synthesis.

1. **Thesis:** An accepted way of seeing the world.
2. **Antithesis:** A challenge to the accepted paradigm.
3. **Synthesis:** A resolution of competing world views which holds each in creative tension.

The synthesis can then be challenged by a new antithesis. This is the iterative process through which we develop new ideas and make progress.

Trust vs. accountability

Let's examine how this approach to the dichotomous mindset plays out when considering how – or whether – teachers (or schools) should be held to account. There are some who have the misguided belief that any attempt to hold teachers accountable for their performance is wrong. Trust, they say, is the vital

---

* Obviously, having your cake and then eating it is child's play; eating and then having it presents far more difficulty.

ingredient. Others will argue that we need robust systems in place to make sure that everyone is doing their job and that no one is shirking their duty. These extremes can cause us to see trust and accountability as polar opposites:

Figure 4.2. Trust vs. accountability

On the face of it, trust and accountability may well seem to be dichotomous. Arguments polarise because the most interesting thinking often happens at the extremes. The middle ground is exactly that: the bland merger of two competing approaches where efforts to bestow trust and monitor performance end up cancelling each other out. The answer is rarely in the middle, but it can come from the integration of apparent opposites.

My suggestion is that we bend these competing concerns back on themselves to be held in creative tension:

Figure 4.3. Trust and accountability held in creative tension

Teachers – and school leaders – do need to be held to account for their decisions, but it's also true that both teachers and school leaders need the freedom to experiment and innovate if they are to be their best. We can combine the best of both of these extremes by holding teachers and school leaders to account for what they have said they will do instead of checking they are complying with what some else thinks is right.

1. **Thesis:** Teachers must be monitored and evaluated to make sure they are making effective professional judgements.
2. **Antithesis:** Teachers perform best when trusted with the freedom to explore how to be their best.
3. **Synthesis:** In order to make sure teachers are incentivised to be their best instead of looking good, they should be held to account for the trust they are given.

It should be clear that the aims of both teachers and school leaders ought to be aligned. Whatever else we might believe is important, everyone working within education wants children to be happy, healthy, safe and successful. There is no one working against these aims. However, how we go about trying to achieve them might be very different.

Let's agree that all teachers and school leaders want, at heart, the same things. The fact that in too many schools there exists an 'us and them' culture, where teachers and school leaders view each other as the enemy, is deeply regrettable. It may seem hopelessly naive to say that school leaders must trust teachers, but it's equally true to say that for a school to be successful teachers have to trust their leaders.

Perhaps the synthesis above could be further refined:

1. **Thesis:** In order to make sure teachers are incentivised to be their best, instead of looking good they should be held to account for the trust they are given.
2. **Antithesis:** School leaders should be accountable for ensuring that teachers are held to account in a way that values their professionalism.
3. **Synthesis:** Teachers and school leaders both want the best for the students in their schools, and for this to happen there must be mutual trust for which both groups must be accountable.

Making accountability intelligent

The biggest mistake we make when holding teachers (or anyone else) to account is telling them what 'right' looks like before the process begins. We're often at pains to say that this is the best way to mark books, teach lessons, manage behaviour or whatever else we want teachers to do. Now, let me show you how ... Then, when we go through a process of quality assurance, what we're actually doing is checking whether the teacher has marked their books, taught their lessons or managed their classes in the way we have told them to (see Figure 4.4). Although this does have the advantage of being relatively easy to check.

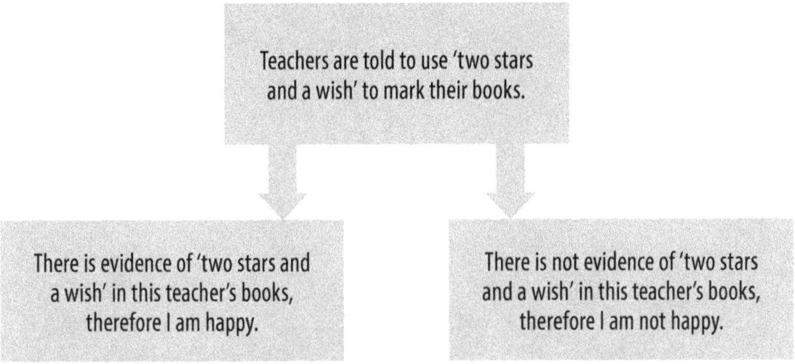

> Teachers are told to use 'two stars and a wish' to mark their books.

> There is evidence of 'two stars and a wish' in this teacher's books, therefore I am happy.

> There is not evidence of 'two stars and a wish' in this teacher's books, therefore I am not happy.

Figure 4.4. Poor accountability

We rarely stop to think whether there might have been a better way or whether the way we have operationalised is actually having the effect we wanted. Although there may be many excellent reasons for marking students' books, to date there has been no meaningful quantitative research on the best way to mark. Astonishingly, as a profession we have no idea whether there might be a 'best way' to mark or even if marking is worth the time and effort.[16] In many ways, educational research is in the same parlous state as medieval medicine. It makes sense for a doctor who believes in the four humours theory of disease to prescribe bloodletting, even though modern doctors now know that, in most cases, it's a terrible idea. But such doctors were victims of survivorship bias: they systematically ignored patients who didn't recover and focused on those who did. This strongly suggests that being overly prescriptive about marking policies is as likely to reduce students' outcomes as not.

Where we have compelling evidence that some education approaches are likely to be harmful they should be proscribed. Additionally, if a school leader believes there is real cause for concern that a teacher's actions are damaging their students, then they are obligated to intervene. It may also be true that the actions of an individual teacher place them in conflict with the explicit aims and values of a school community. These are all instances which require teachers to be treated differently and will be addressed in the next chapter.

A better accountability process might proceed as in Figure 4.5.

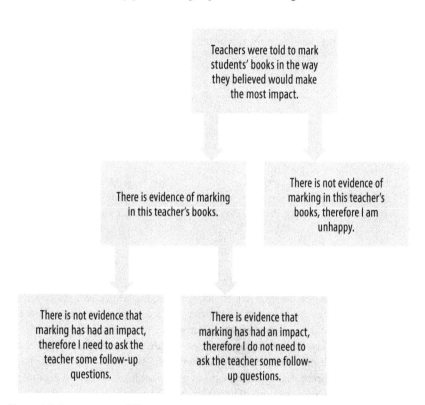

Figure 4.5. Better accountability

This process trusts that teachers will use their professional judgement to mark their students' books in the way they deem most efficient and effective. It acknowledges that the teacher might know better than the person holding them to account. However, it still assumes that a teacher must mark books in order to be a good teacher. Is this actually the case? How do we know? There are certainly some parts of the world where this isn't an expectation in the same way that it is in the UK.

An even better kind of accountability process for book monitoring might look like Figure 4.6.

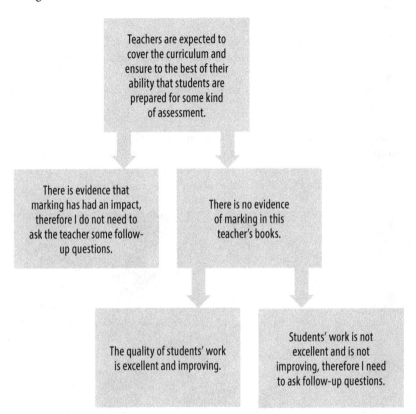

Figure 4.6. Intelligent accountability

Here, teachers are trusted to fulfil their responsibilities in the way they deem best. That may or may not include books being marked, but the teacher who chooses not to mark will be expected to justify the decisions they have made. If they give a reasoned and plausible answer, then we should wait to see what happens. If they say, "Well, I just couldn't be bothered," then we might need to remove some of the presumption of trust from the process.

In one school I have worked with, teachers were told that the school expected a minimum standard of grammatical knowledge. Teachers were asked to self-assess themselves, given a variety of means to address any deficit and told they would be held to account for their choices. Teachers were then left alone and trusted to act as professionals. This seems an eminently fair and sensible way to get what we want.

If schools were routinely led like this, teachers would not be forced into doing things which don't seem worthwhile, school leaders would be allowed to act more humanely and, maybe, it would result in a surplus model of school improvement in which happier, more autonomous professionals were trusted and respected.

In order to embed a system of intelligent accountability, we need to forego the need to compel teachers to do what we think is best in favour of allowing them to do what they think is best. But, wait, what about those teachers we can't trust? How do they fit into this? That is the subject of the next chapter.

Summary of Chapter 4

- Accountability processes can lead to unsustainable workload burdens that make it harder for teachers to be effective.
- If we are not held accountable for our behaviour, we are less likely to behave morally.
- Poor accountability processes result in teachers trying to look their best rather than trying to be their best.
- We are prone to thinking in false dichotomies. Instead of looking for weak compromises between competing extremes, we should be working out if polarised positions can be held in creative tension.
- Using the process of thesis, antithesis and synthesis can help us to make better decisions and arrive at stronger conclusions.
- Intelligent accountability makes teachers accountable for the trust we place in them.
- Accountability is intelligent if:
  - Teachers know how they will be held accountable before judgements are made.
  - The views of the people holding teachers to account are unknown.
  - Teachers believe that those holding them to account are well informed and interested in accuracy.

CHAPTER 5
EQUALITY, FAIRNESS AND AUTONOMY

It is better that some should be unhappy, than that none should be happy, which would be the case in a general state of equality.

Samuel Johnson, *The Life of Samuel Johnson* (1791)

What is fair?

In the interests of egalitarianism, we might suggest mothers and fathers should be allowed to take the same amount of parental leave after the birth of a child. At first glance, this might even seem fair, but it doesn't take much to see that women go through far more before, during and after childbirth; it's clearly fairer for them to have a longer leave of absence. Taken to extremes, the faulty logic which privileges equality over fairness would do away with wheelchair access, subtitles and guide dogs for the blind. After all, why should blind people get a dog if we can't all have one? Obviously, this conception of equality is as absurd as it is unfair.

Economist Stephen Moore argues that while economic policy needs to "help expand opportunities and raise the earnings of those stuck at the bottom", the welfare state might not be the most reliable way of going about this. Moore believes economic growth best advances opportunity and prosperity for the poor and middle classes. He says:

the free enterprise system is the on-ramp to economic progress and rising incomes ... [T]he poor are always and everywhere better off in economically free countries than in nations that are not free. So, in other words, if we judge society by how well it serves the poor, then free enterprise is far and away the greatest anti-poverty program known to man.[1]

Whether you accept this as a just economic position is one thing, but it does seem to be the case that all too often well-intentioned social policies which attempt to place equality before fairness end up perpetuating the very conditions they aim to solve. Why might this be?

There are times when people should be treated equally. In fact, there are laws to enforce it. Maybe the most useful way to think about this is to contrast equality of opportunity with equality of outcome. It's hard to argue that people should not have the same opportunities; in education, all teachers should have the same opportunity to be treated with respect and be given the same rights. Such things should not depend on inherent qualities possessed by individuals.

But, equally clearly, although all teachers should have the same opportunity to apply for a position, it doesn't follow that they're all equally likely to be appointed; being able to apply is an opportunity but getting the job is an outcome. The basic rule of thumb is that opportunities should be given equally, whereas outcomes should be based on what is most fair.

Many people believe differential pay causes resentment and envy within the workforce and ultimately lowers performance. For instance, if you work in a supermarket, everyone at the same grade gets paid the same regardless of their talents. Johannes Abeler and colleagues argue that, in fact, "the use of equal wages elicits substantially lower efforts" from workers.[2] Hard-working employees are infuriated at seeing their efforts go unrecognised and unrewarded. If everyone is paid equally, despite different experiences, efforts and expertise, everyone slacks off. Something similar happens in education.

This is not to argue that teachers should be paid differently – there's good reason to think that performance related pay has little or no effect in education[3] – but that they should be treated according to their means.

Balancing prescription and autonomy

If a school is judged to be good, it is treated differently to a school judged to be underperforming. We might quibble about whether these judgements are reliable, but the idea that schools should be treated according to their needs is well established. It's hardly a very great stretch to see that the same principle ought to be applied to teachers.

So, how might this work in practice? Despite the fact that it's much harder to identify good teachers than we tend to believe (see Chapter 6 for details), every head teacher I've ever spoken to has a pretty good idea who their most hard-working, trustworthy teachers are. More often than not they are confident that they know who needs to be supported and who can be trusted to think critically and follow the spirit rather than the letter of a policy. If all teachers were equally experienced, equally hard-working and equally effective then it would make sense to treat all teachers in exactly the same way. Obviously enough, all teachers are different. They are effective at different things. If we try to make all teachers do the same things we will, inevitably, reduce the effectiveness of very many.

Head teacher Matthew Evans presents a useful analogy:

Imagine a square, within which there is another, smaller, square shaded blue: the blue box. The blue box represents prescription and the larger white space within the square represents autonomy. How big is the blue box? What is in it? Why? A respectful accountability system engages teachers in a discussion about the blue box.[4]

Let's return to the example of the marking policy discussed in the previous chapter. While the most skilled and experienced of teachers should be left to make their own judgements of what best to do, the least experienced teachers will need some structure to prevent them from going astray. But, as with all scaffolding, the aim should be to remove this structure when it becomes unnecessary.

With this in mind, we announce our marking policy to all staff. We make it clear that the point of marking is to support students to engage with high quality content to their best of their ability. We also intend to ask teachers to self-identify how they want to be held to account from the following options:

1. No structure needed. Students' books to be reviewed after a four-week period, and if all is well, once per term thereafter. If there are concerns then the staff member will move to option 2.
2. Some guidance and support needed. Students' books to be reviewed once every four weeks. If, after a term, all is well, the staff member will be given the option to move to option 1. If there are concerns, the staff member will move to option 3.

3.   Clear guidance and regular support needed. Students' books reviewed fortnightly by a line manager. If, after a term, all is well, the staff member will be given the option to move to option 2. If there are concerns, the staff member's performance will be reviewed by a senior leader.

Everyone can choose to be in option 1, but you have to make the case that this is where you belong and then *earn the right to stay there*. It might be the case that an individual has made an inappropriate choice and you need to intervene from the outset. This requires clarity and straight-talking: tell them exactly why they have not yet earned the right to choose as they might wish and spell out precisely what they would need to do to earn that trust. Some teachers might make choices that give you pause for thought. So, pause and think! My advice is that when you are unsure you ought to extend the benefit of the doubt, but to be clear that teachers will be held to account for their choices.

Might this not be a more effective way to hold teachers accountable? As Aristotle never said, "The worst form of inequality is to try to make unequal things equal."[5]

Earned autonomy

We are obsessed with autonomy in education and a whole lot of unhelpful mythology has arisen about how vital it is for teachers' professional integrity. Right from the beginning of our careers, we are told that we know our students best and therefore only we should be able to make decisions about how and what to teach them.

It's not that this kind of professional freedom isn't to be welcomed, but that it has be balanced against responsibility and expertise. Early career teachers don't yet know enough to make wise decisions and, regrettably, this continues to be true for too many teachers throughout their professional lives. This is not due to any deficit inherent to teachers themselves, but because they are systemically failed.

Like all novices, new teachers need instruction to be matched to their level of proficiency. Rather than discussing how best to manage an unruly classroom, most new teachers need to be told – and shown – how to do it. A novice doesn't need to be introduced to a range of methods; they need to become proficient in one method. Then, having mastered this, they might have the bandwidth to experiment with other approaches.

At worst, new teachers are told nothing about effective instruction, and the best many get is the equivalent of window shopping: look at all the lovely things you could be doing. While teachers might argue that they want autonomy, a frightening number simply rely on downloading ready-made lesson resources with no sense of quality control.

The same is true of school leadership: leaders scour inspection reports or look to neighbouring schools and, through the process of mimetic isomorphism, blindly copy what they assume has been successful elsewhere with little or no understanding of how, why or even if what they're copying is likely to be effective in their own school. Again, this is not the fault of individual leaders; it is the result of a systemic failure to explicitly state what school leaders need to know. In order to earn autonomy – whether as teachers or as school leaders – we must demonstrate that we are educated enough to make consistently good bets.

We're not all the same – we have different talents, passions and failings. Some teachers need support in some areas, others will need support in other areas. When everyone is treated equally, some are given unfair and unnecessary advantages, while others are unable to participate. When people are treated fairly they are supported according to their needs.

Figure 5.1 neatly demonstrates the difference between fairness and equality.

Figure 5.1. Equality vs. fairness
Source: Craig Froehle.

When working out how we should treat teachers fairly, the most sensible approach is one of earned autonomy. There will be times when it's right and reasonable to remove freedoms and impose tight constraints in order to support those who struggle, but does it sound like a good idea to make *all* staff feel this way? Mastery should earn autonomy.

There is good evidence that people prefer fair inequality over unfair equality – inequality should be meritocratic. For instance, while we are happy to share windfalls equally, we resent equal sharing of anything that requires effort.[7] So, if all teachers are given an unexpected reward just because you're feeling benevolent, no one is likely to object. However, if all teachers are expected to work for a benefit but all are rewarded despite their unequal efforts, those who have worked hardest are likely to be the most resentful and those who have made least effort will think you're a mug.

For instance, some head teachers make the decision that all staff can pass through pay progression thresholds regardless of their efforts. What does this say to the most diligent staff? Will they feel their efforts are valued? And what will it say to those who haven't worked hard? We seem to have evolved an aversion to free-riders – individuals who take from the group without contributing – and, where groups are self-organising, free-riders tend to be penalised harshly. If schools treat everyone equally, regardless of perceived merit, it seems unlikely that such decisions will motivate anyone to be their best in the future.

But let's move away from financial incentives. What if the reward for hard work is greater trust and increased autonomy? What if, no matter how hard a teacher works, no matter how successful their efforts are, they are still expected to follow the same constraints designed to support the least effective teachers? These problems are avoided if teachers are allowed to earn autonomy. Teachers who, for one reason or another have not yet earned the autonomy to make their own decisions may not be happy, but they'll understand, especially if it's made clear how they can earn greater autonomy.

Earned autonomy is fair.

Of course, if we are working as part of collective within a school, with shared aims and values, complete autonomy is neither desirable or possible. The point is that while senior leaders often have a great deal of latitude about how they choose to spend their working day, classroom teachers have little or no choice.

Some of this is an inevitable result of how schools are run: if the timetable says you are teaching in period 1, you can't reasonably choose to do some curriculum planning instead. But just as senior leaders are trusted to make good choices about how they spend their time within the constraints they face, so too should teachers be able to earn the right to be trusted to make good choices about how best to teach their subjects to their classes.

Problems with performance management

Teachers sometimes spend so much time and effort proving what they have done or will do, that there is little space left over to actually do what needs to be done. In the one-size-fits-all approach to staff appraisal, everyone is treated according the lowest common denominator. If some staff don't mark their books then, in the interests of equality, everyone is scrutinised in the same way. But treating everyone the same isn't fair. If some colleagues need support, give it to them. If others merit freedom, they should have it. There will be times when it's right and reasonable to remove freedoms and impose tighter constraints, but when all staff are treated identically everyone is demotivated.

Daniel Pink argues that financial incentives don't really work when we're performing complex tasks like teaching.[8] He suggests that extrinsic rewards essentially lead to short-term thinking. They act to snuff out intrinsic motivation, diminish performance, crush creativity and encourage cheating, shortcuts and unethical behaviour. It's not just financial incentives that can backfire. When teachers are forced to work towards meaningless imposed targets over which they have little control – especially targets related to student outcomes – even if they meet those targets, they are unlikely to develop professionally because they won't know how (or even whether) their actions had any impact on outcomes. Teachers are much more likely to be motivated by autonomy, purpose and mastery.

Mastery is about getting better at something we feel is important and worthwhile. As we become proficient in the basics, tasks require less effort and become more enjoyable. Teaching requires persistence, determination, hard work and resilience in the face of setbacks; if the basics are mastered, teaching becomes easier and more enjoyable and teachers can work on refining ever more complex behaviours and routines. Performance management is much more likely to result in teachers thriving if it is centred on asking teachers what they want to work on and then, if they have earned the autonomy to be trusted, holding them to account for working on their priorities.

The greater the range of options teachers have in how to conduct their professional lives, the more invested they're likely to be in those choices. Classroom teachers necessarily lack choice about much of their working lives; they operate according to a strict timetable and have little or no choice about who and when they teach. Lacking autonomy is stressful. The more agency you have in how to divide up your time and prioritise tasks, the easier it is work effectively. Senior leaders have much more freedom to decide how to spend their time as their working day is gradually freed from the rigidity of timetabling. In contrast, teachers can rarely even choose when to have a cup of coffee or go to the toilet! This being the case, it makes sense to extend to teachers as much autonomy as possible at the level of what and how they teach – but, of course, this autonomy must be earned through trust. If teachers are given too much freedom before they've mastered the basics, there's a good chance they will make poor choices. The key to successful autonomy is intelligent accountability.

Purpose is what keeps us going. We need purpose as well as pleasure to feel fulfilled. When performance management targets are imposed on teachers, their professional life becomes a routine of continually being asked to reach for something that is both meaningless and out of reach. If we seek to motivate teachers with a combination of carrots and sticks, teaching is reduced to doing what you're told, covering your back and explaining why things went wrong. But if teachers feel a sense of purpose in sharing the breadth and beauty of their subjects, they are much more likely to work conscientiously and strive to improve, as well as being less burdened by anxiety. Having a purpose imbues teachers with the desire to improve for its own sake.

Suggestions for better performance management

- Performance management should be 'high challenge, low threat': teachers are most likely to improve when they are excited by challenges, trusted to make sensible choices and held to account for doing what they have said they will do.
- Be prepared: know the teachers you are responsible for as well as possible.
- Negotiate teachers' targets: if they have earned your trust, allow them freedom to choose how to develop; if they are still earning autonomy, insist on as few constraints and guidelines as is possible.
- Ask teachers what support they need and, where practical, provide it.

- Make sure targets can be achieved by teachers through their own efforts. Teachers should not be set targets relating to student outcomes because it is students who achieve these outcomes, not teachers.
- If teachers have not met their targets, ask them why. If they have made reasonable efforts but still fallen short, maybe they require more support or maybe the target was impractical.
- Always give credit for sincere effort.
- Consider setting team targets to encourage departments or groups to work together more closely and share expertise.

How to treat teachers fairly

Every head teacher or senior leader I've ever spoken to has a clear sense of which teachers they think are great and which they have concerns about. As such, it's very easy for school leaders to sort teachers into one of the four quadrants in Figure 5.2.

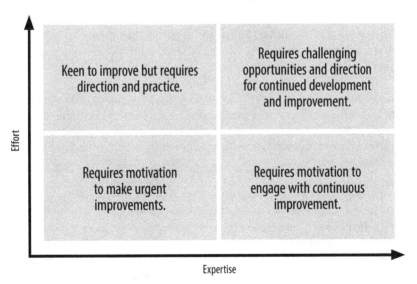

Figure 5.2. Teacher effectiveness matrix

Caveat: It's important to make clear that this is a very imprecise model. As the mathematician George Box reputedly said, "All models are wrong but some are useful." By placing an individual into one of these four broad quadrants, we shouldn't make the mistake of thinking that this is a static position. Individuals' performance may vary widely depending on the context. Furthermore, it has absolutely no statistical validity and ought never to be used in a punitive way or to hold teachers to account. Rather, it should only be viewed as a fast and dirty way of ascertaining how to help teachers at different point in their careers improve.

Let's consider each group in turn.

Top right: highly motivated, highly competent teachers

These teachers need both to be recognised and challenged. It's no good telling them they're outstanding and leaving it at that. Some who are considered outstanding stop improving just because no one is sure what to suggest. Others settle into self-satisfied complacency and overconfidence.

Andy Hargreaves and Michael Fullan and point out the dangers of 'balkanized' teacher cultures forming in schools made up of separate and sometimes competing groups:

> Innovative teachers who see themselves as being ahead of or above their colleagues can also segment themselves in ways that hinder whole-school development. Indeed, this is one of the classic reasons for the fading and failure of innovative schools and programmes over time – a sheer inability to manage envy![9]

The language of labelling in education is rarely, if ever, a good thing – whether we are labelling students or teachers. Remember the danger of personalising the activity. Just like children who exceed our expectations and deserve more than "Good work, keep it up", these teachers will continue to grow and develop if we provide new challenges and fresh horizons. Yes, of course, we want them to be involved in system improvement and to spread good practice, but only to the extent that we don't ask them to do more than they're currently doing.

Too often, the only solution is to promote highly effective teachers out of the classroom where their skills and knowledge are so badly needed. Maybe instead we need to consider how to keep them there as much as we can. They should be offered both challenging opportunities to develop and asked to embrace situations where they might struggle. Offer them secondments either within or outside the school; suggest sabbaticals to help them develop further; ask them to take on challenges outside their current area of expertise so they know what it's like both to fail and improve.

Top left: highly motivated but novice teachers

Teachers who already have the motivation to improve are a relatively simple nut to crack. Any school leader worth their salt already knows who they are; there is nothing to be gained from making them even less effective by scrutinising them further. If we're serious about helping these teachers to improve, we should think about what they're best at. Most support focuses on improving what a teacher is perceived to be bad at, and, consequently, is pretty dispiriting. What if instead we started by focusing on and growing teachers' individual 'bright spots'? Then we at least have a chance of getting them to believe they can be better. Dylan Wiliam points out that:

> it could well be that their students will benefit more by having their teachers become outstanding at things they are already good at, rather than worrying too much about weaknesses. The aim of professional development is not to make every teacher into a clone of every other teacher [back to the goal displacement effect of consistency] but rather to support each teacher in becoming the best teacher he or she can be.[10]

Before worrying about anything else, sort out the basics. If behaviour is a problem, senior leaders should take responsibility for the fact that children think it's acceptable to misbehave in any lesson in your school, no matter who the teacher is. In good schools this doesn't happen. Make sure groups are functional and that systems are in place to deal with problems; help teachers set up routines to ensure high expectations. Never, ever tell a teacher that poor behaviour is their fault. While it's true that a well-planned lesson can contribute to good behaviour, it is most certainly not true that good planning can solve behaviour problems.

We learn most by observing others and then having an opportunity to ask questions and discuss assumptions. If we want to help struggling teachers improve, free them up to observe colleagues. Absolutely don't expect them to do this in their limited non-contact time; senior leaders should cover lessons so that actual support is provided.

Use observations as an opportunity to explore mistakes. It's right that we should have the highest expectations, but this doesn't mean we should smash people when they fail to live up to them. We would never take this approach with children but it seems pretty standard with teachers. The message must be that it is OK to make mistakes. It is sometimes said that mistakes in teaching will cost lives. This is nonsensical and dishonest. We can all always try again and fail better next lesson. Supporting teachers with this message is more likely to lead to something sustainable rather than simply expecting them to get a 'good' at the end of a short-term intervention programme. School leaders need to take responsibility for showing people how to do something rather than just telling them how to do something.

Bottom right: highly competent but demotivated teachers

There are many teachers who are misunderstood and unappreciated. Maybe they're unable or unwilling to 'turn it on' for a one-off observation. Maybe their methods are out of step with the schools' views about the 'best' way to teach. Maybe their face just doesn't fit. Sadly, it's unlikely that any support will be useful if you're seen as too quirky, too out-of-place or just too long in the tooth. It is lamentably easy to destroy a good teacher through such 'support'.

These are teachers who, year on year, get great results. Parents love them and students acknowledge them as living legends. But maybe they roll their eyes in staff meetings. Maybe they've seen it all before, bought the T-shirt and can't be bothered to waste time doing it again. For senior leaders trying to introduce a new initiative, this can be annoying to say the least. But what if they're right? What if they have precious wisdom to share? What if they're so used to no one ever listening that they've given up trying to contribute? Hargreaves and Fullan suggest that "too often the sage criticisms of top-down leadership and quick-fix systems made by experienced teachers are dismissed as alienated grumblings of high-priced old curmudgeons".[11]

In many ways, these old lags are my favourite group of teachers with whom to work. They tend to be so used to being disregarded and overlooked that they may well be suspicious if you start showing your face in their classroom. You have to earn their trust by asking questions about their practice and making it clear you're there to learn. These teachers have a wealth of untapped expertise and you will learn much from listening to them. They are also likely to be some of the most honest individuals within the organisation because they are not tempted to act as echo chambers for management.

One of the most effective ways of working with this group of teachers is to shine a light on what they're doing well by making the rest of the staff aware of it. Send other teachers to watch and learn, praise them in staff briefings, and get them involved in new initiatives from the outset by asking them what has been tried before and what went wrong. (These are ideal candidates to involve in pre-mortem meetings.) These teachers often possess extremely healthy professional scepticism which should be encouraged (no matter how annoying you might find it!).

We should always remember the importance of mutual respect. Just as teachers need to respect the wider perspective of – and weight of responsibility borne by – senior leaders, leaders should never disrespect teachers because they choose not to be senior leaders. Mutual respect should be based on the fact that both groups care about their students and have their best interests at heart.

In terms of helping you to acquire sufficiently realistic knowledge to inform your decision-making, you can be fairly confident that – if you've got this group on board – what you are aiming for will stand a stronger chance of working.

Bottom left: demotivated, incompetent teachers

Some of these individuals are toxic and give us all a bad name. They don't mark their books, they resort to videos at the slightest provocation and they give kids a thoroughly raw deal. Thankfully, they're relatively rare, but I'm sure every school has one or two. And as with other categories of teachers, everyone will know who they are. How you decide to deal with them is up to you. Is it worth the effort of trying to save them or should they be fired as soon as is expedient? That's a judgement call. But we should work with everyone who is willing to improve. Simply forcing them out and giving them a glowing reference is just shuffling the deck and being dishonest. For the whole system to improve, we need these teachers to be better if they're planning to stay in education.

Caveat: The categorisation of teachers outlined above is fine for informal processes as long as they're coupled with the belief that all teachers can improve and that the school environment is one of the major factors shaping teacher effectiveness.

But we have no reliable mechanisms for reliably identifying effective and ineffective individuals (as we'll explore in Chapter 6). No matter how confident you may be that a particular teacher is ineffective, this must not be used to make high stakes judgements about pay or progression.

Trust and fairness

One point to note is that due to the hierarchal nature of schools, it's possible to do all of the above and still be unfair. The philosopher Immanuel Kant argued that we are all moral equals, with both rights and responsibilities. As such, we should all – teachers and leaders – be held accountable according to the same principles. As a school leader, you have the power to control teachers in ways that they cannot reciprocate. Intelligent accountability means that teachers should be held to account using principles that are suitable for everyone, leaders included.

This is a high bar. It's easy to argue that our particular circumstances are unique and that we should be excused for treating teachers unfairly. But if we are ever tempted to act in ways that those we have power over cannot, then we are open to accusations of bullying. To rise above this, we must explicitly reject any forms of coercion or intimidation.

In schools where trust has been eroded, it is often because senior leaders are acting on principles that cannot be principles for all. As Onara O'Neill puts it, "they breach and neglect fundamental duties and in so doing violate others' rights and undermine ... the placing of trust".[12]

When teachers feel victimised they are less likely to be honest about the problems they face; they will cover up their mistakes and shift the blame on to others, often students. They will refuse to speak their mind and any sense of professionalism will be eaten away. Far too many teachers work in schools where this is a daily reality.

It's hard to hear that your actions might result in teachers feeling victimised, but if you treat others in ways they cannot treat you, why would they ever place their trust in you? Upholding teachers' rights to be treated fairly is a responsibility of leadership. The corresponding responsibility for teachers is that they respect your right to give them reasonable instructions. The mechanism is precarious: if either side neglects their responsibilities, no one's rights are protected. In Table 5.1, teachers' and leaders' rights and responsibilities have been expanded to reflect the points made here.

	Teachers	Leaders
Rights	• To be treated with respect. • To be trusted as acting in the best interests of students. • To be held to account fairly, using principles applied to all.	• To be treated with respect. • To be trusted as acting in the best interests of the school. • To have reasonable instructions complied with.
Responsibilities	• To cooperate with all reasonable expectations. • To commit to continual improvement. • To be honest about mistakes and avoid blaming others.	• To remove all demands that get in the way of teachers teaching effectively. • To avoid coercion and intimidation. • To be fair in applying the principles of accountability.

Table 5.1. Teachers' and leaders' rights and responsibilities

Both teachers and leaders can be too passive in expecting their rights to be met. Leaders expect to exercise their right to tell teachers what to do; teachers expect their right to be treated reasonably will be respected. To have our rights respected we must first meet our responsibilities. Only when we are active in being professionally responsible can we ensure that trust and fairness are balanced.

Treat consistency with caution

Superficially, the idea that everybody should be singing from the same hymn sheet makes sense – a choir singing from different hymn sheets would create a cacophony – but if we stretch the metaphor a little we can see that while a choir may be singing the same hymn, different choristers will be singing different parts and in different keys. Their hymn sheets will be different. It's important to avoid the goal displacement effect and to remember that mastery and effectiveness, not consistency per se, are the desired outcomes. After all, who wants a consistency of mediocrity?

As Yuval Noah Harari puts it, "Just as when two clashing musical notes played together force a piece of music forward, so discord in our thoughts, ideas and values compel us to think, re-evaluate and criticise. Consistency is the playground of dull minds."[13] In Harari's view, inconsistency is the engine room of creativity and innovation. The ability to grapple with competing, contradictory ideas is the hallmark of maturity and sophistication.

However, Emerson expressed the idea better when he said, "A foolish consistency is the hobgoblin of little minds, adored by little statesmen and philosophers and divines."[14] It's not consistency per se that cause problems but foolish consistency. Hargreaves and Fullan suggest that "collaborative cultures require

107

broad agreement on values, but they also tolerate and to some extent actively encourage disagreement within these limits … because purposes, values, and their relationship to practice are always up for discussion".[15]

There's a delicate balance to be struck between giving teachers freedom and giving them constraints. If teachers have carte blanche to do as they please, the result might be chaotic. On the other hand, if teachers are simply expected to follow instructions the order produced may be stultifying. But if everyone is aligned towards a clear purpose, and if everyone understands their responsibility in fulfilling that purpose, individual eccentricities and divergent thinking can still result is better collective action.

Who knows how best to teach the Year 9 history curriculum to 9X3? Who's the expert at teaching phonics to Year 1? Who would you want to make decisions about what texts to choose for an A level literature class composed of students with a wide range of abilities? If, as a school leader, your answer is, "Me" or "I don't know", then shame on you. Although you should make every effort to become as expert as possible in every aspect of the curriculum, the (often unacknowledged) experts are experienced subject teachers.

Tacit knowledge and cargo cult teaching
Several years ago, I spent a day with a English department discussing how to improve the teaching of English. To most of the younger members of the department much of what I told them was new, unfamiliar and, dare I say it, exciting. One older teacher spent a good deal of the time staring at me quizzically. When I'd finished my presentation she came over for a chat. She told me that she already did many of the things I was suggesting but hadn't known she was doing them – she was 'just teaching'.

It became clear that she was considered a maverick by her head of department, a liability by some members of the leadership team and a legend by her students. What I found most fascinating was that whereas a lot of what I know is filtered through education theory and psychology, most of what she knew was tacit. She hadn't realised how much of an expert she was. As Dylan Wiliam points out, "this dimension of tacit knowledge has been shown to be important in a number of areas of expertise".[16]

One way towards greater consistency might be to get all the younger teachers to spend as much time as possible watching their more experienced colleagues to benefit from their wisdom and practical knowledge. However, there is a risk that junior colleagues end up mimicking their performance without understanding why what they see is successful. This can result in cargo cult teaching.

Cargo cults grew up on some of the Melanesian islands during the first half of the 20th century. Amazed islanders watched as Westerners arrived on their islands, built landing strips and then unloaded precious cargo from the aeroplanes which duly landed. That looks easy enough, some canny shaman must have reasoned: if we knock up a bamboo airport then the metal birds will come and lay their cargo eggs for us too. Despite the islanders' best efforts, no cargo arrived. Not only had they no understanding of global geopolitics and modern science, but they had fundamentally misunderstood the causal relationship between cargo and airports.

Richard Feynman famously appropriated the cargo cult metaphor to describe bad science. He referred to the social sciences as cargo cult science because "they follow all the apparent precepts and forms of scientific investigation, but they're missing something essential, because the planes don't land".[17] Melanesian islanders had lots of theories about how to attract cargo but made very little progress. As a result, most cargo cults died out fairly quickly because it was really hard to continue fooling themselves: the planes didn't land. We don't always have this advantage in education because, depending on the kind of 'cargo' we desire, it can be much easier to convince ourselves that it has arrived.

Many poor ideas are perpetuated because they *seem* to work – students are engaged, work is completed, feedback is given, classrooms are calm, questions have been asked and answered, the curriculum has been covered. These visible elements of teaching are often poor proxies for learning.

A teacher I once worked with observed the fact that I would address the class from different positions in the room at different points in the lesson. He decided to imitate this but, because he didn't understand why I did what I did, he ended up confusing the students as they tried to follow his random perambulations around the room. It became clear what had gone wrong after the lesson, but because I'd never really considered why I moved around the room, I was unable to explain why what I did worked and what he had done didn't. Much of teachers' – and leaders' – professional knowledge is tacit.

Once a skill has been acquired, we stop being able to see the joins between the items of knowledge that went into its creation. Our actions begin to feel intuitive and effortless. The more expert we become, the more invisible and automatic our skills become until, eventually, we are no longer able to see how we acquired them. Everything we know explicitly depends on a more tacit understanding. Eventually, we may start to believe that the skill which for us has become so natural and straightforward can be taught to others as a complete edifice. This is like presenting someone with a meal and telling them to cook their own without giving them the ingredients or a recipe. It's possible for another expert to see how this might be done, but frustratingly difficult for a novice. The idea that skill can be imparted without the hard work of teaching all the requisite knowledge is an illusion born from being unable to remember how we went about acquiring our own expertise.

In the case of the teacher I'd been working with, once he started to mimic me in moving around the classroom, he found it difficult to stand still in one place. Eventually, I duct-taped an X on the floor and told him he must 'master the X' before he was allowed to move anywhere else. This seemed to help.

The point is, no matter how excellent our model, getting all teachers to act with consistency may be a conveniently straightforward way to check compliance, but it's likely to backfire when applied thoughtlessly. Some teachers are sufficiently expert that it's sensible to allow them to experiment and innovate. Other teachers need to be told what to do because they haven't yet mastered the basics. Consistency – making all teachers do the same things regardless of their level of expertise – inevitably reduces all to the lowest common denominator.

Making consistency work

One way to ascertain the effectiveness of a school's leadership is to check to what extent teachers are following school policies. If teachers are found to be following policies, then apparently the school is considered well led. Not unreasonably, this might lead some to conclude that the most effective way to run a school is to mandate what teachers should be doing and then enforce compliance through lesson observations and book audits. This would be a mistake.

Firstly, this approach falls into the error of unintelligent accountability explored in Chapter 4. As a model, it has a built-in insufficiency and goal displacement effect because it privileges compliance over intelligence. Once again, the collective knowledge of the organisation is diminished; therefore, decisions are not grounded in honesty and lack expertise and realism. Collective knowledge and responsibility are weakened. Secondly, it runs the risk of over-sufficiency which wastes organisational time and reduces the autonomy and mastery of teachers.

While it might seem reasonable that teachers should be held to account for carrying out agreed tasks, who gets to decide that these tasks are worth carrying out? We should always negotiate what is non-negotiable. If teachers don't know why they're being asked to work 60 hours a week (and worse, if school leaders don't know either), then surely it's reasonable to negotiate? Should English teachers have same set of expectations as PE teachers? Should all maths teachers be treated equally? Who says so? Unless you're prepared to negotiate what's non-negotiable, you're no better than a thug wielding a cudgel.

Focusing on the process rather than the outcome results in goal displacement and increases the risk of learned helplessness. Where the emphasis in a school is on processes rather than outcomes, it becomes inadvertently or deliberately focused on compliance rather than mastery. Of course, there are those who will argue that compliance leads to mastery, but they are at risk of a forming false syllogism.

Mastery in any complex activity tends to require knowledge and independent critical thought – the professional scepticism referred to in Chapter 1. It is therefore unlikely that thoughtless compliance will lead to mastery. This explains the 'mystery' of why non-compliant teachers tend to (inconveniently) gain good results.

Accountability for process will lead to people following a process. This will improve outcomes only if you know for sure that the process will lead to the desired outcome. In contrast, accountability for outcome is more likely to lead directly to the desired outcome.

Aim to be a 'responsive' leader when seeking collective organisational knowledge: ask teachers what they think – as graduate professionals they really ought to have something to offer. Suggest some ways of working and ask them to think critically about what might not work or be unrealistic. Anyone considering asking teachers to change what they do should read the list of ideas on page 30–34 and encourage teachers to ask thoughtful, intelligent and awkward questions. If these questions aren't asked at the outset, it's harder to avoid the best case fallacy.

Rather than all teachers doing everything in the same way, what most sensible school leaders want is that all teachers take a consistent stance concerning the aims and values of the school. Diversity of opinion is a strength – there's plenty of room within the system for all sorts of schools to flourish – but institution level alignment matters. Leaders need to be clear about what they stand for, seek consensus from staff, make the most intelligent and educated bets available, and remain humble enough not to get sucked into sinking additional costs into failing ideas.

Imposing consistency invites dissent and division, whereas aligning your actions to shared beliefs and values is more likely to result in the kind of consistency that helps teachers to thrive.

The process of seeking alignment
- Senior leaders determine the aims and values of the school.
- Consensus is sought by explaining the rationale behind these decisions.
- Constructive criticism and professional scepticism are encouraged so that weak points can be identified in advance.
- Best bets are selected to advance the agreed values and purposes of the institution.
- Middle leaders – if they have earned autonomy – are trusted to interpret these bets with their teams in the ways that best suit their areas of responsibility. If they have not yet earned this autonomy, they are supported in doing so.
- Teachers are trusted to implement the approaches that have been agreed that best suit their students. If they have not yet earned this autonomy, they are supported in doing so.
- Everyone is held to account for what they have agreed is the best way of implementing the shared aims and values of the school.

When teachers are allowed to earn the autonomy to develop and apply their own expertise, they are more likely to be invested in the decisions to which they contribute than those that are made remotely and handed down without negotiation. Teachers, and especially subject leaders, really ought to be more expert in their subjects than senior leaders.

Allowing each subject leader to determine, in consultation with their team, the most effective approaches in their subject area is likely to be a good bet. When teachers have been consulted and consensus sought, compliance is less likely to be an issue. Of course, that is not to say that subject leaders are not capable of dreaming up doctrinaire, workload heavy policies and procedures, but when the principles of intelligent accountability are combined this becomes less likely. If subject leaders earn the autonomy to be trusted and then held to account for this trust, all should be well.

Even where alignment has been sought and the principles of intelligent accountability applied, some things are more likely to benefit from being negotiated than others. Essentially, where a choice is binary – either a thing is done or it isn't – it might profit from being a non-negotiable fact of school life, but where choices distribute along a continuum – a thing can be done well or badly – it is likelier to gain from being negotiated.

Head teacher Michael Tidd says:

[C]hoosing a blunt tool such as 'non-negotiables' to tackle … poor performance is both a weakness of leadership and a barrier to excellence for those teachers who work day-in, day-out to achieve their best for their students. For every poor teacher who will use the loophole, there are many, many more who are weighed down by rules which prevent them from providing even better feedback, or planning even better lessons.[18]

If you do an internet search for 'non-negotiables in schools' you'll find some quite extraordinary lists of things which are considered non-negotiable, but in practice would be either impossible or foolish to do in all instances. Table 5.2 is a suggested list of the sorts of things which could be non-negotiable and things which really should be negotiated.

Can or should be non-negotiable	Should be negotiated
Teachers are punctual for lessons.	How teachers begin a lesson.
Teachers uphold the school's rules.	How questions are asked.
Senior leaders support teachers in upholding the school rules.	Whether lessons should end with a plenary.
All staff interact politely and respectfully.	How lessons are planned.
Entry and exit routines into classrooms are orderly.	How feedback is given to students.
High standards of behaviour are expected.	How students' work is marked.
Students follow teachers' instructions.	The content of lessons.
Statutory obligations are followed.	How policies are interpreted.
	How work is displayed in classrooms.

Table 5.2. Things which should and should not be negotiated

Teachers will have signed up to do what is best for their students in their subject areas. Thoughtless consistency makes for a dull, repetitive rhythm. Instead, we should embrace the potential of discord, dissonance and uncertainty. Often harmony, or at least euphony, relies on thoughtful discord.

Treating teachers equally comes with a huge opportunity cost. Being fair is hard. Anything you ask teachers to do just for the sake of accountability is time that cannot be spent doing something more worthwhile. Although setting up a surplus model and trusting teachers to make the most of the support we provide and to work towards being the best they can be is scary, it's the only way that school improvement can be made sustainable.

Having explored each of the principles of intelligent accountability, in the following chapter we turn our attention to the specifics of how we might go about helping teachers to improve.

Summary of Chapter 5

- Although the aims of equality are well intentioned they inevitably result in people being treated unfairly.
- Treating teachers fairly means giving them the support and freedoms they need to be most effective.
- The more teachers are trusted, the greater autonomy they ought to be allowed.
- Autonomy must be earned; it should be clear to all teachers how it can be earned.
- Teachers can be loosely categorised according to perceptions about their effort and expertise: high effort and high expertise, low effort and high expertise, high effort and low expertise, low effort and low expertise.
- There is no sufficiently reliable process to confidently identify the most or least effective teachers: remember that you should cultivate uncertainty and embrace your ignorance.
- Rights and responsibilities must be balanced; teachers and school leaders must be subject to same principles of accountability.
- Consistency can be overrated; negotiate your non-negotiables.
- It is more reasonable to make some things non-negotiable than others: anything that requires teachers' judgement and expertise is best left negotiable.

CHAPTER 6
IMPROVING TEACHING

The art of progress is to preserve order amid change, and to preserve change amid order.

Alfred North Whitehead, *Process and Reality: An Essay in Cosmology* (1929)

Improving the quality of teaching – both *how* teachers teach and *what* they teach – in schools is one of our best bets for improving the quality of education. Effective teaching here should be taken to mean that teachers make intelligent decisions about how to ensure students learn what they intend them to learn. As we'll see, a big problem with many approaches to school improvement is that identifying effective teachers is far less straightforward than is often supposed. The deficit model approach is to get rid of ineffective teachers and replace them with better ones. However, even if we knew how to identify effective teachers before they joined the profession (we don't), by attempting to get rid of the least effective current teachers we would, inadvertently but inevitably, end up firing a significant number of the most effective teachers.

As outlined in Chapter 2, if we were to shift our thinking slightly and say instead that it's not the quality of teachers but the quality of *teaching* that makes a difference, we might think and behave differently.[1] There is, as Graham Nuthall has argued, no such thing as a universally good or bad teacher.[2] Any teacher can teach badly and most can teach well. Teachers are not equally effective with all students. Context matters. A few teachers have the good fortune to thrive within deficit models, but many more are ground down and spat out. While all teachers will never be equally effective, many more would be likely to thrive in a surplus model.

One of the great advantages of thinking in terms of teaching rather than teachers is that we are more likely to stop looking for – or at – individuals and instead start thinking about behaviours and the activity of teaching. If our purpose is not to evaluate teachers' performance but instead to help them improve, then the tools of accountability start to look very different.

But let's begin by reviewing some of the evidence on identifying effective teachers.

Do we know who the best teachers are?

Obviously enough, not all teachers are equal. Studies have found that who you are taught by matters. For instance, if teachers are divided into three groups (more effective, average and less effective), students taught by the most effective third of teachers make 40% more progress than those taught by the average teachers, whereas students taught by the least effective teachers make 30% less progress. Students taught by the most effective teachers make twice the progress of those taught by the least effective teachers.[3]

Another study compared student outcomes over a 12-year period and found that students taught by effective teachers made 50% more progress in maths and 40% more progress in reading per year than those taught by average teachers.[4] The most effective teachers are, on average, four times as effective as the least effective teachers. If students are assigned to 50 different teachers all teaching the same subject, those taught by the most effective teachers will learn in six months what those taught by average teachers will learn in a year. Students taught by the least effective teachers would take two years to learn the same content.[5]

Such findings make the deficit model seem much more appealing. Surely, things would improve if we just got rid of the bottom third of teachers and replaced them with effective teachers? This is all well and good, but how would we go about it? Perhaps we could raise the entry requirements for teacher training and turn away the bottom third of all new entrants to the profession? Such a policy could, over a 30-year period, make a significance difference to students' outcomes.[6] Sadly, as yet, no one has been able to work out how to identify more and less effective teachers in advance. In an interview situation, a coin toss would result in hiring the best candidate 50% of the time; using the most robust predictive analyses we could perhaps improve this to 57%.[7]

So, how do we know which ones are any cop? As we saw in the previous chapter, everyone in a school community thinks they know who is doing a decent job. And, in fact, this hunch is borne out by research. When head teachers are asked to rate the effectiveness of their staff on a scale of 0 (inadequate) to 10 (exceptional) the average rating is just over 8, with around 10% of teachers being rated as less than 6.5 and about 10% rated as 10. When head teachers' hunches are matched against sophisticated, long-term value-added measures of students' progress, it turns out that head teachers are around three times more accurate than could be accounted for by chance. And when it comes to identifying the least and most effective teachers, the results are even better.[8] But the depressing truth is that, despite this, head teachers are still wrong far too often to justify high stakes decisions (and the world of employment law does not lend itself to hunches, even when these are relatively knowledgeable and realistic).

Contrary to our intuitions, while we have robust evidence that on average some teachers are more effective than others, we have no real way of identifying with sufficient evidence who the most and least effective individuals are. By placing teachers into four categories ('most effective', 'above average', 'below average' and 'least effective') and then tracking student outcomes from year to year, we know that 57% of teachers judged to be least effective in one year will be also be least effective in the following year. But 20% will be either most effective or above average. Conversely, 36% of teachers judged to be most effective in one year will still be equally effective next year, but the exact same percentage – 36% – will be below average or least effective in the following year.[9]

Other studies provide similar findings. For instance, by comparing different modelling techniques for analysing value-added data, 9% of teachers identified as being least effective under a traditional random effects model are rated as most effective using a fixed effects model.[10] Similarly, 4–15% of teachers rated as most effective in one year are identified as least effective in the following year.[11]

While these percentages are far greater than those produced by random chance, they are woefully insufficient for making high stakes decisions about pay or employment.

The input/output problem

The problem with using exam results to judge teachers is that results are achieved by children, not teachers. We have a natural tendency to look for explanations in the stable characteristics of individuals and to underestimate situational variability, which may lead us to over-interpret value-added measures as a property of the teacher.[12] For instance, those teachers who teach the highest attaining students are significantly more likely to perform well in value-added measures, and are more than twice as likely to be judged favourably in classroom observations.[13] Essentially, teachers perform better on all metrics when assigned higher performing students to teach. The fact that teachers are often assigned classes on a non-random basis further biases estimates of teachers' performance. This can lead to a vicious downward spiral: if you are given lower performing students to teach, you will, on average, perform worse on estimates of your own performance and, subsequently, will be more likely to be assigned lower performing students.[14]

Students' performance tells us relatively little about what a teacher has done. There are some children who will make limited progress whatever you do and some who will fly despite you. Teaching is leading the horse to water; learning is having a drink.

As Graham Nuthall has observed:

Student learning is a very individual thing. Students already know at least 40–50% of what teachers intend them to learn. Consequently they spend a lot of time in activities that relate to what they already know and can do. But this prior knowledge is specific to individual students and the teacher cannot assume that more than a tiny fraction is common to the class as a whole. As a consequence at least a third of what a student learns is unique to that student, and the rest is learned by no more than three or four others.[15]

Teacher input does not inexorably lead to student output. Despite teachers' best efforts some students won't learn. Students will react to teaching in their own individual ways. It seems not to matter what teachers do. Sometimes students are keen to learn and anxious to please; sometimes they're not. Clearly, teaching must have some effect on student outcomes but quantifying its impact is extraordinarily difficult, with some estimates suggesting teaching probably only accounts for around 30% of the variance in such outcome measures.[16]

Dylan Wiliam uses the analogy of a set of weighing scales that is accurate to plus or minus 50 pounds. If we used these scales to weigh a group of teachers, we'd have enough information to see that some teachers are, on average, heavier than others. We'd even be able to see that male teachers are, on average, heavier than female teachers. But we'd be nowhere near able to identify the precise weight of any individual teacher.[17]

Natural volatility

In addition to all this, we have the problem of natural volatility. One of the most beguiling assumptions in teaching is that children succeed in school because of what schools and teachers do. We feel this to be true because we're acutely aware of all the things we've done: all the hours of teaching, marking, planning, pastoral support and everything else we do. We *just know* these things are what make the difference to young people's lives.

Typically, schools spend a good deal of time looking at data. Our assumption that we're making a positive difference is based on the idea that if the numbers go up, we're making more of an impact and if they go down, our impact is less. This is very intuitive but also highly problematic. There is plenty of evidence that the ratio of signal to noise makes it meaningless to describe schools or teachers as effective by analysing data.[18] The concept of 'natural volatility' is well established, but is all too often unknown in schools.

Amanda Spielman, now head of Ofsted but formerly the chair of Ofqual, presented the following data at the 2014 researchED conference:

Subject	Standard deviation of change in % A*–C, 2013–2014
Single sciences	9–10
Mathematics	12
Geography and history	13
English literature	14
MFL	14–15
English language	15.5
Science/additional science	18–19

Table 6.1. Volatility in GCSE subjects, 2013–2014

That results are subject to natural volatility essentially means that results can go up or down (sometimes by as much as 19%[19]) and have absolutely nothing to do with actions taken by teachers or school leaders.

There will always be uncertainty about three things: (1) how individual students will perform in examinations, (2) how particular cohorts are composed and (3) how school populations change over time. This means we can never be sufficiently sure that results going up or down can be attributed to school or teacher effects. Sometimes – often – stuff just happens. Natural volatility is both well known and predictably unpredictable.

Unless a school consistently records 100%, there will never be a meaningful pattern in any historical data. This is because the information is based on children's results, and children are complicated and individual and the population in any given school is too small to make meaningful generalisations. Long-term trends in something as complex as educational outcomes are always random.

What does your data tell you? Not as much as you think it does.

Could students be achieving successful outcomes despite what you're doing? Very possibly. Rather than looking to the false reassurance of positive data trends, we should instead think about other sources of information. For instance, everyone knows there is a gap in performance between students of different socio-economic profiles. According to the Organisation for Economic Co-operation and Development, a student's socio-economic profile is the factor most likely to affect outcomes – the wealthier a student's background, the more likely they are to do well.[20]

Now look again at your exam data: how are the very poorest students doing? The likelihood is that most of your positive results derive from those students most likely to do well regardless of anything you did. Results could even be due to students receiving additional tuition. The Sutton Trust's report *Extra Time* notes that "private tuition is the hidden secret of British education. Within an educational 'arms race' that entrenches advantage for those who can afford private school fees or homes close to good comprehensives and grammars, it has remained largely in the shadows."[21] Equally, the positive performance of the least advantaged is more likely to be due to teacher and school effects – left to their own devices, and without recourse to additional tuition, these students are much more likely to fail.

Now, how confident are you that you're doing the best for these students?

We might improve what we do in schools if we assumed:

1. The factor most likely to influence children's educational attainment is their socio-economic profile.
2. Schools systematically privilege the most privileged and disadvantage the least advantaged.

3. The success of children from more advantaged backgrounds is just as likely to be despite, not because of, actions we've taken.

These assumptions may not be true – and they're certainly not fated – but, in the spirit of professional scepticism, they are healthy to make.

If the performance of the children from the most disadvantaged backgrounds seems to be steadily improving, then maybe we can infer that what we're doing really is making a genuine difference. If their performance is static or on a downward trend, we ought to assume that we're not serving any of our students well.

Students' socio-economic profiles are just a proxy. How much your parents earn does not directly cause you to do better in examinations. To really think about how we might better serve students we need to consider what the proxy represents. In my view, the most significant difference between students is the quality and the quantity of what they know. Children from wealthier backgrounds are statistically more likely to have greater knowledge of the world, and it is this background knowledge that is strongly predictive of GCSE results.

Improving exam results is not the same as improving teaching

One final point to make about using teachers' test scores to judge their effectiveness is that we are unlikely to improve teaching by seeking to raise test scores. Examination results are a proxy for what students have learned. A percentage or a grade tells us relatively little about the specifics of what students can and cannot do. What these numbers are good at telling us is how students have performed relative to each other.

The aims of education should relate to students' mastery of curriculum content, not to the grade they are awarded for having done so. But, as ever, the knife-edge of unintelligent accountability makes it difficult for schools to focus on what really matters. The grades and numbers consume us and we lose sight of what they are meant to represent. When this happens, the temptation to 'game' results can be overwhelming; after all, if school leaders are held to account for the wrong things, then no one should be surprised that perverse incentives drive unethical behaviour.

The messy narrative of what children are actually learning is so much harder to measure than a percentage or grade. Nevertheless, we still attempt to measure it and the judgemental observation of lessons is an almost ubiquitous element of educational life.

The problems with lesson observations

Although much progress has been made since Ofsted finally stopped judging lessons in 2014, there are still schools – labouring under the misapprehensions of the deficit model – where observations of teachers' lessons are used to make judgements about their effectiveness.

Of all the imperfect methods we could use to evaluate teacher effectiveness, graded lesson observations are the least sufficient and most unreliable. The multi-million dollar MET Project (which has utilised much more rigorous training and externally validated observation protocols than it would ever be possible to replicate in schools) has made some worrying findings: if a lesson is given a top grade by one observer, there is a 78% chance that a second observer will give a different grade. And if a lesson is given a bottom grade, there is a 90% chance that a second observer will give a different grade![22]

Worse, receiving a favourable judgement from a lesson observation doesn't seem to correlate well with actually being an effective teacher. Michael Strong and colleagues found that fewer than 1% of lessons judged inadequate are genuinely inadequate when compared to the value-added scores of students in these teachers' classes. Additionally, only 4% of lessons judged outstanding actually produce outstanding learning gains. Overall, 63% of judgements will be wrong.[23] We would get a more statistically valid and less biased assessment if we flipped a coin. At least that would be fairer. When lessons are graded, the observer looks for those things she approves of and is critical of anything else, regardless of the impact on students.

Charlotte Danielson's Framework for Teaching[24] is often cited as a way to improve observation, but, like all such scales, it quickly runs into difficulties. One of Danielson's scales is 'Engaging Students in Learning' which makes judgements on degrees of students' initiative, self-direction and expression that are ultimately used to determine a teacher's level of effectiveness. As Eric Kalenze says, "for a teacher's rating to progress up and up through this domain element's levels of performance, students must be observed exercising more and more control of the classroom environment. (If we take this to a logical conclusion, the perfect Danielson teacher is one who does no actual teaching whatsoever.)"[25]

Lesson observers are also likely to overestimate the importance of the role of teachers' fundamental character traits and underestimate the importance of the situation and context.[26] We tend to reach for a dispositional explanation for events, as opposed to a contextual explanation. We like to believe that we're objective and reasonable in the way we treat others, but it's incredibly difficult to evaluate teachers' performance in a way that is both valid and reliable. It's so much easier to go with our gut and assume we *just know* who is good and who requires improvement.

This kind of labelling is a seductively simple shortcut to explaining complexity. But the way we act is at least as dependent on the circumstance we're in as the people we are. Is a teacher effective because they feel supported, or are they hard-working and talented? Might a teacher be ineffective because they feel under threat, or are they feckless and unprofessional? It's relatively easy to do well when everyone around you is supportive and believes in you – success breeds success – and it becomes easier to think of some teachers as outstanding than to honestly scrutinise their performance. Likewise, reputations can be easily crushed. If a member of staff is perceived as underperforming, how do we react? Do we give them our trust and support? Or do we put them on capability?

Effective classroom observation

Despite the evidence which indicates that classroom observation may be a poor means of establishing teacher effectiveness, when conducted in a high trust environment it can be a valuable means of professional development.

In fact, there are compelling reasons to believe that observations are crucial to teachers' development. Susan Rosenholtz's study of 'moving' and 'stuck' schools found that teacher isolation and uncertainty were associated with 'learning impoverished' settings where teachers learned little from their colleagues.[27] If teachers do not have the opportunity to routinely see – and be seen by – their colleagues it's not hard to see how they can become professionally isolated.

Before discussing how to make classroom observation more effective we need to refocus on what it means for accountability to be intelligent.

Principles of intelligent accountability
1. We must know we will be accountable before we are judged.
2. The audience's views must be unknown.
3. We must believe the audience is well informed and interested in accuracy.

As long as these are held in mind when planning, enacting and following up on observations, all should be well. Beyond that, the following advice may also be useful.

'Looking at' not 'looking for'
When we enter another teacher's classroom looking for certain elements to be present, we warp our ability to see what's going on. What's more, if teachers know what we're looking for, then we violate the second principle of intelligent accountability. Instead, if you're in the privileged position of being able to observe a fellow professional, go in with the mindset that you are there to learn: be responsive rather than directive. Look at what is happening and make notes about what you see and questions that arise. When you have the opportunity to discuss the lesson with the teacher, the discussion should be framed using questions like these:

- Why did you ...?
- Were there any surprises?
- How might you have done that differently?
- Can you explain what was happening when ...?
- Were you aware of ...?
- What do you think the impact of X might be?
- Where does this lesson fit into your sequence of teaching?
- What have students done in order to get to this point?
- What did they already know?
- How will you develop what students have done so far?
- What will happen next lesson in light of this lesson?
- How do you know if students are making progress?

Using *any* kind of generic observation checklist is "not even wrong".[28] Even if you have ironclad evidence that you're looking for the right things, you're missing the point. Rob Coe and colleagues observe that "effective pedagogy ... [consists] of more than just a set of classroom techniques, but ... [depends] on the ability to make complex judgements about which technique to use when".[29] The point is this: how teachers teach is only the tip of a very large iceberg; the question of real importance is whether *how* they're teaching is matched to *what* they're teaching. As Michael Young explains:

> It is why the term pedagogy, which describes the professional practice of teachers, is so important but so often undervalued ... pedagogy refers to the theory and practice involved in taking students beyond their experience and helping them to acquire new knowledge. ...
>
> It is the knowledge that teachers want students to acquire that defines the curriculum, how they do this is what we refer to as pedagogy and how they reflect on whether they are successful is always part of any teacher's pedagogy.[30]

Actually listen to the answers and try to learn from them. If the teacher being observed asks for or is interested in your opinions, wait for them to ask you. Otherwise, try to keep your judgements to yourself. This is hard, but if you accept the reality that you are not necessarily the expert you think you are and that the teacher you've observed will know their class and their subject better than you, all should be well. At some point you might be tempted to share what you would have done. Resist this temptation. It is a pointless piece of self-indulgence to try to download your preferences as 'expertise' on to another teacher. They won't thank you for it, it won't change their practice and it's probably unhelpful.

Make it reciprocal

We learn more from observing than we do from being observed. It's also generally true that those who observe most teach least. Therefore, the most useful thing school leaders with lighter teaching loads can do is to use their time to cover colleagues so they can observe each other. Why doesn't this happen? Because we're obsessed with the idea that 'we know best'. But even if this is true and we do actually know best, what benefit is that to the teachers we lead and the students for whom we are responsible? If we're serious about professional development, we need to lay the groundwork for an enquiry model of observation which allows teachers to investigate and reflect on aspects of their own teaching.

If classroom observation is reciprocal – I'll watch you, you watch me – then we remove the power imbalance of being the observer and the observed. This not only makes the coaching process much more collaborative, but it also builds the trust teachers need to fulfil the third principle of intelligent accountability.

Susan Rosenholtz's study of 'moving' and 'stuck' schools found that teacher isolation and uncertainty were associated with "learning impoverished" settings where teachers learned little from their colleagues.[31]

Show, don't tell

Explaining something to someone who doesn't share your knowledge base is challenging and all too often results in vague maxims and proxies which necessarily omit the crucial details that need to be demonstrated rather than explained. But if we show teachers how they could improve, rather than simply telling them what to do, we sidestep the difficulty of being unable to put our expertise into words.

We are well aware of the benefits of modelling new ideas and procedures with students, but we rarely apply the same principle to teachers' professional development. If teachers have an opportunity to see effective teaching modelled by another teacher, they are more likely to understand how new techniques can be implemented.

In addition, watching someone else teach your class can be much more interesting and instructive than observing another class being taught: teachers can spot dynamics of which they were only peripherally aware and make connections that are only half-formed. When teachers watch someone else teach their class, things that seemed mysterious or confusing suddenly become clear.

This is not to claim that the person teaching the model lesson knows best or that such lessons always proceed according to plan. They often don't. It's refreshing for teachers to see that no one will get it right all the time and that we all, inevitably and invariably, make mistakes. Senior leaders making themselves vulnerable in this way builds trusts and credibility.

Focus on instructional support

As we've seen, some aspects of teaching are 'kind' and others are 'wicked'. Providing effective emotional support (motivating and engaging students) and effective classroom organisation are essential; if we neglect them we have chaos. Teachers can get away with low quality instructional support if they're skilled at engaging students and making them behave. Because the goal of effective instruction is to get students to remember things in the future and to transfer their abilities between different contexts, it's hard to see the effects in the here and now.

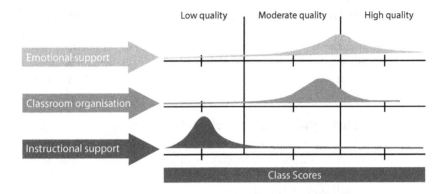

Figure 6.1. Average ratings of interactions in pre-kindergarten to third grade classrooms
Source: B. K. Hamre, S. G. Goffin and M. Kraft-Sayre, *Classroom Assessment Scoring System (CLASS) Implementation Guide: Measuring and Improving Classroom Interactions in Early Classroom Settings* (2009), p. 17. Available at: https://www.boldgoals.org/wp-content/uploads/CLASSImplementationGuide.pdf.

Instructional support includes dimensions such as the kinds of structuring, explaining, questioning, interacting, embedding and activating outlined on page 134–136. One of the reasons that many teachers stop improving in this area is because they achieve a level of competence with which they are comfortable. It takes a rare individual to independently decide to leave this comfort zone. But we only improve through deliberate practice, and that means doing things which we can't currently do.

The current vogue in education is for observations to focus on students' learning. Well, the bad news is that doing this encourages teachers to prioritise short-term approaches because we are focused on current performance rather than long-term learning.

It's more productive, especially if we want to concentrate on improving instructional support, to observe what the teacher is doing. This leads to more nuanced post-observation discussions because a teacher is much better placed to discuss their own actions and judgements rather than speculate on the unknowable nature of their students' learning. And if our focus is guided practice, then it becomes essential to watch what teachers are doing to be able to give the feedback and support to embed improvement.

By foregrounding teaching rather than teachers we can isolate the elements that require work and practise them over and over. The thinking is that we get good at what we practise. If we've practised an instructional technique then we're much more likely to use it. This is where classroom observation can be used to focus on guided practice of these instructional techniques that are likely to have the most impact.

How else can we judge teacher effectiveness?

If you can't sufficiently rely on lesson observations or results, how can you judge teacher effectiveness? In addition to classroom observation and value-added measures of data, the Sutton Trust's report, *What Makes Great Teaching?*, reviews evidence on the following means of judging teacher effectiveness: student ratings, principal (or head teacher) judgement, teacher self-reports, analysis of classroom artefacts and teacher portfolios.[32] Each of these suggestions come with costs and benefits. Combined, all might give us a more rounded view of teachers' effectiveness, but singly each can be open to abuse. For instance, many teachers will recoil in horror at the idea of students being asked to rate them; there's the very real danger that this would quickly turn into a popularity contest as often happens in higher education, with the 'coolest' profs getting the highest ratings regardless of how effectively they teach. There is evidence which suggests that when surveys are used wisely, students respond "to the range of items with reason, intent, and consistent values".[33] However, it also seems to be true that student ratings of teacher behaviour are highly correlated with value-added measures of student cognitive and affective outcomes.[34] So, students who are performing well and feeling good rate their teachers highly. No surprises there.

When students complain about a teacher their main concerns tend to be poor behaviour management and poor explanations. There may be teachers who are so ineffective at managing students that they have no business working in a school but, for the most part, this is an area where intelligent leadership can make a huge – and fairly rapid – difference. Helping teachers to refine the quality of their explanations is a tougher nut to crack and probably requires subject specific coaching to help unpick common misconceptions and build up a wide range of analogies for helping students to understand abstract concepts. Overall, student evaluations can be a useful self-improvement tool but provide weak evidence of teachers' effectiveness.[35]

Of the remaining methods, the analysis of classroom artefacts (students' work) and teacher portfolios are interesting ideas, but difficult to implement. The report is fairly damning of the validity and reliability of head teacher judgements, and teacher self-assessment is unlikely to gain much traction: "Yeah, I think I'm doing great, actually, thanks for asking."

Combining each of these measures might allow us to reliably judge teacher effectiveness, but at a considerable cost. It may be possible, through a rigorous application of some sort of combination of aggregated value-added scores, highly systematised observation protocols (probably about 6–12 observations per teacher per year) and carefully sampled student surveys to give this summative judgement the degree of reliability it would need to be anything other than arbitrary.[36] The problem is that for summative measures of effective teaching to achieve that rigour and reliability, they would become so time-consuming, unrealistic and expensive that the opportunity costs would far outweigh any possible benefits.

Book monitoring

One popular approach in schools to hone in on teacher effectiveness is to regularly monitor the quality of students' work and teachers' feedback. Regrettably, there's very little in the way of robust evidence on whether this can provide reliable information about teaching quality, but there's good reason to exercise caution.

In Chapter 4, we considered how intelligent accountability could be used to design an approach to marking that might result in teachers being more motivated to be their best rather than just look good, but can we take a similarly intelligent approach to evaluating the quality of work in students' books?

The answer, of course, is yes. There's nothing wrong with observing lessons, work scrutiny or any of the other practices used to peer inside the black box of teaching quality; the problems stem from how the information gleaned is then used. If I monitor students' exercise books with a checklist of criteria, I will be viewing students' work and teachers' interactions through a set of predefined parameters which will inevitably distort what I see.

Here's an example of the sort of checklist a school might use to monitor students' books:

1. Teachers must have a **secure overview** of the starting points, progress and context of all students.
2. Marking must be **primarily formative** including use of a **yellow box** which is *clear* about what students must act upon and *selective marking*, where relevant.
3. Marking and feedback must be **regular.**
4. The **marking code** must be used.[37]

Number 1 is a clear statement of what the role of a teacher entails and as such seems an excellent way to hold teachers to account. However, the second principle of intelligent accountability is undermined by predetermining what 'good' looks like in points 2-4. Why must a yellow box be used? Why can't marking be irregular if it's frequent?* What's the reasoning for one marking code being superior to another? These sorts of impositions result in teachers marking books not for the students' benefit, but for the convenience of auditors. This isn't a learning policy, it's managerialism. Rather than creating unnecessary workload, it would be better to simply say either, "We trust you to have a secure overview of the starting points, progress and context of all students, and how you go about doing that is up to you." Or, for teachers who have not yet earned autonomy to be trusted, "We will specify how you should monitor the starting points, progress and context of your students until you have earned the autonomy to no longer need this structure."

It comes down to whether you're more interested in getting what you want or trusting people to do what's best. Instead of looking for items on a checklist, we should be looking at what is there and asking questions about why it's there and what it represents. As I've argued, accountability works if those being held to account are prompted to try to be their best instead of trying to look good. When teachers are told what good looks like, they know that anything which deviates from this expectation is likely to be viewed with suspicion and be subject to misunderstanding. The safe option is to cover your back, give the observer what they want and regularly festoon your books with yellow boxes.

The point is that none of this matters. The only thing worth checking for is the quality of students' work.

---

* In fairness, there's often a confusion between frequency and regularity. Charitably, we should assume that frequency is implied.

	Is students' work of sufficient quality? (yes/no)	Is there evidence that the teacher is monitoring and reviewing students' progress? (yes/no)
Teacher 1	No	Yes
Teacher 2	Yes	No
Teacher 3	No	No
Teacher 4	Yes	Yes

Table 6.2. The results of a work scrutiny

Consider the evidence in Table 6.2. Teacher 1's students have produced work which is untidy and lacking in quality. Teacher 2's classes, on the other hand, have produced some great stuff but it hasn't been marked. Teacher 3's classes are turning out rubbish work which is also going unmarked, and the students of Teacher 4 are working well *and* their work is being marked. What does this tell you? Which outcome do you prefer? What assumptions are you in danger of making? What questions would you want to ask?

The last two cases present few difficulties. It seems reasonable to intervene with Teacher 3: her lack of marking suggests she may not even be aware that there is an issue with the quality of students' work. Even if we assume that there are other methods by which the teacher might be giving feedback, clearly these are not working. In the case of Teacher 4, both teacher and students seem to be doing exactly what's expected and required. Case closed.

But what about the first two teachers? What has our scrutiny actually revealed? I'd want to have a chat with Teacher 2 to find out how this magic is being worked. It would be interesting to compare students' work across subjects to see whether they're all simply highly motivated young people who do what's required despite feckless teachers. I might want to speak to some of the students to ask about the conditions under which their work was produced and to find out whether they've been receiving feedback through means other than marking. But, if the work is good, the last thing I would want to do is sanction the teacher.

Teacher 1, though, is a cause for concern. Despite students' work being marked, it's just not good enough. Is this because students are ignoring their teacher's earnest efforts? Might it be that the presence of marking isn't providing useful feedback? If the teacher is working hard to mark, but the quality of work isn't improving, maybe the teacher needs some support? Or perhaps the situation will right itself given time and should just be earmarked for further monitoring? It should always be remembered that treating teachers equally is fundamentally unfair.

Both of these cases reveal circumstances where book monitoring could go wrong. It's far harder to assess the quality of work than it is the quality of marking, and so we have an entirely natural tendency to do what's easier. If we're just looking to see whether a marking policy has been followed, Teacher 1 might get a gold star despite the poor quality of the work. And I can well imagine a scenario where Teacher 2 is forced to comply with a marking policy despite the successes of the students.

Another related point is about who's doing the book monitoring. Senior leaders will not have sufficient expertise in all subjects to be able to do this work effectively. For instance, I was once told by a senior leader that the work my Year 7 English class had produced wasn't sufficiently challenging. When I asked why, he told me this was because they'd been studying The Lady of Shalott, a poem he'd seen being taught in a primary school he'd visited. I had to explain that Tennyson's poetry was also on the syllabus for my A level class and that literary works can, and often should, be used with a broad range of different age groups. Ideally, work monitoring should be carried out by subject leaders and, ideally, be made transparent in departmental meetings, with all members of a subject team holding each other to account.

The standard to which we should hold teachers is this: is students' work sufficiently good? If the answer is no, then whatever teachers are doing isn't working. But if the answer is yes, no other questions need to be asked.[38]

Do teachers plateau or continue to improve?

The quantity and complexity of the decisions and responses teachers make in the course of a day is daunting. As useful as it would be to think deeply about and reflect thoroughly on each of these interactions, there is rarely time to stop and stare. In order to function we have to rely on our intuition. Most of what we do in the classroom we do because 'it works'. How do we know it works? Because it feels right.

The trouble is, our intuitions may not be reliable. This doesn't chime with what we intuitively believe about intuition. We tend to think that as we become more experienced, we acquire expertise: the more you teach, the better your intuitive judgements will be. This is an attractive idea, but not necessarily one rooted in reality. As we saw in Chapter 2, experience doesn't always result in expertise, but it does usually result in increased confidence. In some fields, the feedback we get doesn't help us to improve the quality of our judgements.

Earlier, we reviewed studies which have indicated that although teachers seem to improve rapidly (in terms of student outcomes) over the first three years of practice, they subsequently plateau and perhaps even begin to decline over time. This is not uncontroversial; there is also research which shows that teachers continue to get better and better with time.

Tara Kini and Anne Podolsky argue that studies which show teachers ceasing to improve have used poor statistical models and that, actually, "Teaching experience is positively associated with student achievement gains throughout a teacher's career" and that, "for most teachers, experience increases effectiveness".[39] John Papay and Matthew Kraft offer a slightly more nuanced picture which finds that teachers vary a great deal over how they improve over time: "Some teachers do plateau, whereas others continue to improve."[40] As we also saw in Chapter 2, schools appear to have an important role to play in this process.

The problem for anyone without a statistical background is that these claims and counter-claims revolve around who has the better maths and methodology. As the mathematician John Ewing says, "Whether naïfs or experts, mathematicians need to confront people who misuse their subject to intimidate others into accepting conclusions simply because they are based on some mathematics."[41] In short, it's almost impossible to work out who is right, but Kini and Podolsky's claims are, in part, based on an erroneous assumption:

[The finding that teachers don't improve with experience] seems counter-intuitive, *given the evidence that professionals in a wide range of contexts improve their performance with experience*. For example, a surgeon's improved performance is associated with increased experience gained at a given hospital. An increase in a software developer's experience working on the same system is associated with increased productivity. What is common sense in the business world – that employees improve in their productivity, innovation, and ability to satisfy their clients as they gain experience in a specific task, organization, and industry – is not the commonly accepted wisdom in public education.[42]

They're correct to say that the idea that experience doesn't lead to expertise is counter-intuitive, but they're wrong about everything else. As we saw in

Chapter 1, surgery, software development and business are all examples of domains where experience does not automatically confer expertise.

Schools matter

School environments have an effect on teacher improvement and, as we saw in Chapter 2, there is evidence that some school environments are more likely to result in teachers continuing to develop expertise over their careers.

The factors most clearly associated with continued teacher improvements

- Consistent order and discipline.
- Opportunities for peer collaboration.
- Supportive head teacher leadership.
- Effective professional development.
- A school culture characterised by trust.
- A fair teacher evaluation process providing meaningful feedback.

It's easy to see that orderly schools with good student behaviour and a supportive approach to school leadership are likely to be conducive to teachers thriving, and there's a growing body of evidence that providing opportunities for peer collaboration is highly correlated with ongoing teacher improvement.[44] Similarly, there's good reason to believe that teacher evaluation is more effective when accountability and trust are combined in the ways discussed in Chapter 4.

What are the best bets for effective teaching?

There is quite a bit of evidence available on what effective teaching is likely to include. According to Rob Coe and colleagues, "Great teaching must be defined by its impact: a great teacher is one whose students learn more."[45] After reviewing the available research, they go on to suggest that there are four distinct dimensions to expert teacher behaviour, subdivided in 17 distinct elements, which stand the best chance of working.

1. Understanding the content

- Having deep and fluent knowledge and flexible understanding of the content you are teaching
- Knowledge of the requirements of curriculum sequencing and dependencies in relation to the content and ideas you are teaching

- Knowledge of relevant curriculum tasks, assessments and activities, their diagnostic and didactic potential; being able to generate varied explanations and multiple representations/analogies/examples for the ideas you are teaching
- Knowledge of common student strategies, misconceptions and sticking points in relation to the content you are teaching

2. Creating a supportive environment

- Promoting interactions and relationships with all students that are based on mutual respect, care, empathy and warmth; avoiding negative emotions in interactions with students; being sensitive to the individual needs, emotions, culture and beliefs of students
- Promoting a positive climate of student–student relationships, characterised by respect, trust, cooperation and care
- Promoting learner motivation through feelings of competence, autonomy and relatedness
- Creating a climate of high expectations, with high challenge and high trust, so learners feel it is okay to have a go; encouraging learners to attribute their success or failure to things they can change

3. Maximising opportunity to learn

- Managing time and resources efficiently in the classroom to maximise productivity and minimise wasted time (e.g. starts, transitions); giving clear instructions so students understand what they should be doing; using (and explicitly teaching) routines to make transitions smooth
- Ensuring that rules, expectations and consequences for behaviour are explicit, clear and consistently applied
- Preventing, anticipating and responding to potentially disruptive incidents; reinforcing positive student behaviours; signalling awareness of what is happening in the classroom and responding appropriately

4. Activating hard thinking

- Structuring: giving students an appropriate sequence of learning tasks; signalling learning objectives, rationale, overview, key ideas and stages of progress; matching tasks to learners' needs and readiness;

scaffolding and supporting to make tasks accessible to all, but gradually removed so that all students succeed at the required level
- Explaining: presenting and communicating new ideas clearly, with concise, appropriate, engaging explanations; connecting new ideas to what has previously been learnt (and re-activating/checking that prior knowledge); using examples (and non-examples) appropriately to help learners understand and build connections; modelling/demonstrating new skills or procedures with appropriate scaffolding and challenge; using worked/part-worked examples
- Questioning: using questions and dialogue to promote elaboration and connected, flexible thinking among learners (e.g., 'Why?', 'Compare', etc.); using questions to elicit student thinking; getting responses from all students; using high-quality assessment to evidence learning; interpreting, communicating and responding to assessment evidence appropriately
- Interacting: responding appropriately to feedback from students about their thinking/ knowledge/understanding; giving students actionable feedback to guide their learning
- Embedding: giving students tasks that embed and reinforce learning; requiring them to practise until learning is fluent and secure; ensuring that once-learnt material is reviewed/revisited to prevent forgetting
- Activating: helping students to plan, regulate and monitor their own learning; progressing appropriately from structured to more independent learning as students develop knowledge and expertise.[46]

There's good reason to believe that by focusing on these elements, teachers would be most likely to increase their effectiveness.

Of course, there needs to be flexibility in how we use this toolkit to help teachers develop. Arguably, teachers are best when they are themselves. If you force an individual to change too much, you're likely to make them less effective. Every teacher's path to improvement will be different because every teacher is differently skilled and will need to work on improving different elements of their craft. This means teachers need choice, but not too much choice. Too much choice leads to teachers heading off down blind alleys and raises the ever present spectre of lethal mutation.

Avoiding lethal mutations

In biology, a lethal mutation is a genetic mutation caused by an unfortunate combination of genes. Individually, these genes would be harmless, but when combined their expression results in the premature death of the organism carrying them.

In education, the term 'lethal mutation' is sometimes used to describe the phenomenon of perfectly sensible approaches to teaching being misunderstood or misapplied, to the point that they become harmful to students' outcomes. Take, for instance, the sorry tale of Assessment for Learning (AfL). Properly understood, the careful application of formative assessment, combined with responsive approaches to teaching, has one of the most positive evidence bases in education research. So much so that, when AfL was publicised by Dylan Wiliam and Paul Black in the 1990s, it was seized on by policy makers and given a huge push to roll it out in schools.

Few instructional approaches have ever been so well supported and widely trialled, but in terms of its effects on student outcomes AfL was a dismal failure. Why? Not because the research was flawed or the strategies too difficult to implement, but because this top-down implementation resulted in lethal mutations.

The underlying principles were ignored in favour of more visible, gimmicky means of operationalising them; a good example of the prioritisation of compliant process over intelligent focus on mastery and expertise. While most teachers were trained in the use of lollipop sticks to select students in class, almost none were introduced to the underlying research. While almost all schools leapt on the idea that students should have a better understanding of their progress relative to their starting point and end goal, this was widely interpreted as needing to write more and more comments in exercise books and issue target grades to students.

The gap between what the evidence indicated and what schools actually did became gradually wider, resulting in a systemically broken approach to teaching becoming mandated in an increasing number of schools. Teachers' workload increased hugely, while students' outcomes flatlined.

Does it do more harm than good to expose teachers to new ideas?

Let's look again at the implementation of AfL. As early as 1981, Brian Simon decried the vacuum left by the historic neglect of pedagogy in England and the concomitant vulnerability to "the winds of fashion – to pedagogical initiatives which 'seemed to work' ".[47]

Into this vacuum, the Department for Education and Skills launched *Pedagogy and Practice*, a sequence of 20 'pedagogically informed' training materials.[48] Of these, Assessment for Learning was unit 12. Ruth Powley points out:

> By dividing 'pedagogy' into twenty chunks, the holistic element of instruction was underplayed. This fashion for 'listing' in education will be familiar to any teacher who has ever attempted to squeeze a series of acronyms: ICT, RWCM, VAK, and PLTS* (I could go on) into their already over-filled lessons in an attempt to 'tick all the boxes' in the lesson plan.[49]

Arguably, the effect of this atomisation was actually to impede effectiveness. Gert Biesta criticised the "cookbook approach" of the National Strategies.[50] Similarly, Robin Alexander criticised the Primary Strategy as "stylistically demeaning, conceptually weak, evidentially inadequate and culpably ignorant of recent educational history".[51] It is important to remember that AfL was packaged as part of this list of pedagogical recipes which drew indiscriminately on pseudoscience as well as reputable research. This was the era in which learning styles and Brain Gym reached their apogee.

The approach advocated by *Pedagogy and Practice* had many faults, but chief among them were that it lacked realism, expertise and honesty. Hargreaves and Fullan go so far as to claim that this "informed prescription" was an attempt to curb the "era of classroom autonomy".[52]

Unaware and uninformed, teachers and school leaders were hostages to learned helplessness and the top-down imposition of 'expertise'. To prevent good ideas from lethally mutating – and to sort the wheat from the chaff – teachers need to be encouraged to express intelligent and informed professional scepticism. Perhaps lethal mutation can only be avoided when teachers are empowered to move away from learned helplessness and ask, with real information to hand, questions such as, "Why will this work?" and "Under what conditions is it more or less likely to work?"

What should professional development look like?

One of the most fundamental principles of effective professional development programmes is that teachers with different levels of expertise require different

---

* Information communication technology; reading, writing, communication and mathematics; visual, auditory and kinaesthetic; and personal learning and thinking skills.

types of professional development. As Robert Coe and colleagues say, "the answer to the question 'What can I best focus on to improve?' is likely to be different for different teachers".[53]

The consensus on what constitutes effective professional development is that it should be sustained, collaborative, subject specific, draw on external expertise, have buy-in from teachers and be practice-based. However, there is reason to doubt that this finding is sufficiently secure as there are numerous examples of programmes incorporating all these aspects which have failed to make any difference to students' outcomes.[54]

Why? Probably because of the necessity to be realistic about the need for sufficient deliberate practice to create habits of mind and action. Trying to alter what teachers do in their classrooms involves dismantling highly automated routines. In order for teachers to change their practice, they need to change their habits.

The approach to teachers' professional development that seems most likely to make a difference to raising attainment is 'instructional coaching', which is characterised by an ongoing cycle of observation and feedback. However, teachers' classroom practice is unlikely to improve without injections of new knowledge, so an individualised coaching programme should be combined with training sessions or courses in which teachers are taught new approaches and given new insights.

The qualities of instructional coaching

- **Individualized** – coaching sessions are one-on-one.
- **Intensive** – coaches and teachers interact at least every couple of weeks.
- **Sustained** – teachers receive coaching over an extended period of time.
- **Context-specific** – teachers are coached on their practices within the context of their own classroom.
- **Focused** – coaches work with teachers to engage in deliberate practice of specific skills.
- **Expert** – coaches should be effective teachers who have received specialist training not simply willing colleagues.[55]

However, this makes a professional development programme much more expensive to run. Schools would either have to train up their most effective teachers as coaches – meaning they are no longer available to teach – or else hire in experts from outside. As we've seen, the best is often the enemy of the good, so in the interests of expediency we might do well to see this final point as something to which we should aspire, but not as a reason for inaction.

Another point to consider is that the research indicates that quality is more important than quantity. In other words, the expertise of the coach and the focus of the coaching seems to have a greater effect on students' outcomes than the total number of coaching hours.[56]

Assuming, then, that the most practical approach to instructional coaching is to employ existing teachers informally, it's worth discussing some principles for effective classroom observation.

Summary of Chapter 6

- The quality of teaching is a more important factor in school improvement than the quality of teachers.
- Although we know being taught by the most effective teachers makes a huge difference to students, we don't have the ability to reliably identify the best individual teachers.
- Judging teachers by students' outcomes is a flawed way to identify the most effective teachers; teaching more able students makes a teacher twice as likely to be labelled as effective.
- Students' results are as much down to natural volatility as they are to any school or teacher factors.
- Lesson observation is even more flawed: on average, 63% of observational judgements will be wrong.
- Teachers don't simply improve with experience: effectiveness begins to plateau after the first three years.
- We only continue improving in 'kind' domains – that is, environments where we get reliable feedback.
- Teaching is, to some extent, a 'wicked' domain, in that teachers don't receive reliable feedback on the quality of their teaching.
- Instructional coaching is a good bet for nudging teacher improvement.

- Teachers will become more effective if the conditions of practice support the development of intuition.
- Attempts to impose top-down improvement programmes are likely to suffer lethal mutation; teachers need to be guided rather than compelled.

CHAPTER 7

INTELLIGENT LEADERSHIP

Leadership should be born out of the understanding of the needs of those who would be affected by it.

Attributed to Marian Anderson,
singer and civil rights activist (1897–1993)

If schools are going to transform themselves into places where teachers can thrive, then we'll need intelligent school leadership. This will include tapping into the collective knowledge available within schools as well as rethinking some of what we think the purpose of school leadership should be.

The illusion of leadership

One person, no matter how heroic a leader they are, cannot bring about genuine school improvement by the force of their will. The illusion of leadership is perpetuated because transforming a school from a disaster zone into a place of order is relatively easily achievable by means of strong leadership. But then what?

Consider the following list of the characteristics of good schools:

- Good behaviour.
- Great exam results.
- A broad, rich, well-planned curriculum.
- A wide range of extracurricular provision.
- A culture where social norms reinforce the benefits of hard work.
- Well-run pastoral systems.
- A sense of respect in the wider community.

- A focus on developing and supporting staff.
- Intelligent accountability systems.
- A belief in the potential of all students.

Sorting out the very worst excesses of students' behaviour has to take priority. This takes effort and commitment but it is not difficult to work out: you stop tolerating bad behaviour and apply simple, fair and consistent consequences (see pages 164–168). I don't underestimate how exhausting this is to implement but the principles are clear. Once the swamp has been drained, teachers can teach and students can learn. Moving from special measures to requiring improvement is – relatively speaking – easy. From that point on, the actions and decisions of heroic leaders have diminishing marginal returns.

Once you've crossed off behaviour, how do you achieve the other items? Do you know how to make sure that results go up in every subject? Do you know what a broad and balanced curriculum looks like in every aspect? Could you personally ensure a wide range of extracurricular activities? Can one person safeguard the welfare of all students? Do you know how to make all teachers perform at their optimal efficiency and effectiveness?

Many of these things cannot be successfully imposed from the top down. You can't force exam results up (although you can try to game the system), and no individual can single-handedly make a curriculum broad and balanced. These are the emergent properties of a well-run school, dedicated to ongoing, iterative improvement. Putting in place a rich curriculum, while also maintaining a focus on exam success, requires collective intelligence and aligned organisational action. For this, the school leader may be an 'architect' or an 'engineer' who can construct their vision with the buy-in of others, but they are unlikely to be a 'bus driver' taking the 'right' people on a predetermined route.

James Meindl refers to 'the romance of leadership'. He observes that "the social construction of organizational realities has elevated the concept of leadership to a lofty status and level of significance. Such realities emphasise leadership, and the concept has thereby gained a brilliance that exceeds the limits of normal scientific inquiry."[1] Meindl argues that 'leadership' has been invented to explain any unusually good or bad performance and to simplify the world into something we feel able to control.

The consequence of this myth of heroic leadership is that we can never measure up. We rarely hear stories of failure, indecision or setbacks, and so when we inevitably experience these things we begin to doubt ourselves and miss the opportunity to learn from failure. The illusion of leadership contains a paradox: what looks like leadership is often ineffective and what looks less like leadership is often more effective.

Schools are complex systems and relational environments. For teachers to thrive, leadership should be nurturing and responsive, privileging autonomy, mastery and purpose. For the most part, school leaders should seek to avoid imposing rigid systems of compliance. However, the one exception to this applies to the most easily improved aspect of a school: student behaviour. Despite the individual complexities of students' lives, getting large groups of children to behave well is not intellectually hard: it is, in the jargon, 'low hanging fruit'.

Intelligent leadership works by creating a high trust surplus culture, holding teachers to account for the good things they've said they want to do. If they do what they've said and prove themselves trustworthy, we give them more trust. If they don't do what they say they will, we tighten the accountability cycle.

An intelligent leader knows that leading by consensus is impossible: nothing gets done and everyone gets frustrated. However, they do seek alignment and collective knowledge, particularly over those areas of school life that are important to teachers. Generally, you will find that teachers don't feel the need to be consulted on how many boilers the school has (as long as classrooms are a sensible temperature), but they do like to be consulted about the length of lessons. Make realistic and wise decisions about when to consult and when to get on with it.

The problem with 'strong' leadership

As Archie Brown points out in *The Myth of the Strong Leader*, "you don't need to go far in contemporary democracies before you find people hankering for a strong leader".[2] Education – like so many other sectors – has succumbed to this wider societal myth. Everyone knows what's needed to turn around a struggling school: strong leadership. In order for it to be deemed necessary for a school to be consigned to special measures, something has to have gone badly wrong. It's more than likely true that poor leadership will be at the heart of the problem. So, the school is taken over and a new 'strong leader' is parachuted in.

The absolute monarchy of headship can encourage some authoritarian behaviour. This sort of outlandishly macho brinkmanship is embodied by the former chief inspector, Sir Michael Wilshaw:

At the start of my tenure as HMCI I think I may have recommended Clint Eastwood as a role model heads should follow. I recalled that scene in *Pale Rider* when the baddies are shooting up the town, the mists dissipate and Clint is there, the lone warrior fighting for righteousness. I also remember that the notion wasn't universally welcomed. But I stand by Clint. If a head finds him or herself in the educational badlands, facing impossible odds and a hesitant posse – then Clint is what is needed.[3]

In Wilshaw's world, schools are the badlands – corrupt and iniquitous – and teachers are the baddies. The hero head is the lone gunman who will impose order. Although he may see violence as a last resort, his word is backed by the gun. Elsewhere, reflecting on his time as a head teacher, Sir Michael has said: "It sounds very arrogant to say I didn't need much help, but I knew all the pitfalls. And I could replicate all the stuff that I had done in Newham in Hackney, with similar sorts of children."[4] He's right, it does sound very arrogant. Sir Michael exemplifies the kind of lucky risk-taker we considered in Chapter 1.

Robert Greenleaf, founder of the Servant Leadership movement, observes that "an important weakness in the concept of the single chief at the top of a managerial hierarchy is that such a person is apt to be a manager and to assume, by virtue of having the position, that he or she has all of the talents it requires".[5] A strong leader can decide that a school will create a new curriculum and direct individuals to make it broad and balanced, but this is unlikely to work. Good work is not produced in this way. Leaders cannot mandate creativity, mastery or excellence; people have to want to do it. They have to feel that their expertise is valued and encouraged. They have to feel that their suggestions and concerns will be listened to, if not acted on. And, most importantly, they have to feel that whoever is holding them to account is both humble and intelligent enough to recognise good ideas, and knowledgeable and realistic enough to recognise bad ones. An intelligent leader creates the conditions for teachers and students to flourish through intelligent accountability. This is no easy trick and it is possibly why truly excellent schools are the exception.

A bad leader tries to make things happen. They impose their vision, set timetables for change, ignore advice and root out dissent. Unwittingly or otherwise, they create conditions that choke trust and engender fear. Layers of management increase, systems of control multiply and policy documents proliferate. Strong leaders increasingly spend their time managing managers. Prescriptive management not only results in a far greater risk of foolish decisions that are not grounded in organisational knowledge, but it also slows down the implementation of even good decisions as problems get bounced around with no one willing to take responsibility in case they are blamed for getting it wrong.

Strong leadership sounds desirable because the alternative offered by a false dichotomy is weak leadership. But perhaps it's not helpful to see leaders as either strong or weak. Nassim Nicholas Taleb contrasts fragility with 'antifragility'. He says:

> Some things benefit from shocks; they thrive and grow when exposed to volatility, randomness, disorder and stressors, and love adventure, risk, and uncertainty. Yet, in spite of the ubiquity of the phenomenon, there is no word for the exact opposite of fragile. Let us call it antifragile. Antifragility is beyond resilience or robustness. The resilient resists shocks and stays the same; the antifragile gets better.[6]

We don't want resilient leaders who resist shocks and stay the same; instead, we want antifragile leaders who improve as they encounter stresses. Where a strong leader stands firm in the face of opposition, an antifragile leader will accommodate pressures. Where a strong leader is prescriptive and uncompromising, an antifragile leader allows teachers to grow and evolve. If we were to approach school leadership in this way, we could make the best use of everyone's talents.

There may be a need for troubleshooting, my-way-or-the-highway leaders, but over the longer term this brand of school leader prevents schools from being sustainably sufficient. Few people want to think of themselves as this sort of leader: we tell ourselves we're nurturing and supportive, but are we?

The problem isn't that this style of leadership doesn't have an impact, it's that it does. Strong leadership always has an impact, but it's often negative. Consider the overwhelming and enormous harm Mao Zedong did to the Chinese people over several decades. Consider Stalin's brutal impact on the lives of millions of Russians. Strong leaders get change, but they don't bring prosperity. Head teacher Matthew Evans observes:

> The problem is that there is too much leadership going on. Leadership simply isn't needed anywhere near as much as we like to think it is. The art of leadership is knowing that it is best used scarcely, and as a last resort. But people hate it when you say this.[7]

They might hate it, but this kind of insistence on the ubiquity of leadership leads to 'leaderism'.

Leaders vs. managers

The title 'leader' has pretty much entirely replaced that of 'manager' in schools. Years ago, schools used to have senior management teams (SMT) whereas today senior leadership teams (SLT) proliferate. On one level, managerialism simply refers to the beliefs and behaviour of managers, but more commonly it is used to refer to the petty tyrannies brought on by an over-reliance on metrics, control and accountability. Understandably, no one wants to be thought of like this and manager has increasingly come to be viewed almost as a term of abuse. Leaders, on the other hand, are clear-eyed superheroes, swooping in to singlehandedly improve underperforming schools. As we'll find out, this view of school leadership – let's call it leaderism – has a pernicious effect on how schools are run. Not only does this have negative consequences for teachers and students, but it's equally unhealthy for leaders themselves.

Leaders are seen as visionaries whose role is to have bold ideas and make decisions. One of the enduringly popular conceptions of the effective leader is getting the 'right' people on the bus (and, of course, getting the 'wrong' people off the bus),[8] but is this what we really want from school leaders? Will schools be improved by new ideas and the 'right' people all being driven in the 'right' direction? Is it really senior leaders who should be making decisions about the curriculum? Are you really the best person to decide how teachers should teach?

What teachers most want from leaders are prompt answers to questions, to know what's possible and what isn't, clarity and help solving problems. I've often encountered school leaders who trot out the maxim, "Don't bring me problems, bring me solutions!" (To my shame, I've said this myself.) But doesn't this just make leadership redundant? If you're not there to solve teachers' problems, what is your role? If teachers are expected to solve all their own problems and simply ask you to arbitrate or rubber-stamp their decisions, you are little more than an administrator.

Arguably, leaderism results in dishonesty and distrust. School leaders have a distorted view of what they are meant to be doing and how to make it possible, and teachers are squeezed into compliantly enacting the will of leadership. All this tends to be done in the name of school improvement, but what does it really mean to improve a school? Leaderism results in authoritarian double-think that blights the lives of teachers while claiming that all is being done 'for the students'. Can we honestly claim that students' education will be improved by staff being overworked and fearful? If we were to view school improvement as the freedom to pursue excellence, then this might make it easier to evaluate whether initiatives are more likely to do harm than good.

All too often, leaderism is responsible for building an architecture of compliance rather than intelligence. Whenever you're tempted to implement a new initiative, ask yourself these two questions:

1. How will this contribute to teachers and students being free to pursue excellence?
2. Will this result in greater compliance or greater collective intelligence?

The failure to consider these questions contributes to the resentments of 'them and us', where teachers and school leaders both view each other as the enemy. When this happens, leaders are trapped in a bubble where their preferences are endlessly mirrored back to them.

The leadership bubble

Some years ago, the English faculty I led was subject to a week-long regime of monitoring and review. Knowing that every member of the department was to be observed and that we would be expected to showcase loads of 'student centred learning', I made sure everyone had planned plenty of group work and took steps to minimise whole class instruction. At the end of the week, the head teacher congratulated me on the quality of all of the lessons he'd seen and how student centred they'd been. Despite this, I could see he was troubled and asked whether anything was wrong. He cleared his throat, looked a bit uneasy and said, "All the lessons I've seen have been amazing, but ... when do you actually teach them stuff?" I just stared at him. Did he really not know? I can't remember what I said at the time but the answer was crystal clear: we actually taught them stuff when no one from the leadership team was watching.

This is one of the fundamental dangers of school leadership: you carry your job title around with you. If you're not very careful, people will show you what they think you want to see and say what they think you want to hear. The only time they're ever honestly themselves is when you're elsewhere.

More recently, I was asked to conduct a teaching and learning review for a school I'd been working with and agreed to spend a day visiting lessons. There was a clear and consistent theme: most lessons were subject to routine, low level disruption. The students' behaviour wasn't usually awful but, taken as a whole, it painted a bleak picture of missed opportunities and wasted time. When it came time to feed back my observations to the head teacher, he simply refused to accept that what I said was true. He explained that the reason he knew it wasn't true was because *he* visited lessons every day and wherever *he* went behaviour was always excellent!

It's difficult to deal with this level of self-deception. I tried pointing out that the difference between his experiences and mine was that he was the figure of ultimate authority in the school and I was just some random bloke. The one thing consistent to all the lessons *he* visited is that the head teacher was always in the room. Sadly, not long afterwards the school failed an inspection and was placed into special measures.

Just in case the message of these two anecdotes isn't clear, here it is: *power insulates you from reality*. If you have power over others they will alter their behaviour to suit your preferences. If you specify exactly what you expect to see, you will be shown exactly what you specify. As we explored in Chapter 3, the very best you will ever get is compliance. Unless you explicitly make the effort to reach beyond this and give people permission to be authentic with you, you are likely to have your preferences mirrored back to you.

Václav Hável, playwright and former president of the Czech Republic, was aware of this tendency for leaders to become blind to reality. He wrote that "being in power makes me permanently suspicious of myself". He says of leaders who begin to lose the battle with the trappings of power: "In attempting to persuade themselves that they are still merely serving ... they increasingly persuade themselves of nothing more than their own excellence."[9] The very concept of leadership inspires a mindset where everything that happens in a school is filtered through a series of dramatic events and heroic interventions. No matter how sincere school leaders are, they always run the very real risk of being seduced by their position. Belief in their own excellence contributes to the bubble senior leaders often occupy.

Let's return to the concept of the 'wicked domain' introduced in Chapter 1 where feedback on performance is absent or biased. This was compared to playing golf in the dark. Occupying a leadership bubble is the equivalent of leading with the lights out. But it's worse than that: because feedback in wicked domains is biased, it leads us to believe that we're experts when we're not. We become ever more overconfident and certain that we're right: a dangerous combination.

Bursting the bubble

Intelligent school leadership relies on judgement and openness to feedback, therefore specify that what you want is knowledge, professional scepticism and honesty. Sadly, this is likely to surprise colleagues who have become accustomed to a compliance culture in education, so we will need to be explicit, persistent and grateful in privileging knowledge and honesty over 'mirroring'.

If you want to break out of the leadership bubble, the solution is to let go of the leadership myths that proliferate in books and training and embrace intelligent accountability. You need people to trust that you are well informed and interested in accuracy, honesty and an exploration of what could be better. In return, you need to allow teachers the autonomy they've earned. If you want teachers to be their best, then you need to hold them to account for doing what they believe is in their students' best interests. You need to listen to them and trust that they know how to do their jobs, and that they know how to teach their subject to their students better than you do. You need to trust that most teachers are doing their best and that they care about their students' welfare and success at least as much as you do. If you don't trust that this is true, then you must tell them so honestly and set out what they need to do to gain your trust and earn greater autonomy.

If teachers can see that you are not seduced by a belief in your own excellence, *and* that you trust them to do their jobs, *and* that you will hold them to account for doing what they believe to be the best way to teach their students, *and*, ideally, that you are an ally who can be of use instead of a threat to be circumvented, then, in return, they will allow you out of your bubble and invite you into their classrooms to celebrate and support, not to censure, what they are doing.

Do we have a deficit model of school leaders?

As professor of public leadership, Barbara Kellerman observes, "the rise of leadership as an object of our collective fascination has coincided precisely with the decline of leadership in our collective estimation".[10] While everyone may be able to bring to mind an inspirational figure who embodies all the virtues we would wish a school leader to possess, it remains a depressing fact that far too many teachers (and school leaders) have to work for some truly terrible bosses.

With all the training that is ploughed into developing great leaders, shouldn't we expect better? Why is it that all the writing, research and training seems to produce such meagre results? Perhaps the answer is, as with politicians, that we get what we deserve. If we privilege learned helplessness, compliance and accountability, how will we attract the potential leaders who thrive in cultures of honesty and mastery?

A classroom teacher once commented to an ambitious young teacher: "You're too good to be a head teacher." Was this an outlier remark, or do we actually have a deficit model for our school leaders – believing that they are ambitious, misguided, misinformed, corrupt and uninterested in collective intelligence?

We need to try harder to understand the systemic processes that produce leaders who fail to meet our hopes and expectations. Rather than giving in to learned helplessness and abdicating responsibility, teachers need to consider what they can do to improve matters. This entails knowing more about the social psychology and educational contexts that reinforce the traits and behaviours which result in leaders being promoted and being successful. What if our preferences for what leaders should be like are in opposition to the traits we actually reward? What if the very school leaders we might want do exist but are failing to seek promotion to the highest offices because they do not want to be part of enforcing a low trust compliance culture?

None of this is to suggest that the school leaders we have are not well intentioned or sincere; on the whole, the overwhelming majority are fiercely determined to do the very best for the young people in their schools. And, to their credit, they have the integrity to work in an imperfect system not of their making.

But good intentions and sincerity are not enough. What is needed is twofold. Firstly, we require a shift of culture from high stakes, low trust, compliant and accountable cultures which are always likely to attract 'controlling' leaders, to high trust, intelligent, knowledge based cultures which are always likely to attract 'responsive' leaders.

Secondly, we need to place greater value on domain specific expertise. Expertise that is specific to a particular domain does not transfer between contexts. The expertise required to manage a premiership football team, run a biscuit factory or a branch of the armed forces is not the same as the expertise required to run a school. Effective school leadership depends on a specific body of knowledge. It is not a generic skill.

Despite this, there are a number of qualities that pretty much everyone thinks are important, whether or not they are characteristic of many or most senior leaders.

What traits should we encourage in school leaders?

The theme of this book is the urgent need for intelligent accountability. We do not have to be victims of learned helplessness. We can have agency, and if we have leaders that we don't like, in politics or education, we cannot simply wash our hands and abdicate responsibility. We should think carefully about the traits we want to encourage, value and privilege in our leaders – traits like humility, love, determination, vision and attention to detail.

Humility

The capacity to admit to mistakes with grace and dignity and to face up to the knowledge that you don't always know best is, I think, the paramount quality a leader can possess; from this humble beginning everything else flows. Being humble is not about being apologetic or meek. There is an important difference between *control* and *strength*. Tensile strength – being antifragile – is recognised as the opposite to brittleness.

Being humble means acknowledging that there are deep wells of collective knowledge and experience in a school, and recognising that everyone is – or should be – an expert in their own subject, classes and areas of responsibility. Humility doesn't mean assuming others know best or are always right; it means assuming that others may know best or might be right, and that collective knowledge always trumps individual preferences and predilections. It's about asking questions and really listening to the replies rather than having your biases confirmed by compliant colleagues. It's about being open to your own biases and seeking to explore them rather than trying to confirm them. It's about facing up to the uncomfortable truth that no matter how much you know and how expert you become, there will always be things you don't know and others who are more expert.

Humility is about accepting that you are part of an organic collective in a symbiotic relationship rather than an individual 'expert' with a mandate. In short, it's about responsive and formative leadership. Some leaders talk about 'leadership through failure' – your ability to encourage and support others by sharing with them, not your superlative strengths and how superior you are to all those around you, but the times when you were less than perfect – to provide encouragement and consolation to others in an imperfect world.

The overwhelming challenge of leadership is knowing you might be wrong but having to make a tough call anyway. I imagine good leaders lose sleep over their decisions. Sometimes you have to exude confidence even when you don't feel it. Rightly or wrongly, we all have core values – principles on which we refuse to compromise – and these are the stars by which we navigate.

In the end, the principle of humility might come down to recognising that you are there to serve. Being in charge can bring its own rewards, but sitting in the big chair is a burden you shoulder in order to make it easier for others to excel.

How do you know if you're humble?

You probably seek to give credit instead of taking it and are likely to be aware of your own deficiencies.

Love

Schools are ultimately and conclusively relational environments. Head teacher John Tomsett says that one of the prerequisites for headship is that you have to love teachers. This means working hard to create the conditions in which teachers can thrive, which in turn means making the terrifying decision to trust. Tomsett writes: "trust is reciprocal; if you trust your teachers, they will grow to trust you. When you have to make difficult decisions, they will trust you."[11]

It probably helps that school leaders love teaching too. Often, the very best school leaders still teach. Being seen to enjoy the thing you're employed to lead others in doing is pretty important. It's much easier to empathise with teachers when you're there in the trenches with them. A good leader doesn't just inflict pain – ordering others over the top; a good leader should share pain.

Teachers are not attracted to the profession by the offer of rich rewards or in the belief that they will bathe in the public's esteem; most teachers see purpose in their work. As such they are led by trifles. Little things matter: a kind word here and an acknowledgement there goes a very long way. Sincere recognition and encouragement are the outward signs of loving teachers. The historian Thomas Carlyle reportedly said, "Tell a person they are brave and you help them become so." It's probably true to add, show a teacher you trust them and they will work hard to repay that trust.

How do you know if you love teachers?

You probably worry about their welfare and think of ways to make their lives easier.

Determination

A determined leader will make sure that things get done. It's all very well trusting teachers, but creating the conditions for growth also means holding them to account. If you're sufficiently humble, you will know how hard this is to do well and you will have developed intelligent accountability systems. A determination not to avoid difficult conversations and a willingness to be disliked is crucial, as long as this is done with love and humility. Popularity is not leadership. Others will respect you for being the one who 'shovels the shit' and makes the tough calls.

Perhaps the area in which school leaders can make the most difference to the quality of teaching and learning in a school is by ensuring that students' behaviour is managed humanely, while still expecting the highest of standards. A good leader will be utterly determined to make their school one in which students enjoy learning, in which there is a culture where hard work and academic success are valued, and where students are supported to struggle, no matter their ability. This means that there must be an intolerance of low level disruption, rudeness, laziness, complacency and low expectations. We should always remember that while social disadvantage is no excuse for bad behaviour, 'no excuses' is no excuse for inflexible tyranny.

How do you know if you're determined?

You probably don't allow your decisions to be eroded by the forces of inertia, pessimism or fatalism.

Vision

Vision has become a widely misunderstood cliché, but in essence, you need to have some idea of where you want to go if you hope to ever get there – a blueprint if you like – because schools don't 'take off' by themselves, any more than planes do. School leadership and aviation require knowledgeable and realistic engineering. A good leader inspires those around them to be their best. They set the destination and the pace and lead the charge. Sitting in an office churning out policy documents is not vision. Vision is catching glimpses of the desired future and working out, through collective knowledge, how to get there.

We need to distinguish between 'leaders with vision' and 'visionaries'. Although usually well intentioned, visionaries can be ruinous. Without humility, love and determination, vision is likely to cause harm. But without vision, you can have all the humility, love and determination in the world but you still might not get anywhere. Vision must be tempered by a thorough appreciation of the human cost.

The future we imagine might be searingly bright, but we must always consider the cost. An overlooked aspect of leadership is recognising that perfection is impossible – that is, knowing when to cut your losses and settling for the least worst option.

How do you know if you have vision?

You probably read a lot, think a lot and talk a lot to others in education, as well as having your own ideas about the future.

Attention to detail

It's not enough to see the big picture; a good leader should also see how the pieces fit together. After all, it only takes one component to be faulty for a complex machine not to work as intended. This is what I'm worst at: I'm always imagining shining cathedrals, but I often lack the patience to worry about the snagging and the fiddly bits. When it comes to the details I'm a bodger. A good leader doesn't lose sight of the day-to-day and the mundane. That doesn't mean they should do everything – in fact, they definitely shouldn't even attempt to do everything – but it does mean they should know who's doing what and ensure that teachers are supported by an effective and efficient infrastructure which frees up capacity for mastery. A good leader ensures that generally things don't go wrong, and can quickly spot where things are going wrong so they can swiftly intervene to put their finger in the damn at just the right moment.

Having focus also means you know that the small things matter. A smile, a frown, a pat on the back can make or break another's day. As a senior leader, what you say and do matters to others. Focusing on the details may not be glamorous but it's usually the difference between success and failure. A good leader should know that if something can be misunderstood or miscommunicated it will be. Ideally, mistakes should be anticipated and countered before they occur. Learning from the ground up is invaluable. A leader who has learned from the ground up will already have made almost all of the mistakes and learned from them.

The importance of clearly and explicitly communicating 'what matters' can't be overemphasised. I regularly have the experience of being told by teachers that they 'wouldn't be allowed' to approach their jobs in new ways because doing so would contravene a policy. When I then speak to school leaders, they're often shocked that their advice or suggestions have been misinterpreted as 'law'. This shouldn't surprise us, so it's always worth erring on the side of charity when considering the actions of others.

How do you know if you're focused?

You've probably seen a few projects through to the point where your ongoing involvement is no longer needed. And you probably know an awful lot of very boring information that someone has to be on top of.

Hollow skills

There's an obvious contradiction here. On the one hand, I've stated that leadership is not a collection of generic skills that can be transferred between different contexts, and on the other, I've listed a fairly generic inventory of qualities that leaders should possess. The first thing to say is that each of these qualities – humility, love, determination, vision and attention to detail – are only meaningful when applied to a specific context. To demonstrate humility, you have to know what you don't know and yet know enough to recognise expertise in others. You can't love in the abstract; you have to have a wide experience of the challenges and joys of teaching. It's no good simply being determined, you have to be determined about something. Whatever you want to achieve as a school leader will be inextricably bound up with your knowledge of education and the specifics of the school you are leading. In order to have a meaningful vision you need to know what is possible and how it can be achieved. And for attention to detail to have any worth, you need to have an in-depth understanding of the details you're focusing on.

In *Leaders with Substance*, head teacher Matthew Evans calls these traits 'hollow skills' – traits that are broadly desirable but meaningless in the abstract.[12] Instead, domain specific skills are acquired by having experience of specific problems and issues. The list of traits above might be best thought of as desirable but insufficient. School leaders also need leadership content knowledge, defined as "that knowledge of subjects and how students learn them that is used by administrators when they function as instructional leaders".[13]

According to James Spillane and Karen Seashore-Louis, "Without an understanding of the knowledge necessary for teachers to teach well – content knowledge, general pedagogical knowledge, content specific pedagogical knowledge, curricular knowledge and knowledge of learners – school leaders will be unable to perform essential school improvement functions such as monitoring instruction and supporting teacher development."[14] Values, personality and belief systems are all important, but if they're *all* you have you will not make wise decisions. As Viviane Robinson says, the most important quality for school leaders is "the integration of knowledge and relationships in a context of school-based problem solving".[15]

Domain specific intelligence

Perhaps the most important quality that school leaders need to possess is intelligence. At its most basic, intelligence is defined as the ability to acquire and apply knowledge and skills. Professor of educational psychology Linda Gottfredson defines it in this way:

> Intelligence is a very general mental capability that, among other things, involves the ability to reason, plan, solve problems, think abstractly, comprehend complex ideas, learn quickly, and learn from experience. It is not merely book-learning, a narrow academic skill, or test-taking smarts. Rather, it reflects a broader and deeper capability for comprehending our surroundings, 'catching on', 'making sense' of things, or 'figuring out' what to do.[16]

The importance of intelligence is certainly borne out by research: according to one study, intelligence topped the list of qualities subjects desired in leaders and was the only attribute included in all subjects' lists.[17] A meta-analysis conducted on the degree to which various character traits correlated with successful leadership also found intelligence to be the most significant variable.[18]

While this might lead some to argue that prospective school leaders should be given mandatory IQ tests to establish their fitness to lead, we should also acknowledge that the predictive values of IQ scores are only ever true on average and that intelligence is a very imperfect proxy for effective school leadership. Would a 20-year-old with a very high IQ score make an effective leader? Rather than intelligent *leaders*, we need intelligent *leadership*.

To this end, Evans argues that school leaders have specific intelligence rather than general intelligence: "leaders who can think in more sophisticated ways about the actual challenges they face".[19] In *Making Kids Cleverer*, I argued that intelligence is made up of both fluid intelligence (our raw reasoning power) and crystallised intelligence (our ability to apply prior knowledge to solve problems), and that our best bet for increasing children's intellectual capacity was to increase their store of crystallised intelligence by expanding the quality and quantity of what they know.[20]

Psychologist Philip Ackerman suggests that the 'dark matter' of intelligence is the specific knowledge needed to perform well in a domain:

[M]any intellectually demanding tasks in the real world cannot be accomplished without a vast repertoire of declarative knowledge and procedural skills. The brightest (in terms of IQ) novice would not be expected to fare well when performing cardiovascular surgery in comparison to the middle-aged expert, just as the best entering college student cannot be expected to deliver a flawless doctoral thesis defense, in comparison to the same student after several years of academic study and empirical research experience. In this view, knowledge does not compensate for a declining adult intelligence; it is intelligence![21]

This suggests that intelligent leadership, rather than being an inherent quality of certain individuals and not of others, is a capacity that expands with the acquisition of knowledge and experience within a domain. If this is true, then effective school leaders grow into their roles as they learn more about the challenges of school leadership. And, regardless of how much you may have learned individually, the collective knowledge distributed throughout a school has the potential to exponentially increase the intelligence of decision-making.

Of course, humility, love, determination, vision, attention to detail and intelligence are not the sole preserve of leaders. If we claim that such qualities are what leadership is, we turn it into a thing separate from other areas of human activity. Everyone in a school benefits from possessing these qualities, not just leaders. The difference is, where these qualities are absent in school leaders, there is a greater capacity for harm.

Why aren't leaders perfect?

Who are these extraordinary men and women? Does this list of qualities reflect anything attainable or is it simply wishful thinking? If you've just read the list above and patted yourself on the back, there's every chance that you lack self-awareness.

Leaders aren't perfect because they're human. Far too much rhetoric is wasted on trying to describe what leaders *should* be like and far too little effort goes into investigating what leaders are *actually* like.

We should understand the divergence between what is good for schools and what is good for school leaders. Schools demand superhuman levels of self-sacrifice but school leaders, just like teachers, are all too human. Human beings are driven by the need for status, recognition and reward. We maximise our own survival chances by making sure we possess what we need to make this survival more likely. Is it any wonder that leaders often put their own needs ahead of the needs of others? This can lead to an inherent tension between what's best for us and what's best for the group.

While it might be true that leaders are more likely than teachers to be motivated by status, recognition and reward, these are not the only motivations of school leadership. In a surplus model of education, there will be leaders who are motivated by the desire to make a difference. As Hargreaves and Fullan observe, "people are motivated by good ideas tied to action; they are energized even more by pursuing action with others ... they are ultimately propelled by actions that make an impact – what we call 'moral imperative realized' ".[22]

If we're going to insist that leaders should be self-effacing, compassionate, authentic and honest, we need to acknowledge that this demand might disbar pretty much everyone from positions of leadership as it is currently conceptualised. As Jeffrey Pfeffer remarks, "neglect of what's good for the individual interests of leaders might be one reason so many recommendations have so little traction in the real world".[23]

Does intelligent accountability work for school leaders?

Let's start from the principle that the best school leaders are teachers, and therefore what works for teachers may stand the best chance of working for the type of school leaders we want.

Firstly, senior leaders need to how they're being held to account. If we apply the same standards that we did to teachers in Chapter 4, accountability must be preannounced. The accountability of school leaders is tricky. Should we look at the school's results? If it's hard to get much reliable data on teacher effectiveness from student outcomes, then meaningful data on leadership – at one more step removed – is even less likely to be a sufficiently valid measure. Maybe leaders should be held to account for staff turnover? If lots of teachers are leaving after a short time, we might conclude that the conditions in a school are not conducive to teachers' well-being. Or perhaps leaders should be accountable for the behaviour of students and the professional culture in their schools? Our best bet might be to combine all of these, along with anonymous surveys from teachers and the rest of the leadership team, on how effective they are considered.

Secondly, we should conceal our preferences in order to prevent compliance and pretence. As with teachers, we must avoid setting down precisely how schools should be led. Instead, we should negotiate with leaders about how they might go about making improvements and then hold them to account for what they've said they will do. Again, as with teachers, autonomy must be earned.

Thirdly, whoever holds leaders to account must be trusted to be knowledgeable and interested in accuracy so that leaders do not become fearful, cynical and risk-averse. One of the issues is that we don't necessarily trust external inspectors. While we may agree that the inspection process has improved for teachers, if anything it's even more high stakes for senior leaders. Not only do we still fear the 'rogue' inspector who will make unreasonable judgements, but there is also reasonable concern that Ofsted are not interested in helping schools to improve (after all, that is not their role) and are more focused on apportioning blame. In this way, school inspection operates on a deficit model rather than a surplus model.

This last point has no easy fix. School governors have a role in supporting their heads and leadership teams, but in order for anything to change – especially if we're more interested in improvement and attracting the leadership we want rather than quality assurance – then we need to adjust the way that schools are held to account.

A curriculum for school leadership

Most of what school leaders need to know is domain specific. The greater part of everything written about leadership is either wishful thinking or dangerously incomplete. As Pfeffer puts it, "much of the oft repeated conventional wisdom about leadership is based on hope rather than reality, on wishes rather than data, on beliefs instead of science".[24] Rather than aping the behaviour of prominent figures from the world of business or sport, in order to be effective school leaders need to know a lot of vital context specific information.

For instance, Robinson discusses the example of a principal who asks teachers for data on their students' achievement and is told that in one class 94% of students have achieved their intended learning outcomes. Even though the teacher assures him that the objectives used were typical for children of that age, because he didn't know enough about the curriculum he was unable to recognise that the outcomes on which the children had been so successful were normally set for students who were about 18 months younger than those in this class.[25] As Table 7.1 shows, generic skills were useless in the absence of the specific ability to apply curriculum knowledge to make sure the information given was accurate.

Leadership skills	Generic	Specific
1. Ask teacher for information about students' achievement	✓	
2. Recognise absence of information about benchmark	✓	
3. Ask follow-up questions of teacher to find out what the benchmark was	✓	
4. Use curriculum and pedagogical knowledge to evaluate the adequacy of teacher's answers		✓

Table 7.1. Skills and knowledge required to monitor and evaluate achievement
Source: V. M. Robinson, Putting education back into educational leadership. *Leading and Managing*, 12(1) (2006), 62–75.

From an instructional point of view, the body of knowledge that a school leader needs includes (but is not limited to): implementing and running systems designed to result in excellent student behaviour and positive staff culture, effective pedagogy, educational research, instructional coaching, understanding data, the recruitment and retention of teachers, overseeing curriculum development and quality assurance, understanding the limits of data and how to use assessment effectively, and how to evaluate the effectiveness of interventions. Some of these items may feel superficially similar to what goes on in the armed forces, premiership football teams or blue-chip businesses, but in fact schools are dramatically different.

The beating heart of a school is the academic development of its students. All other concerns are secondary to the quality of education a school provides. However, creating a culture in which teachers thrive and seek to become masters of their profession is probably our best bet for ensuring that students make progress.

Eliminating unnecessary workload

Why are so many teachers expected, if not compelled, to do so many things which don't contribute to improving children's educational outcomes? An awful lot of teachers' workload is 'over-sufficient' for the convenience of managers and the sake of compliance, rather than the education of children.

Marking, planning and data collection are all convenient proxies. Teachers' work is scrutinised in an effort to ascertain whether it is effective – for example:

- Does marking follow policy guidelines?
- Is planning in the form and style mandated?
- Is data accurate, timely and being acted on expediently?

Like all proxies, these things are not the 'thing itself'. We look at marking, planning and data because it's hard to tell whether teachers are effective at getting students to learn the things they're required to learn. It's much easier to check whether teachers are compliant. There's nothing wrong with this per se. In fact, as long as we recognise and remember that proxies are merely proxies and refuse the temptation of turning them into high stakes accountability measures, all would probably be well. But that is not what happens.

Teachers are routinely held accountable for the ease with which school leaders are able to check compliance. If managers can see at a glance that marking is in line with expectations, planning looks good and data is in on time and following an upward trend, then there's no need to look in depth at what teachers are teaching, how well they're teaching it and whether they might be able to teach it more effectively.

If we're serious about wanting to eliminate unnecessary workload and ensure that the education of children is the priority of teachers, then a clear principle for senior leaders to follow is: *The primary role of school leadership is to remove extraneous demands on teachers so they can focus on planning and teaching the very best curriculum possible.*

If you're doing anything that interferes with this responsibility, take a long, hard look at yourself. If you want to spend your time checking proxies, that's up to you. But to compel teachers to spend their time making this process easier robs time from what matters most to students, especially the most disadvantaged students.

If you're not the one teaching the students, why are you looking at planning and marking? Could you free up time for your teachers so that they can look at their planning and marking? This is a good way to ensure that practice is sufficient without becoming over-sufficient. Sometimes, ironically, it can be school leaders who exhort staff to do less and conscientious colleagues who demand to 'proofread' students' work or plan individual lessons. Having time to consider planning and marking pays off because it fosters intelligent discussion and debate about what would make it less time-consuming and more efficient and effective.

Creating a culture of high expectations

One of the most important ways for leaders to ensure that teachers can focus on teaching is to make sure that schools are orderly and students are well behaved. One school of thought suggests that the person with primary responsibility for students' behaviour is the classroom teacher. If you believe that good behaviour is a product of good teaching, then you're also likely to believe that poor behaviour is a result of poor teaching. From this, it logically follows that students only misbehave for bad teachers.

While teachers are responsible for holding children to account for unacceptable behaviour, school leaders are responsible for implementing and maintaining the systems that make it possible for teachers to do this. If senior leaders fail to support teachers' attempts to enforce school rules – or worse, if they blame teachers for students' decisions not to comply – then children will learn that there are some teachers for whom good behaviour is not an expectation.

As the UK government adviser on school behaviour, Tom Bennett, observes: "There are two schools in every school: the school of the high-status staff member, with the luxury of time and authority to cushion them from the worst classes; and the school of the supply teacher and NQT, who possess neither."[26]

As long as students toe the line for experienced and senior teachers, they have carte blanche to blight the lives of newly qualified and supply teachers.

As explained previously, schools have an important role in teachers' improvement. One of the factors that can make a real difference to whether or not teachers thrive is the attitude school leaders take to students' behaviour. John Papay and Matthew Kraft interviewed teachers in two different schools serving similar students but with very different school cultures:

> In one school, teachers were expected to deal with student behavioral challenges individually, in their classroom or in the hallways. The lack of consistent policies, consequences, and follow-through by school administrators left teachers frustrated. Many said that the school's lack of order and discipline made them less effective instructors. By contrast, teachers in the other high school found that the administration's efforts to create clear policies and enforce them consistently had helped create an environment conducive to learning.[27]

Schools represent a microcosm of wider society. As well as the expectation that they provide an academic education, schools are also a training ground for civilised discourse and cultural participation. The children are the governed and the adults are the proxies for government: enacting laws, maintaining order and ensuring justice. Because children are still learning about how to fit in we cut them a lot of slack. We help them to manage their reactions when they feel angry, hurt or disappointed, and generally hold them to lower standards than those to which they will be held when they enter the adult world.

Relationships between adults and children within school communities matter as much as they do anywhere else. Children will like some teachers more than others; teachers may also have favourites. This will, no doubt, affect the quality of interactions between them and children will probably learn more from those teachers they respect and who they believe respect them. The point is this: *the quality of children's education should not rest on the quality of their individual relationships with their teachers.*

We tend to accept that teachers ought to provide the same education to all their students, regardless of whether or not they like some children more than others. Likewise, we expect that children should treat all adults (and all other children) with the same basic respect regardless of their relationship. We might be nicer to those we like, but if there's not an expected standard of decency for all, then children will quickly learn that they are allowed to choose where and how they behave based on their whims and preferences. This is not a good life lesson.

Sadly, though, it is an attitude that is encouraged in some schools. I recently encountered a school leader saying that at his school there are no behaviour problems in either the English or maths departments because the teachers in those departments give up their lunchtimes to work on their relationships with students. I think there's a lot wrong with this view.

If teachers need to give up their lunch break in order for this to happen, we can infer that good behaviour is not the norm. The implication is that behaviour is worse in areas of the school where teachers don't make this sacrifice. If this is the case, then the senior leaders in this school have abnegated their responsibility to maintain an effective behaviour policy. If there are pockets of good behaviour in a school, this will be due to pockets of effective leadership – either by classroom teachers or middle leaders. Good schools are ones where students and teachers can expect a minimum standard of respect whoever they are and whoever they interact with. This depends on school leaders doing the hard work of ensuring these standards are met. When basic respect is guaranteed, relationships can flourish and schools can become the purposeful and productive communities we would all wish them to be.

No one wants to compel, force or otherwise browbeat children into a compliant, cowering mass (although this is not a particular risk with your average group of teenagers). We all want to be greeted by a sea of happy, eager faces clamouring to learn the wonderful complexities of our subjects. The question is, how do we accomplish that aim? Do we do it by destroying some teachers and prioritising what children want, or do we calmly, patiently and implacably expect children to follow reasonable instructions?

Here are five principles which might help us in our endeavours to create a warm but strict school culture:[28]

Five principles for creating a culture of high expectations
1. **Limit the rules.** If there are too many rules – or if they are too complicated – they become hard to follow. We all naturally want to follow the easiest and most direct path,

and behaviour policies should take account of this. What
are the fewest possible rules you need? Rules should be
based on common sense and natural justice. Young people
have a strongly developed sense of fairness. Where a rule is
essentially fair, a student may still break it but they are less
likely to argue with consequences being applied.

2. **What we permit we promote.** Whatever students see enacted
around them will come to be seen as normal. Rules are only
as effective as our determination to enforce them. Students
will always take their cues from our actions, not our words.

3. **Certainty not severity.** The certainty that a consequence
will be applied for misbehaviour is far more important than
that the consequence is severe. What is important is that we
should use the minimum compulsion necessary. What is the
least severe sanction that might be sufficiently effective?

4. **Don't do it alone.** If you're operating in isolation, without
the support of your school, everything is harder. If children
don't obey the school's rules, it is everyone's collective
responsibility to do something about it. This only works if
there is a system designed to support teachers.

5. **Act as a proxy for the real world.** School is a relatively safe
environment to fail in. The punishments for mistakes are
infinitely less harsh than those children will experience when
they're adults. If we baulk at our duty to help socialise our
students, we will be setting them up for a life of misery.

Of course, we should work hard to grapple with the heart-breaking cankers of
some children's lives. We should be compassionate and understanding. But we
should also be firm and consistent. Blaming teachers for children's decisions
to misbehave undermines everyone and runs the risk of being both inexpert
and dishonest.

If you genuinely believe that teachers are responsible for the behaviour in
their classroom, then logically it makes sense to believe that school leaders are
responsible for the behaviour in their school. To hold teachers to some 'higher'
standard on this is intellectually dishonest. All too often, arguments over whose
'fault' behaviour is can be attributed to a lack of knowledge and expertise.
Teachers and school leaders who are experts in behaviour management don't

usually sit around debating who is responsible. They don't need to: they know that they are responsible and get on and deal with it. Managing behaviour is not the most intellectually challenging task that teachers or school leaders face, but it does require all involved to have expertise. If this is missing, don't waste time debating it; take knowledgeable and realistic action to address this insufficiency.

Getting the measure of metrics

Whether we're tracking student data, evaluating teacher effectiveness or checking stock in the stationery cupboard, we'll be generating data using metrics. Metrics can be great, but their downside is that we can be so preoccupied with seeing only what is right in front of us that it's all too easy to miss anything peripheral. What we believe we can do with the data we generate matters. All school leaders should become familiar with these two important rules:

1.	Campbell's law: "The more any quantitative social indicator is used for social decision-making, the more subject it will be to corruption pressures and the more apt it will be to distort and corrupt the social processes it is intended to monitor."
2.	Goodhart's law: "When a measure becomes a target, it ceases to be a good measure."

It's hard to argue that metrics haven't led to major improvements in education from when I started teaching in the late 1990s. Back in the day, nobody asked me to look at any kind of data and I had literally no idea of my students' prior attainment and only the vaguest notion of how well they did in national exams. Consequently, lots of children did very badly and no one took any responsibility. Times changed. Education became increasingly focused on gathering performance data and pressure was put on schools to make sure exam results went up. And they did. Then came concerns about the curriculum narrowing and distortion, grade inflation, gaming and malpractice.

Did the metrics help? Well, maybe. Perhaps they helped to address some of the most egregious incompetence in the system, but then, as Goodhart's law kicked in, they became increasingly unreliable.

While metrics can be useful, more often than not they do far more harm than good, resulting in perverse incentives, unintended consequences and what Jerry Muller calls 'metric fixation'.[31]

Basically, metrics can be useful in a low stake, high trust environment. Where this is absent, any attempts to measure student outcomes result in, at best, gaming and, at worst, cheating. Similarly, attempts to measure teacher effectiveness usually result in turning biases into numbers which, in turn, end with anything from resentful compliance to unfair dismissal.

Availability bias and bad data

What's more likely to kill you: a shark or a hot water tap? We've all heard stories of killer sharks, but as yet Spielberg hasn't made a thriller about killer plumbing. We reason based on the information most readily available to us. We assume that the risk of dying in a plane crash is greater than the risk of dying on our sofa because plane crashes are so much more dramatic. But we're wrong.

This is the *availability bias*. We make decisions based on the most readily available information in the belief that because it's readily available, it's more likely to be accurate. Sometimes the information we can draw to mind might be accurate, but sometimes it's not. Ignorance isn't bliss; it's scary. We are often most terrified by the unknown. But if something feels familiar, no matter how bad it is, we can cope. We prefer erroneous information to no information at all.

In order to feel certain about our decisions we surround ourselves with data. But although you can't have information without data, you can most definitely have data without information. Data is uniquely comforting because it's just so quantifiable. If you can turn something into a percentage or a bar graph, it must be objectively true. The problem is, it's remarkably easy to make up data. This leads us to do all kinds of foolish things in schools.

Consider this entirely fictitious scenario: a school leadership group is considering moving away from lesson grading in the light of a landslide of disconfirming evidence. They accept that lesson grading is invalid and unreliable, and that taking a lesson study approach is more likely to support the professional development of teachers. But, and it's a big but, what about Ofsted? Those pesky inspectors are expecting to see a neat spreadsheet which shows the percentage breakdown of teaching which is outstanding, good and requiring improvement. How will they react if this data is not on hand? How can we be accountable without numbers? And that's the problem.

If we accept the findings of the MET Project (see pages 122–123), we know that judgements made in the classroom about how students are learning is guesswork at best. Any attempt to turn this information into data is witchcraft.

But it's so comforting. Many school leaders have been seduced into the easy certainties of grading lesson observations, aggregating the grades and then proudly declaring that teaching in their school is 80% good or better. But this is meaningless. Assigning numerical values to our preferences and biases gives them the power of data, but they're still just made up.

We fall into the same bear trap when setting targets for students. We tell students they need to know their target grades as if they are certainties. While target grades may not be simply plucked from the air like lesson observation grades, they are based on statistical probabilities that may have some validity when applied to large cohorts but which are reduced to meaningless nonsense when applied to individuals.

But no data is bad in and of itself. Just as guns don't kill people, data doesn't distort the curriculum or warp decisions about what to teach: we do that. We are comforted by the illusion of knowing. But we don't really know. And any accountability system which allows people to either input numbers they've made up or extrapolate data which is wrestled into meaning something it was never intended to mean is doomed to fail. But what's worse is that many schools, teachers, parents and children aren't even aware of the failure.

A measurement checklist

1. What kind of information are you thinking of measuring?
When we try to measure anything that can be influenced by the process of measurement, reliability suffers. Teachers and students are self-conscious agents and, if rewards or sanctions are tied to the measurement process, behaviour will be distorted. That said, if teachers and students agree with and approve of what is being measured, the more likely they are to behave in ways that increase the validity of the measurement.

> **Tip:** If you want to measure something inanimate, go for it. If you want to measure some aspect of human performance, gain consensus first and avoid tying your metric to rewards or punishments.

2. How useful is this information?
If data is the solution, what's the problem? Just because you can measure something doesn't mean you should. Muller suggests that ease of measurement tends to be inversely proportional to usefulness.[32] Ask yourself, why do I want

this information? What am I going to do with it? How is this data likely to affect my decision-making? What would I do differently if I didn't have this data?

Tip: Think carefully about how collecting data will improve the experience of students and teachers. If you're not sure it will, don't measure it.

3. How useful are more metrics?

Measures of human performance are most useful at revealing outliers. A good metric might reveal misconduct or ineptitude, but may still do a very poor job when it comes to providing meaningful information about good or average performance. Most schools are small enough that school leaders already know where there is poor performance. Introducing a metric to measure what you already suspect wastes the time of the majority. Measure to the least degree that you need to.

Tip: Treating all teachers or students equally is always and automatically unfair. If you know someone is doing a good job, don't interfere. If you know someone is struggling, invest your efforts in helping them to improve.

4. What are the costs of not relying on standardised measurement?

Every head teacher I've ever spoken to has a pretty good idea of what's going on in their school. If a teacher always seems to be missing from duty, if parents continually request a particular teacher does or does not teach their child, these are useful sources of data. Does it matter if these intangibles fail to show up on test scores? Maybe. If a teacher is well loved but gets poor results you might want to intervene, but you should probably intervene differently than you would for a teacher who gets poor results and is roundly despised. Everyone loves a graph, but what is it actually telling you?

Tip: Don't just look at metrics – compare with more informal sources of knowledge.

5. To what purposes will the measurement be put? To whom will the information be made transparent?

Muller points out that transparency can have a dark side. If we know that data collected on us will be made publicly available, then what could be potentially useful is much more likely to distort behaviour. Arguably, it's the high stakes nature of Ofsted inspections that causes most of the perverse incentives and unintended consequences. If their inspections were not made publicly available, maybe school leaders would have an easier job of improving schools. Similarly, while schools should be held to account for student outcomes, does it help to make these outcomes public? What if individual teachers' results were published in the same way? Metrics that might really help to improve performance if only used internally can backfire badly when they become too transparent.

Tip: Think carefully about what you intend to do with the information you gather. If your purpose is to improve a school, then it's probably not a good idea to disseminate information beyond those who absolutely need to know.

6. What are the costs of acquiring data?

Information is never free. Time spent gathering data is time that cannot be spent on improving performance. Data collection leads to processing, analysis and presentation. Before long, the opportunity costs far outweigh the gains and quickly become a distraction. Is there a different way of interpreting the data? How can I verify the quality of the data I'm being shown, and what are its margins for error?

Tip: Think about what else teachers could do with the time they currently spend collecting, processing and analysing data.

7. Why are performance metrics being demanded?

Muller suggests that the demand for metrics often stems from ignorance. If you're new to a school, you may think that it's an important exercise to collect lots of data to find out about it. New heads often spend a great deal of time observing their teachers. All this comes with costs paid for by other people. Time spent finding out about a school is time that cannot be spent on improving it. You may think it's important to collect all of this data, but someone else will almost certainly already know what you don't.

Tip: Wherever possible, promote from within rather than hiring externally.

8. How and by whom are the measures of performance developed?

There's good evidence that metrics are far more likely to be effective if those being measured have had significant input into developing the metrics they will be subject to. Anything imposed from above will be resisted, gamed and complied with in the dullest possible manner. When teachers are told to mark books in a particular way or start lessons with a particular set of routines, they may well have a better way which they are now prevented from implementing. You will have sacrificed quality for the hollowest form of consistency. Instead, involve as many different people as possible in designing the processes you'll use for assuring quality. Remember that consistency should not be an end itself, especially if it stifles mastery and autonomy.

Tip: Think carefully about how those you're responsible for managing might react when measures are imposed. Ask teachers what they think they should be doing and hold them to account for what they've said they will do.

9. Even the best measures are subject to corruption or goal diversion

Where there are rewards or punishments there will be drawbacks. All too rarely do those in authority consider the possible consequences of imposing metrics. If you expect teachers to welcome students to each lesson at the classroom door, will this make them more likely to ignore bullying or other social problems because they just don't have time to deal with them? If you ask teachers to record behaviour infractions on a computer system, will they end up ignoring bad behaviour because they haven't got the time to log every incident? These unintended consequences don't mean that we shouldn't measure or check anything, but they do mean we should think carefully about what we might be incentivising people to do.

Tip: Try to anticipate problems and think, "What would I do if was a busy, main scale teacher on a six period day and someone asked me to comply with this system?"

10. What are the limits of what is possible?

Not every problem has a solution and an even smaller number of problems can be solved with metrics. Not everything can be improved through measurement and not everything that can be measured can be improved. Often, by gathering data we end up making problems seem more pressing without actually coming any closer to a solution. Metrics have their uses but they are but a single arrow in your leadership quiver. Human conversations, patience, humility and warmth may go a long way to smoothing over what databases and spreadsheets only exacerbate. What are the limitations of data? What doesn't it show?

Tip: Be clear on what you can and can't solve. You can almost always find ways to make the lives of those you lead more pleasant.

In no way should this list be seen as anything other than scratching the surface of what school leaders need to know in order to create the conditions for teachers to thrive; it should be seen as necessary but insufficient. You also need to know enough about every aspect of the curriculum to be able to hold subject specialists to account intelligently.

Summary of Chapter 7

- Too much training in leadership is based on faulty intuition and wishful thinking; better leadership development requires a greater understanding of, and engagement with, research and evidence.
- Leadership is a domain specific not a domain general skill: school leaders need to be more expert in education.
- The primary role of school leadership is to remove extraneous demands on teachers so they can focus on planning and teaching the very best curriculum possible.
- The traits that we would like leaders to possess are often at odds with the traits that get leaders promoted and make them successful.
- What seems to make leaders successful is often illusory. Successful leaders have been lucky in the past but will eventually regress to the mean.
- Senior leaders are likely to occupy a bubble where they only see and hear what those around them think they want to see and hear.

- The constant drive to make schools outstanding can easily undermine efforts to be effective.
- Leaders need to be particularly aware of the limitations and effects of using metrics to measure performance.
- We are likely to make decisions on the data we have available, whether or not it is reliable or valid.
- Predicting individual students' outcomes is a very poor use of data.
- Remember Goodhart's law: when a measure becomes a target, it ceases to be a good measure.

CONCLUSION

The perils and pitfalls of school leadership are many and various. It's staggeringly easy to rush to judgement and make snap decisions which can have disastrous long-term effects on teachers and students alike. Always remember that it is far easier to destroy a school than it is to improve one.

School leadership may be the most important factor in determining children's – especially disadvantaged children's – life chances. You face an awful weight of responsibility and children's lives hang in the balance with every decision you make.

But don't let this put you off. My hat is off to you: you are doing a job I don't have the patience, determination or wisdom to do. All you really have to do is to remember that your job is to make teachers' lives easier so that they can get on with the hard work of teaching students to be rounded, successful individuals, ready to participate in society.

The trouble is that we find it so easy to lose sight of this simple aim. It's hard not to feel important when you get your first leadership role and your own office. If you're lucky enough to have your own personal assistant then you probably feel like a minor deity at times. But big chairs, sharp suits and new initiatives don't make effective leaders.

If this book has accomplished anything, I hope it is to remind you that you exist to serve and that you are only as effective as your ability to tap into the collective knowledge of your school and the wider educational community. If you can maintain your focus on creating the conditions for teachers to thrive, you won't go far wrong.

Intelligent accountability: a summary

- You will never have enough information to make perfect decisions. To improve the odds of making better decisions, you must seek out collective sources of knowledge.
- Work to make your school operate on a surplus model. Assume teachers are well intentioned and look around to see how you can make it easier for them to make better decisions.
- When teachers are trusted to act as professionals, they are more likely to be their best.
- Accountability is essential but only if you make teachers aware when judgements are being made. Try to conceal your preferences and prove that you are knowledgeable and interested in accuracy.
- Treating teachers equally is unfair. Allow those who have earned it as much autonomy as possible and work with those who haven't to earn it in the future.
- Help to create the conditions for teachers to develop expert intuitions by focusing on what they need to learn and the best bets for helping them learn it.
- The single most important aspect of your job is to make it as easy as possible for teachers to teach. All else flows from that.

178

APPENDIX: THE ORIGINS OF INTELLIGENT ACCOUNTABILITY

I first started using the term 'intelligent accountability' in training for school leaders in 2015, and, as far as I knew, I had come up with something original and new. As is usually the case, I was mistaken. In researching this book, I've unearthed a trail of evidence that makes it clear that I'm far from being the first person to explore these ideas.

In their 2000 paper 'Validity and accountability in high-stakes testing', Mary Lee Smith and Patricia Fey say:

> To call for accountability is to assert a political right – to demand that a particular individual or institution assume some responsibility and demonstrate it in a certain form. Although there are many varieties of accountability in education (moral, professional, fiscal, market, bureaucratic, and legal), the term has come to mean the responsibility of a school (district, teacher, or student) to parents, taxpayers, or government (federal, state, city, or district) to produce high achievement test scores.[1]

In the book based on her 2002 Reith Lectures series, *A Question of Trust*, Onara O'Neill discusses accountability and trust as mutually dependent concepts and is, as far as I can tell, the first to use the term intelligent accountability. She says:

> Perhaps the present revolution in accountability will make us all trustworthier. Perhaps we shall be trusted once again. But I think this is a vain hope – not because accountability is undesirable or unnecessary, but because currently fashionable methods of accountability damage rather than repair trust. If we want greater accountability without damaging professional performance we need intelligent *accountability*.[2]

The following year, former Secretary of State for Education David Miliband referred to intelligent accountability in a speech on workforce reform:

> I have a very clear view of the right focus for education policy. It is to help build capacity at school level for effective education. It is a vision rooted in an expansive and I believe exciting view of teacher professionalism at

the heart of education reform. To stretch and emphasise the point, it puts bottom-up teacher professionalism at the centre of reform, rather than top-down prescription.

From Ministers, this vision requires clarity on outcomes. It requires consistency and coherence in priorities and approach, with the effect on teaching and learning the judge and jury of policy. It requires alignment of activity – so that the left hand of government knows what the right hand is doing, and vice versa. It requires a real commitment to freedom and flexibility at the front line, combined with an intelligent accountability framework to incentivise and reward good performance. And of course it requires a commitment to the long term.[3]

Regrettably, at no point did he spell out what an 'intelligent accountability framework' might contain.

In his 2010 book, *All Systems Go*, Michael Fullan lays out what he thinks intelligent accountability should mean: "Intelligent accountability in essence involves building cumulative capacity and responsibility that is both internally held and externally reinforced." He argues that intelligent accountability possesses the following characteristics:

1. It relies on incentives more than on punishment.
2. It invests in capacity building so that people are able to meet the goals.
3. It invests in collective (peer) responsibility – what is called 'internal accountability'.
4. It intervenes initially in a nonjudgmental manner.
5. It embraces transparent data about practice and results.
6. It intervenes more decisively along the way when required.

With the exception of point 5 (which I argue against in Chapter 7), this list is broadly similar to the arguments I make here. I can only say that I had not read Fullan's book before writing my own and, I hope, I have added substantially to his ideas.

ENDNOTES

Introduction

1. D. Wiliam, *Leadership for Teacher Learning: Creating a Culture Where All Teachers Improve So That All Students Succeed* (West Palm Beach, FL: Learning Sciences International, 2016), p. 6.
2. Quoted in M. Hood and H. Fletcher-Wood, *Teaching Teachers: The Bets of American Teacher Educators* (2018), p. 1. Available at: https://www. ambition.org.uk/research-and-insight/teaching-teachers-bets-american-teacher-educators.
3. T. Sowell, *The Vision of the Anointed: Self-Congratulation as a Basis for Social Policy* (London: Hachette UK, 2019), p. 136.

Chapter 1

1. N. Silver, *The Signal and the Noise: The Art and Science of Prediction* (London: Penguin, 2012), p. 45.
2. The metaphor of the island of knowledge comes from a quotation attributed to Ralph W Sockman: "The larger the island of knowledge, the longer the shoreline of wonder." In S. Ratcliffe (ed.), *Oxford Essential Quotations*, 4th edn (Oxford: Oxford University Press, 2016).
3. U. S. Department of Defense, DoD News Briefing – Secretary Rumsfeld and Gen. Myers [news transcript] (12 February 2002). Available at: https://archive.defense.gov/Transcripts/Transcript.aspx?TranscriptID=2636.
4. J. Surowiecki, *The Wisdom of Crowds: Why the Many Are Smarter Than the Few* (London: Abacus, 2005).
5. M. Syed, *Rebel Ideas: The Power of Diverse Thinking* (London: Hachette UK), p. 24.
6. B. Russell, *Proposed Roads to Freedom: Socialism, Anarchism and Syndicalism* (New York: Henry Holt and Co., 1919), p. 147.
7. S. Weil, *Gravity and Grace*, tr. A. Wills (Lincoln: Bison Books, 1997), p. 128.
8. I go into a lot more detail about cognitive biases in education in my book, *What If Everything You Knew About Education Was Wrong?* (Carmarthen: Crown House Publishing, 2015).
9. K. A. Ericsson, Deliberate practice and the acquisition and maintenance of expert performance in medicine and related domains. *Academic Medicine*, 79(10 Suppl.) (2004), 70–81.
10. R. Dawes, House of Cards (New York: Simon & Schuster, 2009).

11. R. M. Hogarth, *Educating Intuition: A Challenge for the 21st Century* (Barcelona: Centre de Recerca en Economia Internacional, 2003).
12. In R. M. Hogarth, T. Lejarraga and E. Soyer, The two settings of kind and wicked learning environments. *Current Directions in Psychological Science*, 24(5) (2015), 379–385, the concept of a wicked domain is expanded to include domains where there is a significant distance between the learning environment and the environment of practice. This obviously applies far less to teaching but, arguably, much more to leadership.
13. Hogarth, *Educating Intuition*, p. 15.
14. There is a caveat here: the least skilled performers, across a range of different domains, don't seem to improve with clear and repeated feedback. This has potential implications for developing teachers and school leaders. See J. Ehrlinger, K. Johnson, M. Banner, D. Dunning and J. Kruger, Why the unskilled are unaware: further explorations of (absent) self-insight among the incompetent. *Organizational Behavior and Human Decision Processes*, 105(1) (2008), 98–121.
15. G. Klein, Sources of error in naturalistic decision making tasks. *Proceedings of the Human Factors and Ergonomics Society Annual Meeting*, 37(4) (1993), 368–371.
16. D. Kahneman and G. Klein, Strategic decisions: when can you trust your gut? *McKinsey* (1 March 2010). Available at: https://www.mckinsey.com/business-functions/strategy-and-corporate-finance/our-insights/strategic-decisions-when-can-you-trust-your-gut.
17. Hogarth, *Educating Intuition*, p. 9; my emphasis.
18. B. K. Hamre, S. G. Goffin and M. Kraft-Sayre, *Classroom Assessment Scoring System (CLASS) Implementation Guide: Measuring and Improving Classroom Interactions in Early Classroom Settings* (2009), p. 17. Available at: https://www.boldgoals.org/wp-content/uploads/CLASSImplementationGuide.pdf.
19. E. L. Bjork and R. A. Bjork, Making things hard on yourself, but in a good way: creating desirable difficulties to enhance learning. In M. A. Gernsbacher, R. W. Pew and L. M. Hough (eds), *Psychology and the Real World: Essays Illustrating Fundamental Contributions to Society*, 2nd edn (New York: Worth, 2011), pp. 59–68.
20. Kahneman and Klein, Strategic decisions.
21. Richard Feynman put it like this: "The first principle is that you must not fool yourself – and you are the easiest person to fool." In *Surely You're Joking, Mr. Feynman! Adventures of a Curious Character* (London: Random House, 1992), p. 343.
22. Kahneman and Klein, Strategic decisions.

23. As an example, Jeremy Clarkson tweeted on 16 August 2018: "Don't worry if your A level grades aren't any good. I got a C and 2 Us. And I'm sitting here deciding which of my Range Rovers to use today." Available at: https://twitter.com/jeremyclarkson/status/1029984945547223040?lang=en.

24. Kahneman and Klein, Strategic decisions.

25. J. Kruger and D. Dunning, Unskilled and unaware of it: how difficulties in recognizing one's own incompetence lead to inflated self-assessments. *Journal of Personality and Social Psychology*, 77(6) (1999), 1121–1134.

26. E. Morris, The anosognosic's dilemma: something's wrong but you'll never know what it is (part 1) [interview with D. Dunning]. *New York Times* (20 June 2010). Available at: https://opinionator.blogs.nytimes.com/2010/06/20/the-anosognosics-dilemma-1.

27. S. Novella, Misunderstanding. *Neurologica Blog* (8 January 2019). Available at: https://theness.com/neurologicablog/index.php/misunderstanding-dunning-kruger.

28. B. Goldacre, *Bad Science: Quacks, Hacks, and Big Pharma Flacks* (Toronto: McClelland & Stewart, 2010), pp. 13–14.

29. D. Didau and N. Rose, *What Every Teacher Needs to Know About Psychology* (Woodbridge: John Catt Educational, 2016), p. 217.

30. Adapted from D. Willingham, Draft bill of research rights for educators (2014). Available at: http://www.danielwillingham.com/daniel-willingham-science-and-education-blog/archives/08-2014.

31. S. M. Koziol Jr and P. Burns, Teachers' accuracy in self-reporting about instructional practices using a focused self-report inventory. *Journal of Educational Research*, 79(4) (1986), 205–209.

32. B. Caplan, *The Case Against Education: Why the Education System is a Waste of Time and Money* (Princeton, NJ: Princeton University Press, 2018), p. 59.

33. L. S. Shulman and S. M. Wilson, *The Wisdom of Practice: Essays on Teaching, Learning, and Learning to Teach* (San Francisco, CA: Jossey-Bass, 2018), p. 504.

Chapter 2

1. This is often attributed to the 2007 McKinsey report by M. Barber and M. Mourshed, *How the World's Best Performing Education Systems Come Out on Top.* Available at: https://www.mckinsey.com/industries/public-and-social-sector/our-insights/how-the-worlds-best-performing-school-systems-come-out-on-top, but a footnote on p. 19 reveals that the quotation actually comes from an unnamed South Korean government official.

2. R. Coe, C. J. Rauch, S. Kime and D. Singleton, Great Teaching Toolkit: *Evidence Review* (2020). Available at: https://www.cambridgeinternational. org/Images/584543-great-teaching-toolkit-evidence-review.pdf.

3. See D. Wiliam at the Schools Network Annual Conference, 20 December 2011. Available at: https://www.youtube.com/watch?v=wKLo15A80lI at 34:50.

4. S. G. Rivkin, E. A. Hanushek and J. F. Kain, Teachers, schools, and academic achievement. *Econometrica*, 73(2) (2005), 417–458.

5. For example, D. Boyd, P. Grossman, H. Lankford, S. Loeb and J. Wyckoff, Overview of measuring effect sizes: the effect of measurement error. Brief 2. *National Center for Analysis of Longitudinal Data in Education Research* (2008). Available at: https://www.urban.org/sites/default/files/ publication/33346/1001264-Overview-of-Measuring-Effect-Sizes-The-Effect-of-Measurement-Error.PDF; D. N. Harris and T. R. Sass, Teacher training, teacher quality and student achievement. *Journal of Public Economics*, 95(7–8) (2011), 798–812; J. P. Papay and M. A. Kraft, The myth of the performance plateau. *Educational Leadership*, 73(8) (2016), 36–42; J. E. Rockoff, The impact of individual teachers on student achievement: evidence from panel data. *American Economic Review*, 94(2) (2004), 247–252; M. Wiswall, The dynamics of teacher quality. *Journal of Public Economics*, 100 (2013), 61–78.

6. M. A. Kraft and J. P. Papay, Can professional environments in schools promote teacher development? Explaining heterogeneity in returns to teaching experience. *Educational Evaluation and Policy Analysis*, 36(4) (2014), 476–500.

7. See, for example, D. A. Garvin, A. C. Edmondson and F. Gino, Is yours a learning organization? *Harvard Business Review* (March 2008). Available at: https://hbr.org/2008/03/is-yours-a-learning-organization; J. R. Hackman and G. R. Oldman, *Work Redesign* (Reading, MA: Addison-Wesley, 1980); R. M. Kanter, *The Change Masters: Corporate Entrepreneurs at Work* (New York: Simon & Schuster, 1984); and D. C. Lortie, *Schoolteacher: A Sociological Study* (Chicago, IL: University of Chicago Press, 1975).

8. S. M. Johnson, M. A. Kraft and J. P. Papay, How context matters in high-need schools: the effects of teachers' working conditions on their professional satisfaction and their students' achievement. *Teachers College Record*, 114(10, special issue) (2012), 1–39.

9. The concept of deficit models and surplus models in education first came, as far as I'm aware, from a blog by Keven Bartle: Deficit or surplus? You decide! *Keven Bartle's Blog* (30 October 2013). Available at: https:// dailygenius.wordpress.com/2013/10/30/deficit-or-surplus-you-decide.

The concept owes a debt to Douglas Mcgregor's theory of contrasting management beliefs and styles which he called Theory X (authoritarian, micromanaging, uses carrots and sticks) and Theory Y (participative, collaborative, trust based).

10. M. Berber, P. Kihn and A. Moffit, Deliverology: from idea to implementation. *McKinsey on Government*, 6 (2011), 32–39

11. Secret Teacher, The exodus of older teachers is draining schools of expertise. *The Guardian* (12 May 2018). Available at: https://www.theguardian.com/teacher-network/2018/may/12/secret-teacher-the-exodus-of-older-teachers-is-draining-schools-of-expertise.

12. Cambridge Assessment, The average age of teachers in secondary schools (July 2016). Available at: https://www.cambridgeassessment.org.uk/our-research/data-bytes/the-average-age-of-teachers-in-secondary-schools.

13. R. Allen and S. Sims, *The Teacher Gap* (Abingdon and New York: Routledge, 2018), p. 52.

14. Department for Education, *Factors Affecting Teacher Retention: Qualitative Investigation.* Research Report (March 2018), pp. 6–7. Available at: https://www.gov.uk/government/publications/factors-affecting-teacher-retention-qualitative-investigation.

15. Voltaire quoted an unnamed Italian poet in his *Dictionnaire philosophique* in 1770: "Il meglio è l'inimico del bene." The line later appeared in his poem 'La Béguele' as "Le mieux est l'ennemi du bien."

16. R. Coe, *Improving Education: A Triumph of Hope Over Experience.* Inaugural lecture of Professor Robert Coe, Durham University, 18 June 2013, p. xii. Available at: http://www.cem.org/attachments/publications/ImprovingEducation2013.pdf.

17. N. C. Soderstrom and R. A. Bjork, Learning versus performance: an integrative review. *Perspectives on Psychological Science*, 10(2) (2015), 176–199 at 176.

18. M. Evans, *Leaders with Substance: An Antidote to Leadership Genericism in Schools.* (Woodbridge: John Catt Educational, 2019), p. 140.

19. See https://www.cdc.gov/injury/features/global-road-safety/index.html.

20. S. Gordon, P. Mendenhall and B. O'Connor, *Beyond the Checklist: What Else Health Care Can Learn from Aviation Teamwork and Safety* (Ithaca, NY: Cornell University Press, 2012), p. 2.

21. J. Nielsen, *The Myth of Leadership: Creating Leaderless Organizations* (London: Hachette UK, 2011), pp. 4–5.

Chapter 3

1. A. Waley, *The Analects of Confucius* (London: Allen & Unwin, 1983), Book XII, Ch. 7, p. 164.
2. The scenario was originally framed by Merrill Flood and Melvin Dresher in 1950. Albert W. Tucker formalised the game with prison sentence rewards and named it 'the prisoner's dilemma'. See W. Poundstone, *Prisoner's Dilemma: John von Neumann, Game Theory and the Puzzle of the Bomb* (New York: Anchor, 1993).
3. O. O'Neill, *A Question of Trust: The BBC Reith Lectures 2002* (Cambridge: Cambridge University Press, 2002), p. vii.
4. The phrase "Bellum omnium contra omnes" was first used by Thomas Hobbes in his 1651 treatise on human nature, *Leviathan*.
5. R. Axelrod and W. D. Hamilton, The evolution of cooperation. *Science*, 211(4489) (1981), 1390–1396.
6. See, for instance, the observer bias entry on the Catalogue of Bias website: https://catalogofbias.org/biases/observer-bias.
7. O'Neill, *A Question of Trust*, p. 18.
8. Health and Safety Executive, Work-related stress, anxiety or depression statistics in Great Britain, 2019. Available at: https://www.hse.gov.uk/statistics/causdis/stress.pdf.
9. Estelle Morris, *Professionalism and Trust: The Future of Teachers and Teaching. A Speech by the Rt Hon. Estelle Morris MP, Secretary of State for Education and Skills to the Social Market Foundation* (November 2001). Available at: https://dera.ioe.ac.uk//10112.
10. Department for Education and Skills, *Time for Standards: Reforming the School Workforce* (London: DfES, 2002).
11. S. Gibson, L. Oliver and M. Dennison, *Workload Challenge: Analysis of Teacher Consultation Responses*. Available at: https://www.gov.uk/government/publications/workload-challenge-analysis-of-teacher-responses.
12. NASUWT, *The Big Question 2019*. Available at: https://www.nasuwt.org.uk/uploads/assets/uploaded/981c20ce-145e-400a-805969e777762b13.pdf.
13. B. Scott and I. Vidakovic, Teacher well-being and workload survey: interim findings. *Ofsted Blog* (30 November). Available at : https://educationinspection.blog.gov.uk/2018/11/30/teacher-well-being-and-workload-survey-interim-findings.
14. D. Jones, D. Molitor and J. Reif, What do workplace wellness programs do? Evidence from the Illinois Workplace Wellness Study. *Quarterly Journal of Economics,* 134(4) (2019), 1747–1791.
15. J. F. Helliwell and H. Huang, Well-being and trust in the workplace. *Journal of Happiness Studies*, 12(5) (2011), 747–767.

16. L. P. Feld and B. S. Frey, Trust breeds trust: how taxpayers are treated. *Economics of Governance*, 3(2) (2002), 87–99.
17. A. Bryk and B. Schneider, *Trust in Schools: A Core Resource for Improvement* (New York: Russell Sage Foundation, 2002).
18. A. Schleicher, *Valuing Our Teachers and Raising Their Status: How Communities Can Help. International Summit on the Teaching Profession* (2018). Available at: https://www.oecd.org/education/valuing-our-teachers-and-raising-their-status-9789264292697-en.htm.
19. J. H. Dyer and W. Chu, The role of trustworthiness in reducing transaction costs and improving performance: empirical evidence from the United States, Japan, and Korea. *Organization Science*, 14(1) (2003), 57–68.
20. S. Bok, *Lying: Moral Choice in Public and Private Life* (New York: Vintage, 1999), p. 13.
21. Bok, *Lying*, pp. 92–106.
22. J. B. Peterson, *Twelve Rules for Life: An Antidote to Chaos* (Toronto: Random House, 2018), p. 230.
23. This phrase comes from R. Scruton, *The Uses of Pessimism: And the Danger of False Hope* (Oxford: Oxford University Press, 2010).
24. D. Wiliam, *Leadership for Teacher Learning: Creating a Culture Where All Teachers Improve So That All Students Succeed* (West Palm Beach, FL: Learning Sciences International, 2016), p. 177.

Chapter 4

1. O. O'Neill, *A Question of Trust: The BBC Reith Lectures 2002* (Cambridge: Cambridge University Press, 2002), p. 50.
2. P. J. DiMaggio and W. W. Powell, The iron cage revisited institutional isomorphism and collective rationality in organizational fields. In J. A. C. Baum and F. Dobbin (eds), *Economics Meets Sociology in Strategic Management (Advances in Strategic Management, Vol. 17)* (Bingley: Emerald Group Publishing, 1983), pp. 143–166. This paper came to recent attention after R. Allen and S. Sims wrote about institutional isomorphism in *The Teacher Gap* (Abingdon and New York: Routledge, 2018), pp. 92–98.
3. M. R. Leary, Sociometer theory and the pursuit of relational value: getting to the root of self-esteem. *European Review of Social Psychology*, 16 (2005), 75–111.
4. J. Haidt, *The Righteous Mind: Why Good People Are Divided By Politics and Religion* (London: Vintage, 2012), p. 91.
5. A. Smith, *The Theory of Moral Sentiments* (London: Andrew Millar; Edinburgh: Alexander Kincaid and J. Bell, 1759). Available at: https://oll.libertyfund.org/titles/smith-the-theory-of-moral-sentiments-and-on-the-origins-of-languages-stewart-ed.

6. J. S. Lerner and P. E. Tetlock, Bridging individual, interpersonal, and institutional approaches to judgment and choice: the impact of accountability on cognitive bias. In S. Schneider and J. Shanteau (eds), *Emerging Perspectives on Judgment and Decision Research* (Cambridge: Cambridge University Press, 2003), pp. 431–457 at 438.

7. J. Baron, *Thinking and Deciding*, 4th edn (Cambridge: Cambridge University Press, 2007).

8. Lerner and Tetlock, Bridging individual, interpersonal, and institutional approaches, p. 23.

9. P. E. Tetlock, Accountability and the perseverance of first impressions. *Social Psychology Quarterly*, 46, (1983), 285–292; and P. E. Tetlock, Accountability: a social check on the fundamental attribution error. Social Psychology Quarterly, 48(3) (1985), 227–236.

10. N. Mero and S. Motowidlo, Effects of rater accountability on the accuracy and favorability of performance ratings. *Journal of Applied Psychology*, 80(4) (1995), 517–524.

11. A. R. Fitzpatrick and A. H. Eagly, Anticipatory belief polarization as a function of the expertise of a discussion partner. *Personality and Social Psychology Bulletin*, 7 (1981), 636–642.

12. P. E. Tetlock and J. I. Kim, Accountability and judgment processes in a personality prediction task. *Journal of Personality and Social Psychology*, 52 (1987), 700–709; and E. P. Thompson, R. J. Roman, G. B. Moskowitz, S. Chaiken and J. A. Bargh, Accuracy motivation attenuates covert priming: the systematic reprocessing of social information. *Journal of Personality & Social Psychology*, 66(3) (1994), 474–489.

13. J. Ross and B. M. Staw, Expo 86: an escalation prototype. Administrative Science Quarterly, 31 (1986), 274–297; J. Ross and B. M. Staw, Organizational escalation and exit: lessons from the Shoreham Nuclear Power Plant. *Academy of Management Journal*, 36 (1993), 701–732; B. M. Staw and L. L. Cummings (eds), *Rationality and Justification in Organizational Life, Vol. II* (Greenwich, CT: JAI Press, 1980); B. M. Staw and F. V. Fox, Escalation: the determinants of commitment to a chosen course of action. *Human Relations*, 30 (1977), 431–450; and B. M. Staw and J. Ross, Understanding behavior in escalation situations. *Science*, 246 (1989), 216–220.

14. Lerner and Tetlock, Bridging individual, interpersonal, and institutional approaches.

15. For further explanation of the idea of cargo cults, see the Cambridge Encyclopedia of Anthropology: https://www.anthroencyclopedia.com/entry/cargo-cults.

16. For a review of the absence of evidence on written marking, see V. Elliott, J. A. Baird, T. N. Hopfenbeck, J. Ingram, I. Thompson, N. Usher, M. Zantout, J. Richardson and R. Coleman, *A Marked Improvement? A Review of the Evidence on Written Marking.* Available at: https://educationendowmentfoundation.org.uk/evidence-summaries/evidence-reviews/written-marking; as well as my critique of it: D. Didau, A marked decline? The EEF's review of the evidence on written marking. *The Learning Spy* (18 May 2016). Available at: https://learningspy.co.uk/assessment/marked-decline-eefs-review-evidence-written-marking.

Chapter 5

1. S. Moore, *Who's the Fairest of Them All? The Truth About Opportunity, Taxes, and Wealth in America* (New York and London: Encounter Books, 2012), p. 22.

2. J. Abeler, S. Altmann, S. Kube and M. Wibral, Gift exchange and workers' fairness concerns: when equality is unfair. *Journal of the European Economic Association*, 8(6) (2010), 1299–1324 at 1302.

3. The EEF Toolkit rates performance related pay as 'low impact': see https://educationendowmentfoundation.org.uk/evidence-summaries/teaching-learning-toolkit/performance-pay.

4. Personal communication, 7 August 2020.

5. It's a great line but, sadly, not something Aristotle ever said. The closest he comes is "equality seems to be just and it is, but not to everyone, only to those who are equal to begin with. And so, inequality seems to be just, and, indeed, it is, but not for all people, only those who are not equal." Read more on the Sententiae Antiquae blog: Fake Aristotle fakely rails against fighting inequality (23 March 2019). Available at: https://sententiaeantiquae.com/2019/03/23/fake-aristotle-fakely-rails-against-fighting-inequality.

6. This image is a metaphor and does not accurately represent reality. It works because the inequality in the image – height – is a quality inherent to the individuals depicted. If you try extending the metaphor too far, it quickly becomes an example of deficit thinking. See: P. Kuttner, The problem with that equity vs. equality graphic you're using. *Cultural Organizing* (29 October 2016). Available at: https://culturalorganizing.org/the-problem-with-that-equity-vs-equality-graphic.

7. C. Starmans, M. Sheskin and P. Bloom, Why people prefer unequal societies. *Nature Human Behaviour*, 1(4) (2017), 0082.

8. D. Pink (2009) *Drive: The Surprising Truth About What Motivates Us* (New York: Penguin, 2011).

9. A. Hargreaves and M. Fullan, *Professional Capital: Transforming Teaching in Every School* (New York: Teachers College Press, 2015), p. 115.
10. D. Wiliam, *Leadership for Teacher Learning: Creating a Culture Where All Teachers Improve So That All Students Succeed* (West Palm Beach, FL: Learning Sciences International, 2016), p. 168.
11. Hargreaves and Fullan, *Professional Capital*, p. 43.
12. O. O'Neill, *A Question of Trust: The BBC Reith Lectures 2002* (Cambridge: Cambridge University Press, 2002), p. 34.
13. Y. N. Harari, *Sapiens: A Brief History of Humankind* (London: Random House, 2014), pp. 183–184.
14. The quotation is from Emerson's 1841 essay, 'Self-Reliance'. See: https://www.gutenberg.org/files/16643/16643-h/16643-h.htm.
15. Hargreaves and Fullan, *Professional Capital*, p. 113.
16. Wiliam, *Leadership for Teacher Learning*, p. 150.
17. R. P. Feynman, *Surely You're Joking, Mr. Feynman! Adventures of a Curious Character* (London: Random House, 1992), p. 340.
18. M. Tidd, 'Non-negotiables' drag us down, without question. *TES* (7 October 2016). Available at: https://www.tes.com/news/non-negotiables-drag-us-down-without-question.

Chapter 6

1. The MET Project showed that an effective teacher in one setting was likely to be effective in a different setting, and because we know it's the same teacher, we can conclude that teacher quality matters. See T. J. Kane, D. F. McCaffrey, T. Miller and D. O. Staiger, *Have We Identified Effective Teachers? Validating Measures of Effective Teaching Using Random Assignment*. MET Project Research Paper (2013). Available at: http://k12education.gatesfoundation.org/download/?Num=2676&f%20ilename=MET_Validating_Using_Random_Assignment_Research_Paper.pdf. It might be fair to say that teacher quality matters because teaching quality matters, but at the moment we're only able to measure teacher quality with very limited accuracy and teaching quality not at all.
2. G. Nuthall, *The Hidden Lives of Learners* (Wellington: NZCER Press, 2001), pp. 26–29.
3. D. Aaronson, L. Barrow and W. Sanders, Teachers and student achievement in the Chicago Public High Schools. *Journal of Labor Economics*, 25(1) (2007), 95–135.
4. J. E. Rockoff, The impact of individual teachers on student achievement: evidence from panel data. *American Economic Review*, 94(2) (2004), 247–252.

5. D. Wiliam, *Leadership for Teacher Learning: Creating a Culture Where All Teachers Improve So That All Students Succeed* (West Palm Beach, FL: Learning Sciences International, 2016), p. 34.
6. E. A. Hanushek, Some simple analysis of school quality. NBER Working Paper No. 10229 (2004). Available at: https://www.nber.org/papers/w10229.pdf.
7. T. Bliesner, Methodological moderators in validating biographical data in personnel selection. *Journal of Occupational and Organizational Psychology*, 69(1) (1996), 107–120.
8. B. A. Jacob and L. Lefgren, Can principals identify effective teachers? Evidence on subjective performance evaluation in education. *Journal of Labor Economics*, 26(1) (2008), 101–136.
9. Aaronson et al., Teachers and student achievement in the Chicago Public High Schools.
10. D. D. Goldhaber, P. Goldschmidt and F. Tseng, Teacher value-added at the high-school level: different models, different answers? *Educational Evaluation and Policy Analysis*, 35(2) (2013), 220–236.
11. D. F. McCaffrey, T. R. Sass, J. R. Lockwood and K. Mihaly, The intertemporal variability of teacher effect estimates. *Education Finance and Policy*, 4(4) (2009), 572–606.
12. M. M. Kennedy, Attribution error and the quest for teacher quality. *Educational Researcher*, 39(8) (2010), 591–598.
13. See J. Cohen and D. Goldhaber, Building a more complete understanding of teacher evaluation using classroom observations. *Educational Researcher*, 45(6) (2016), 378–387; M. P. Steinberg and R. Garrett, Classroom composition and measured teacher performance: what do teacher observation scores really measure? *Educational Evaluation and Policy Analysis*, 38(2) (2016), 293–317; and G. Whitehurst, M. M. Chingos and K. M. Lindquist, *Evaluating Teachers with Classroom Observations: Lessons Learned in Four Districts* (2014). Available at: https://www.brookings.edu/wp-content/uploads/2016/06/Evaluating-Teachers-with-Classroom-Observations.pdf.
14. D. Kalogrides, S. Loeb and T. Béteille, Systematic sorting: teacher characteristics and class assignments. *Sociology of Education*, 86(2) (2013), 103–123.
15. G. Nuthall, *The Hidden Lives of Learners*, p. 12.
16. C. Chapman, K. Lowden, H. Chestnutt, S. Hall, S. McKinney, M. Hulme and N. Friel, *The School Improvement Partnership Programme: Using Collaboration and Enquiry to Tackle Educational Inequity. Report to Education Scotland* (2015). Available at: http://eprints.gla.ac.uk/112298/1/112298.pdf.
17. Wiliam, *Leadership for Teacher Learning*, p. 41.

18. See S. Gorard, R. Hordosy and N. Siddiqui, How unstable are 'school effects' assessed by a value-added technique? *International Education Studies*, 6(1) (2012), 1–9; and McCaffrey et al., The intertemporal variability of teacher effect estimates.

19. C. Crawford and T. Benton, *Volatility Happens: Understanding Variation in Schools' GCSE Results*. Cambridge Assessment Research Report (2017). Available at: http://www.cambridgeassessment.org.uk/Images/372751-volatility-happensunderstanding-variation-in-schools-gcse-results.pdf.

20. I. Peña-López, *PISA 2015 Results (Volume II): Policies and Practices for Successful Schools* (2016), p. 70. Available at: https://www.oecd-ilibrary.org/education/pisa-2015-results-volume-ii_9789264267510-en.

21. J. Jerrim, *Extra Time: Private Tuition and Out-of-School Study, New International Evidence* (2017), p. 2. Available at: https://www.suttontrust.com/wp-content/uploads/2017/09/Extra-time-report_FINAL.pdf.

22. K. Mihaly, D. F. McCaffrey, D. O. Staiger and J. R Lockwood, *A Composite Estimator of Effective Teaching*. MET Project Report (2013). Available at: http://k12education.gatesfoundation.org/resource/a-composite-estimator-of-effective-teaching.

23. M. Strong, J. Gargani and Ö. Hacifazlioğlu, Do we know a successful teacher when we see one? Experiments in the identification of effective teachers. *Journal of Teacher Education*, 62(4) (2011), 367–382.

24. See https://danielsongroup.org/framework.

25. E. Kalenze, *Education is Upside-Down: Reframing Reform to Focus on the Right Problems* (London: Rowman & Littlefield, 2014), p. 44.

26. Mary Kennedy's research into the evaluation of teachers provides reasonable evidence that observers routinely fall into the fundamental attribution error: M. Kennedy, Attribution error and the quest for teacher quality. *Educational Researcher*, 39(8) (2010), 591–598.

27. S. J. Rosenholtz, *Teachers' Workplace: The Social Organization of Schools* (New York: Addison-Wesley Longman, 1989), p. 83.

28. The exact quote comes from Peierls' biography of the physicist Wolfgang Pauli: "Quite recently, a friend showed him the paper of a young physicist which he suspected was not of great value but on which he wanted Pauli's views. Pauli remarked sadly, 'It is not even wrong.'" See R. E. Peierls, Obituary: Wolfgang Ernst Pauli, 1900–1958. *Biographical Memoirs of Fellows of the Royal Society*, 5(60) (1960). Available at: https://royalsocietypublishing.org/doi/10.1098/rsbm.1960.0014.

29. R. Coe, C. Aloisi, S. Higgins and L. E. Major, *What Makes Great Teaching? Review of the Underpinning Research* (2014), p. 20. Available at: https://www.suttontrust.com/wp-content/uploads/2014/10/What-Makes-Great-Teaching-REPORT.pdf.
30. M. Young, D. Lambert, C. Roberts and M. Roberts, *Knowledge and the Future School: Curriculum and Social Justice* (London: Bloomsbury, 2014), pp. 19, 43.
31. S. J. Rosenholtz, *Teachers' Workplace: The Social Organization of Schools* (New York: Addison-Wesley Longman, 1989), p. 83.
32. R. Coe, C. Aloisi, S. Higgins and L. E. Major, *What Makes Great Teaching? Review of the Underpinning Research* (2014). Available at: https://www.suttontrust.com/wp-content/uploads/2014/10/What-Makes-Great-Teaching-REPORT.pdf.
33. K. D. Peterson, C. Wahlquist and K. Bone, Student surveys for school teacher evaluation. *Journal of Personnel Evaluation in Education*, 14(2) (2000), 135–153 at 150.
34. L. Kyriakides, Drawing from teacher effectivess research and research into teacher interpersonal behaviour to establish a teacher evaluation system: a study on the use of student ratings to evaluate teacher behaviour. *Journal of Classroom Interaction*, 40(2) (2005), 44–66.
35. Measures of Effective Teaching (MET) Project, *Asking Students About Teaching: Student Perception Surveys and Their Implementation*. Policy and Practice Brief (2012). Available at: http://k12education.gatesfoundation.org/resource/asking-students-about-teaching-student-perception-surveys-and-their-implementation.
36. D. Muijs, L. Kyriakides, G. Van der Werf, B. Creemers, H. Timperley and L. Earl, State of the art: teacher effectiveness and professional learning. *School Effectiveness and School Improvement*, 25(2) (2014), 231–256.
37. This example is taken from a blog post by R. McGill: Reflections on whole-school marking. *@Teacher Toolkit* (25 November 2015). Available at: https://www.teachertoolkit.co.uk/2015/11/25/worksampling.
38. For advice on marking and feedback policies see: D. Didau, What do students think about marking? *The Learning Spy* (3 March 2019). Available at: https://learningspy.co.uk/featured/what-do-students-think-about-marking.
39. T. Kini and A. Podolsky, *Does Teaching Experience Increase Teacher Effectiveness? A Review of the Research* (2016), p. 1. Available at: https://learningpolicyinstitute.org/sites/default/files/product-files/Teaching_Experience_Report_June_2016.pdf.

40. J. P. Papay and M. A. Kraft, The myth of the performance plateau. *Educational Leadership*, 73(8), (2016), 36–42 at 39. Available at: https://scholar.harvard.edu/mkraft/publications/myth-teacher-performance-plateau.

41. J. Ewing, Mathematical intimidation: driven by the data. *Notices of the AMS*, 58(5) (2011), 667–673 at 667.

42. Kini and Podolsky, *Does Teaching Experience Increase Teacher Effectiveness?*, p. 3; my emphasis.

43. Papay and Kraft, The myth of the performance plateau.

44. For details on the effects of peer collaboration on teacher improvement see: C. K. Jackson and E. Bruegmann, Teaching students and teaching each other: the importance of peer learning for teachers. *American Economic Journal: Applied Economics*, 1(4) (2009), 85–108; and M. Ronfeldt, S. O. Farmer, K. McQueen and J. A. Grissom, Teacher collaboration in instructional teams and student achievement. *American Educational Research Journal,* 52(3) (2015), 475–514.

45. R. Coe, C. J. Rauch, S. Kime and D. Singleton, *Great Teaching Toolkit: Evidence Review* (2020), p. 10. Available at: https://www.cambridgeinternational.org/Images/584543-great-teaching-toolkit-evidence-review.pdf.

46. Coe et al., *Great Teaching Toolkit*, p. 6.

47. Quoted in R. Alexander, Brian Simon and pedagogy: contribution to the celebration of the life and work of Brian Simon (1915–2002) (8 June 2002). Available at: http://robinalexander.org.uk/wp-content/uploads/2019/12/Simon-memorial.pdf.

48. Department for Education and Skills, *Pedagogy and Practice: Teaching and Learning in Secondary Schools* (2004). Available at: http://www.teachersity.org/resources/Pedagogy-and-practice-teaching-and-learning-in-secondary-schools-en.pdf.

49. R. Powley, *Powerful Pedagogy: Teach Better Quicker* (Abingdon and New York: Routledge, 2018), pp. 2–3.

50. G. Biesta, Why 'what works' won't work: evidence-based practice and the democratic deficit in educational research. *Educational Theory*, 57(1) (2007), 1–22 at 11.

51. R. Alexander, Still no pedagogy? Principle, pragmatism and compliance in primary education. *Cambridge Journal of Education*, 34(1) (2004), 7–33 at 7.

52. A. Hargreaves and M. Fullan, *Professional Capital: Transforming Teaching in Every School* (New York: Teachers College Press, 2015), p. 49.

53. Coe et al., *Great Teaching Toolkit*, p. 14.

54. S. Sims and H. Fletcher-Wood, Characteristics of effective teacher professional development: what we know, what we don't, how we can find out (2018). Available at: https://pdfs.semanticscholar.org/ce5e/ffd7f798b46c8e84311674e31f8c89f6b77c.pdf.

55. Adapted from M. A. Kraft, D. Blazar and D. Hogan, The effect of teacher coaching on instruction and achievement: a meta-analysis of the causal evidence. *Review of Educational Research*, 88(4) (2018), 547–588.

56. K. S. Yoon, T. Duncan, S. W. Y. Lee, B. Scarloss and K. L. Shapley, *Reviewing the Evidence on How Teacher Professional Development Affects Student Achievement*. REL 2007 – No. 033 (2007). Available at: https://ies.ed.gov/ncee/edlabs/regions/southwest/pdf/rel_2007033_sum.pdf.

Chapter 7

1.   J. R. Meindl, S. B. Ehrlich and J. M. Dukerich, The romance of leadership. *Administrative Science Quarterly*, 30(1) (1985), 78–102 at 80.

2.   A. Brown, *The Myth of the Strong Leader: Political Leadership in the Modern Age* (New York: Basic Books, 2014), p. ix.

3.   J. Espinoza, "Be tough like Clint Eastwood and devious like Frank Underwood," chief inspector tells teachers. *The Telegraph* (25 May 2016). Available at: https://www.telegraph.co.uk/education/2016/05/25/be-tough-like-clint-eastwood-and-devious-like-frank-underwood-ch.

4.   L. McInerney, Sir Michael Wilshaw [interview]. *Schools Week* (15 September 2015). Available at: https://schoolsweek.co.uk/sir-michael-wilshaw.

5.   R. Greenleaf, *Servant Leadership: A Journey Into the Nature of Legitimate Power and Greatness* (Mahwah, NJ: Paulist Press, 2002), p. 101.

6.   N. N. Taleb, *Antifragile: Things That Gain from Disorder* (New York: Random House, 2012), p. 1.

7.   Personal communication, 7 August 2020.

8.   J. Collins, *Good to Great: Why Some Companies Make the Leap snd Others Don't* (New York: Random House, 2001).

9.   V. Hável, *The Art of the Impossible: Politics as Morality in Practice* (New York: Knopf, 1997, p. 73.

10. B. Kellerman, *Hard Times: Leadership in America* (Palo Alto, CA: Stanford University Press, 2014), p. 3.

11. J. Tomsett, *This Much I Know About Love Over Fear: Creating a Culture for Truly Great Teaching* (Carmarthen: Crown House Publishing, 2015), p. 187.

12. M. Evans, *Leaders with Substance: An Antidote to Leadership Genericism in Schools* (Woodbridge: John Catt Educational, 2019).

13. M. K. Stein and B. S. Nelson, Leadership content knowledge. *Educational Evaluation and Policy Analysis*, 25 (2003), 423–448 at 445.

14. J. P. Spillane and K. Seashore-Louis, School improvement process and practices: professional learning for building instructional capacity. In J. Murphy (ed.), *The Educational Leadership Challenge: Redefining Leadership for the 21st Century* (Chicago, IL: University of Chicago Press, 2002), pp. 83–104 at p. 97.

15. V. M. Robinson, From instructional leadership to leadership capabilities: empirical findings and methodological challenges. *Leadership and Policy in Schools*, 9(1) (2010), 1–26 at 24.

16. L. S. Gottfredson, Mainstream science on intelligence: an editorial with 52 signatories, history, and bibliography. *Intelligence*, 24 (1997): 13–23 at 13.

17. R. G. Lord, R. J. Foti, and C. L. De Vader, A test of leadership categorization theory: internal structure, information processing, and leadership perceptions. *Organizational Behavior and Human Performance*, 34(3) (1984), 343–378.

18. R. G. Lord, C. L. De Vader and G. M. Alliger, A meta-analysis of the relation between personality traits and leadership perceptions: an application of validity generalization procedures. *Journal of Applied Psychology*, 71(3) (1986), 402–410.

19. Evans, *Leaders with Substance*, p. 55.

20. D. Didau, *Making Kids Cleverer: A Manifesto for Closing the Advantage Gap* (Carmarthen: Crown House Publishing, 2019).

21. P. L. Ackerman, Domain-specific knowledge as the 'dark matter' of adult intelligence: Gf/Gc, personality and interest correlates. *The Journals of Gerontology Series B: Psychological Sciences and Social Sciences*, 55(2) (2000), P69–P84 at P83.

22. A. Hargreaves and M. Fullan, *Professional Capital: Transforming Teaching in Every School* (New York: Teachers College Press, 2015), p. 7.

23. J. Pfeffer, *Leadership BS: Fixing Workplaces and Careers One Truth at a Time* (New York: Harper Business, 2015), p. 21.

24. Pfeffer, *Leadership BS*, p. 1. I'm not going to waste your time debunking leadership myths here; reading Pfeffer's book should more than satisfy anyone's urge to find out more.

25. V. M. Robinson, New understandings of educational leadership. *Leading & Managing*, 12(1) (2004), 62–75.

26. T. Bennett, Two schools bad, one school good: ideas for improving school behaviour. *TES* (2 May 2014). Available at: https://www.tes.com/news/blog/two-schools-bad-one-school-good-ideas-improving-school-behaviour.

27. J. P. Papay and M. A. Kraft, The myth of the performance plateau. *Educational Leadership*, 73(8) (2016), 36–42 at 40–41.

28. 'Warm/strict' is technique 60 in D. Lemov, *Teach Like a Champion 2.0: 62 Techniques That Put Students on the Path to College* (San Francisco, CA: Jossey-Bass, 2015). The five principles discussed are adapted from J. B. Peterson, *Twelve Rules for Life: An Antidote to Chaos* (Toronto: Random House, 2018), p. 142.

29. D. T. Campbell, Assessing the impact of planned social change. *Evaluation and Program Planning*, 2(1) (1979), 67–90.

30. M. Strathern, 'Improving ratings': audit in the British University system. *European Review*, 5(3) (1997), 305–321.

31. J. Muller, *The Tyranny of Metrics* (Princeton, NJ: Princeton University Press, 2018).

32. Muller, *The Tyranny of Metrics*.

Appendix

1. M. L. Smith and P. Fey, Validity and accountability in high-stakes testing. *Journal of Teacher Education*, 51(5) (2000), 334–344 at 335.

2. O. O'Neill, *A Question of Trust: The BBC Reith Lectures 2002* (Cambridge: Cambridge University Press, 2002), p. 58.

3. D. Miliband, Workforce reform: no turning back. *The Guardian* (17 June 2003). Available at: https://www.theguardian.com/education/2003/jun/17/schools.uk7.

4. M. Fullan, *All Systems Go: The Change Imperative for Whole System Reform* (Thousand Oaks, CA: Corwin, 2010), p. 66.

BIBLIOGRAPHY

Aaronson, D., Barrow, L. and Sanders, W. (2007). Teachers and student achievement in the Chicago Public High Schools. *Journal of Labor Economics*, 25(1), 95–135.

Abeler, J., Altmann, S., Kube, S. and Wibral, M. (2010). Gift exchange and workers' fairness concerns: when equality is unfair. *Journal of the European Economic Association*, 8(6), 1299–1324.

Ackerman, P. L. (2000). Domain-specific knowledge as the 'dark matter' of adult intelligence: Gf/Gc, personality and interest correlates. *The Journals of Gerontology Series B: Psychological Sciences and Social Sciences*, 55(2), P69–P84.

Alexander, R. (2002). Brian Simon and pedagogy: contribution to the celebration of the life and work of Brian Simon (1915–2002) (8 June). Available at: http://robinalexander.org.uk/wp-content/uploads/2019/12/Simon-memorial.pdf.

Alexander, R. (2004). Still no pedagogy? Principle, pragmatism and compliance in primary education. *Cambridge Journal of Education*, 34(1), 7–33.

Allen, R. and Sims, S. (2018). *The Teacher Gap*. Abingdon and New York: Routledge.

Ariely, D. (2008). *Predictably Irrational: The Hidden Forces that Shape Our Domains*. London: HarperCollins.

Axelrod, R. and Hamilton, W. D. (1981). The evolution of cooperation. *Science*, 211(4489), 1390–1396.

Barber, M., Kihn, P. and Moffit, A. (2011). Deliverology: from idea to implementation. *McKinsey on Government*, 6, 32–39.

Barber, M. and Mourshed, M. (2007). *How the World's Best-Performing School Systems Come Out on Top*. Available at: https://www.mckinsey.com/industries/public-and-social-sector/our-insights/how-the-worlds-best-performing-school-systems-come-out-on-top.

Bartle, K. (2013). Deficit or surplus? You decide! (30 October). *Keven Bartle's Blog*. Available at: https://dailygenius.wordpress.com/2013/10/30/deficit-or-surplus-you-decide.

Baron, J. (2007). *Thinking and Deciding*, 4th edn. Cambridge: Cambridge University Press.

Bennett, T. (2014).Two schools bad, one school good: ideas for improving school behaviour. *TES* (2 May). Available at: https://www.tes.com/news/blog/two-schools-bad-one-school-good-ideas-improving-school-behaviour.

Biesta, G. (2007). Why 'what works' won't work: evidence-based practice and the democratic deficit in educational research. *Educational Theory*, 57(1), 1–22.

Bjork, E. L. and Bjork, R. A. (2011). Making things hard on yourself, but in a good way: creating desirable difficulties to enhance learning. In M. A. Gernsbacher, R. W. Pew and L. M. Hough (eds), *Psychology and the Real World: Essays Illustrating Fundamental Contributions to Society*, 2nd edn. New York: Worth, pp. 59–68.

Bliesner, T. (1996). Methodological moderators in validating biographical data in personnel selection. *Journal of Occupational and Organizational Psychology*, 69(1), 107–120.

Bok, S. (1999). *Lying: Moral Choice in Public and Private Life*. New York: Vintage.

Box, G. E. P. (1976). Science and statistics. *Journal of the American Statistical Association*, 71(356), 791–799.

Boyd, D., Grossman, P., Lankford, H., Loeb, S. and Wyckoff, J. (2008). Overview of measuring effect sizes: the effect of measurement error. Brief 2. *National Center for Analysis of Longitudinal Data in Education Research*. Available at: https://www.urban.org/sites/default/files/publication/33346/1001264-Overview-of-Measuring-Effect-Sizes-The-Effect-of-Measurement-Error.PDF.

Brown, A. (2014). *The Myth of the Strong Leader: Political Leadership in the Modern Age*. New York: Basic Books.

Bryk, A. and Schneider, B. (2002). *Trust in Schools: A Core Resource for Improvement*. New York: Russell Sage Foundation.

Cambridge Assessment (2016). The average age of teachers in secondary schools (July). Available at: https://www.cambridgeassessment.org.uk/our-research/data-bytes/the-average-age-of-teachers-in-secondary-schools.

Campbell, D. T. (1979). Assessing the impact of planned social change. *Evaluation and Program Planning*, 2(1), 67–90.

Caplan, B. (2018). *The Case Against Education: Why the Education System is a Waste of Time and Money*. Princeton, NJ: Princeton University Press.

Chapman, C., Lowden, K., Chestnutt, H., Hall, S., McKinney, S., Hulme, M. and Friel, N. (2015). *The School Improvement Partnership Programme: Using Collaboration and Enquiry to Tackle Educational Inequity*. Report to Education Scotland. Available at: http://eprints.gla.ac.uk/112298/1/112298.pdf.

Chi, M. T., Feltovich, P. J. and Glaser, R. (1981). Categorization and representation of physics problems by experts and novices. *Cognitive Science*, 5(2), 121–152.

Coe, R. (2013). *Improving Education: A Triumph of Hope Over Experience*. Inaugural lecture of Professor Robert Coe, Durham University, 18 June 2013. Available at: http://www.cem.org/attachments/publications/ImprovingEducation2013.pdf.

Coe, R., Aloisi, C., Higgins, S. and Major, L. E. (2014). *What Makes Great Teaching? Review of the Underpinning Research*. Available at: https://www.suttontrust.com/wp-content/uploads/2014/10/What-Makes-Great-Teaching-REPORT.pdf.

Coe, R., Rauch, C. J., Kime, S. and Singleton, D. (2020). *Great Teaching Toolkit: Evidence Review*. Available at: https://www.cambridgeinternational.org/Images/584543-great-teaching-toolkit-evidence-review.pdf.

Cohen, J. and Goldhaber, D. (2016). Building a more complete understanding of teacher evaluation using classroom observations. *Educational Researcher*, 45(6), 378–387.

Collins, J. (2001). *Good to Great: Why Some Companies Make the Leap and Others Don't*. New York: Random House.

Crawford, C. and Benton, T. (2017). *Volatility Happens: Understanding Variation in Schools' GCSE Results*. Cambridge Assessment Research Report. Available at: https://www.cambridgeassessment.org.uk/Images/372751-volatility-happens-understanding-variation-in-schools-gcse-results.pdf.

Dawes, R. (2009). *House of Cards*. New York: Simon & Schuster.

Department for Education (2018). *Factors Affecting Teacher Retention: Qualitative Investigation*. Research Report (March). Available at: https://www.gov.uk/government/publications/factors-affecting-teacher-retention-qualitative-investigation.

Department for Education and Skills (2002). *Time for Standards: Reforming the School Workforce*. London: DfES.

Department for Education and Skills (2004). *Pedagogy and Practice: Teaching and Learning in Secondary Schools*. Available at: http://www.teachersity.org/resources/Pedagogy-and-practice-teaching-and-learning-in-secondary-schools-en.pdf.

Didau, D. (2015). *What If Everything You Knew About Education Was Wrong?* Carmarthen: Crown House Publishing.

Didau, D. (2016). A marked decline? The EEF's review of the evidence on written marking. *The Learning Spy* (18 May). Available at: https://learningspy.co.uk/assessment/marked-decline-eefs-review-evidence-written-marking.

Didau, D. (2019). *Making Kids Cleverer: A Manifesto for Closing the Advantage Gap*. Carmarthen: Crown House Publishing.

Didau, D. (2019). What do students think about marking? *The Learning Spy* (3 March). Available at: https://learningspy.co.uk/featured/what-do-students-think-about-marking.

Didau, D. and Rose, N. (2016). *What Every Teacher Needs to Know About Psychology*. Woodbridge: John Catt Educational.

DiMaggio, P. J. and Powell, W. W. (2000). The iron cage revisited institutional isomorphism and collective rationality in organizational fields. In J. A. C. Baum and F. Dobbin (eds), *Economics Meets Sociology in Strategic Management*

(*Advances in Strategic Management, Vol. 17*). Bingley: Emerald Group Publishing, pp. 143–166.

Dobelli, R. (2013). *The Art of Thinking Clearly: Better Thinking, Better Decisions.* London: Hachette UK.

Dweck, C. S. and Leggett, E. L. (1988). A social-cognitive approach to motivation and personality. *Psychological Review*, 95(2), 256–273.

Dyer, J. H. and Chu, W. (2003). The role of trustworthiness in reducing transaction costs and improving performance: empirical evidence from the United States, Japan, and Korea. *Organization Science*, 14(1), 57–68.

Ehrlinger, J., Johnson, K., Banner, M., Dunning, D. and Kruger, J. (2008). Why the unskilled are unaware: further explorations of (absent) self-insight among the incompetent. *Organizational Behavior and Human Decision Processes*, 105(1), 98–121.

Elliott, V., Baird, J. A., Hopfenbeck, T. N., Ingram, J., Thompson, I., Usher, N., Zantout, M., Richardson, J. and Coleman, R. (2016). *A Marked Improvement? A Review of the Evidence on Written Marking.* Available at: https://educationendowmentfoundation.org.uk/evidence-summaries/evidence-reviews/written-marking.

Ericsson, K. A. (2004). Deliberate practice and the acquisition and maintenance of expert performance in medicine and related domains. *Academic Medicine*, 79(10 Suppl.), 70–81.

Espinoza, J. (2016). "Be tough like Clint Eastwood and devious like Frank Underwood," chief inspector tells teachers. *The Telegraph* (25 May). Available at: https://www.telegraph.co.uk/education/2016/05/25/be-tough-like-clint-eastwood-and-devious-like-frank-underwood-ch.

Evans, M. (2019). *Leaders with Substance: An Antidote to Leadership Genericism in Schools.* Woodbridge: John Catt Educational.

Ewing, J. (2011). Mathematical intimidation: driven by the data. *Notices of the AMS*, 58(5), 667–673.

Feld, L. P. and Frey, B. S. (2002). Trust breeds trust: how taxpayers are treated. *Economics of Governance*, 3(2), 87–99.

Feynman, R. P. (1992). *Surely You're Joking, Mr. Feynman! Adventures of a Curious Character.* London: Random House.

Firestone, W. A. and Riehl, C. (eds) (2005). *A New Agenda for Research in Educational Leadership.* New York: Teachers College Press.

Fitzpatrick, A. R. and Eagly, A. H. (1981). Anticipatory belief polarization as a function of the expertise of a discussion partner. *Personality and Social Psychology Bulletin*, 7, 636–642.

Fullan, M. (2010). *All Systems Go: The Change Imperative for Whole System Reform.* Thousand Oaks, CA: Corwin.

Garvin, D. A., Edmondson, A. C. and Gino, F. (2008). Is yours a learning organization? *Harvard Business Review* (March). Available at: https://hbr.org/2008/03/is-yours-a-learning-organization.

Gibson, S., Oliver, L. and Dennison, M. (2015). *Workload Challenge: Analysis of Teacher Consultation Responses.* Available at: https://www.gov.uk/government/publications/workload-challenge-analysis-of-teacher-responses.

Goldacre, B. (2010). *Bad Science: Quacks, Hacks, and Big Pharma Flacks.* Toronto: McClelland & Stewart.

Goldhaber, D. D., Goldschmidt, P. and Tseng, F. (2013). Teacher value-added at the high-school level: different models, different answers? *Educational Evaluation and Policy Analysis*, 35(2), 220–236.

Gorard, S., Hordosy, R. and Siddiqui, N. (2012). How unstable are 'school effects' assessed by a value-added technique? *International Education Studies*, 6(1), 1–9.

Gordon, G., Mendenhall, P. and Blair O'Connor, B. (2012). *Beyond the Checklist: What Else Health Care Can Learn from Aviation Teamwork and Safety.* Ithaca, NY: Cornell University Press.

Gottfredson, L. S. (1997). Mainstream science on intelligence: an editorial with 52 signatories, history, and bibliography. *Intelligence*, 24: 13–23.

Greenleaf, R. K. (2002). *Servant Leadership: A Journey Into the Nature of Legitimate Power and Greatness*. Mahwah, NJ: Paulist Press.

Hackman, J. R. and Oldham, G. R. (1980). *Work Redesign*. Reading, MA: Addison-Wesley.

Haidt, J. (2012). *The Righteous Mind: Why Good People Are Divided By Politics and Religion*. London: Vintage.

Hamre, B. K., Goffin, S. G. and Kraft-Sayre, M. (2009). *Classroom Assessment Scoring System (CLASS) Implementation Guide: Measuring and Improving Classroom Interactions in Early Classroom Settings*. Available at: https://www.boldgoals.org/wp-content/uploads/CLASSImplementationGuide.pdf.

Hanushek, E. A. (2004). Some simple analysis of school quality. NBER Working Paper No. 10229. Available at: https://www.nber.org/papers/w10229.pdf.

Harari, Y. N. (2014). *Sapiens: A Brief History of Humankind*. London: Random House.

Hare, R. D. (1993). *Without Conscience: The Disturbing World of the Psychopaths Among Us*. New York: Pocket Books.

Hargreaves, A. and Fullan, M. (2015). *Professional Capital: Transforming Teaching in Every School*. New York: Teachers College Press.

Harris, D. N. and Sass, T. R. (2011). Teacher training, teacher quality and student achievement. *Journal of Public Economics*, 95(7–8), 798–812.

Hável, V. (1997). *The Art of the Impossible: Politics as Morality in Practice*. New York: Knopf.

Heath, D. and Heath, C. (2011). *Switch: How to Change Things When Change is Hard*. London: Random House.

Health and Safety Executive (2019). Work-related stress, anxiety or depression statistics in Great Britain, 2019. Available at: https://www.hse.gov.uk/statistics/causdis/stress.pdf.

Helliwell, J. F. and Huang, H. (2011). Well-being and trust in the workplace. *Journal of Happiness Studies*, 12(5), 747–767.

Hogarth, R. M. (2003). *Educating Intuition: A Challenge for the 21st Century*. Barcelona: Centre de Recerca en Economia Internacional.

Hogarth, R. M., Lejarraga, T. and Soyer, E. (2015). The two settings of kind and wicked learning environments. *Current Directions in Psychological Science*, 24(5), 379–385.

Hood, M. and Fletcher-Wood, H. (2018). Teaching teachers: the bets of American teacher educators. Available at: https://www.ambition.org.uk/research-and-insight/teaching-teachers-bets-american-teacher-educators.

Jackson, C. K. and Bruegmann, E. (2009). Teaching students and teaching each other: the importance of peer learning for teachers. *American Economic Journal: Applied Economics*, 1(4), 85–108.

Jacob, B. A. and Lefgren, L. (2008). Can principals identify effective teachers? Evidence on subjective performance evaluation in education. *Journal of Labor Economics*, 26(1), 101–136.

Jerrim, J. (2017). *Extra Time: Private Tuition and Out-of-School Study, New International Evidence*. Available at: https://www.suttontrust.com/wp-content/uploads/2017/09/Extra-time-report_FINAL.pdf.

Johnson, S. M., Kraft, M. A. and Papay, J. P. (2012). How context matters in high-need schools: the effects of teachers' working conditions on their professional satisfaction and their students' achievement. *Teachers College Record*, 114(10, special issue), 1–39.

Jones, D., Molitor, D. and Reif, J. (2019). What do workplace wellness programs do? Evidence from the Illinois Workplace Wellness Study. *Quarterly Journal of Economics*, 134(4), 1747–1791.

Kahneman, D. and Klein, G. (2009). Conditions for intuitive expertise: a failure to disagree. *American Psychologist*, 64(6), 515–526.

Kahneman, D. and Klein, G. (2010). Strategic decisions: when can you trust your gut? *McKinsey* (1 March). Available at: https://www.mckinsey.com/

business-functions/strategy-and-corporate-finance/our-insights/strategic-decisions-when-can-you-trust-your-gut.

Kalenze, E. (2014). *Education is Upside-Down: Reframing Reform to Focus on the Right Problems*. London: Rowman & Littlefield.

Kalogrides, D., Loeb, S. and Béteille, T. (2013). Systematic sorting: teacher characteristics and class assignments. *Sociology of Education*, 86(2), 103–123.

Kane, T. J., McCaffrey, D. F., Miller, T. and Staiger, D. O. (2013). *Have We Identified Effective Teachers? Validating Measures of Effective Teaching Using Random Assignment*. MET Project Research Paper. Available at: http://k12education. gatesfoundation.org/download/?Num=2676&f%20ilename=MET_Validating_ Using_Random_Assignment_Research_Paper.pdf.

Kanter, R. M. (1984). *The Change Masters: Corporate Entrepreneurs at Work*. New York: Simon & Schuster.

Kellerman, B. (2014). *Hard Times: Leadership in America*. Palo Alto, CA: Stanford University Press.

Kennedy, M. M. (2010). Attribution error and the quest for teacher quality. *Educational Researcher*, 39(8), 591–598.

Kini, T. and Podolsky, A. (2016). *Does Teaching Experience Increase Teacher Effectiveness: A Review of the Research*. Available at: https://learningpolicyinstitute. org/sites/default/files/product-files/Teaching_Experience_Report_June_2016. pdf.

Klein, G. (1993). Sources of error in naturalistic decision making tasks. *Proceedings of the Human Factors and Ergonomics Society Annual Meeting*, 37(4), 368–371.

Klein, G. A. (2017). *Sources of Power: How People Make Decisions*. Cambridge, MA: MIT Press.

Koziol, S. M., Jr and Burns, P. (1986). Teachers' accuracy in self-reporting about instructional practices using a focused self-report inventory. *Journal of Educational Research*, 79(4), 205–209.

Kraft, M. A. and Papay, J. P. (2014). Can professional environments in schools promote teacher development? Explaining heterogeneity in returns to teaching experience. *Educational Evaluation and Policy Analysis*, 36(4), 476–500.

Kraft, M. A., Blazar, D. and Hogan, D. (2018). The effect of teacher coaching on instruction and achievement: a meta-analysis of the causal evidence. *Review of Educational Research*, 88(4), 547–588.

Kruger, J. and Dunning, D. (1999). Unskilled and unaware of it: how difficulties in recognizing one's own incompetence lead to inflated self-assessments. *Journal of Personality and Social Psychology*, 77(6), 1121–1134.

Kuttner, P. (2016). The problem with that equity vs. equality graphic you're using. *Cultural Organizing* (29 October). Available at: https://culturalorganizing. org/the-problem-with-that-equity-vs-equality-graphic.

Kyriakides, L. (2005). Drawing from teacher effectivess research and research into teacher interpersonal behaviour to establish a teacher evaluation system: a study on the use of student ratings to evaluate teacher behaviour. *Journal of Classroom Interaction*, 40(2) (2005), 44–66.

Leary, M. R. (2005). Sociometer theory and the pursuit of relational value: getting to the root of self-esteem. *European Review of Social Psychology*, 16, 75–111.

Lemov, D. (2015) *Teach Like a Champion 2.0: 62 Techniques That Put Students on the Path to College* (San Francisco, CA: Jossey-Bass).

Lerner, J. S. and Tetlock, P. E. (2003). Bridging individual, interpersonal, and institutional approaches to judgment and choice: the impact of accountability on cognitive bias. In S. Schneider and J. Shanteau (eds), *Emerging Perspectives on Judgment and Decision Research*. Cambridge: Cambridge University Press, pp. 431–457.

Lord, R. G., De Vader, C. L. and Alliger, G. M. (1986). A meta-analysis of the relation between personality traits and leadership perceptions: an application of validity generalization procedures. *Journal of Applied Psychology*, 71(3), 402–410.

Lord, R. G., Foti, R. J. and De Vader, C. L. (1984). A test of leadership categorization theory: internal structure, information processing, and leadership perceptions. *Organizational Behavior and Human Performance*, 34(3), 343–378.

Lortie, D. C. (1975). *Schoolteacher: A Sociological Study*. Chicago, IL: University of Chicago Press.

McCaffrey, D. F., Sass, T. R., Lockwood, J. R. and Mihaly, K. (2009). The intertemporal variability of teacher effect estimates. *Education Finance and Policy*, 4(4), 572–606.

McGill, R. (2015). Reflections on whole-school marking. *@Teacher Toolkit* (25 November). Available at: https://www.teachertoolkit.co.uk/2015/11/25/worksampling.

McInerney, L. (2015). Sir Michael Wilshaw [interview]. *Schools Week* (15 September). Available at: https://schoolsweek.co.uk/sir-michael-wilshaw.

Measures of Effective Teaching (MET) Project (2012). *Asking Students About Teaching: Student Perception Surveys and Their Implementation*. Policy and Practice Brief. Available at: http://k12education.gatesfoundation.org/resource/asking-students-about-teaching-student-perception-surveys-and-their-implementation.

Meindl, J. R., Ehrlich, S. B. and Dukerich, J. M. (1985). The romance of leadership. *Administrative Science Quarterly*, 30(1), 78–102.

Mero, N. and Motowidlo, S. (1995). Effects of rater accountability on the accuracy and favorability of performance ratings. *Journal of Applied Psychology*, 80(4), 517–524.

Mihaly, K., McCaffrey, D. F., Staiger, D. O. and Lockwood, J. R. (2013). *A Composite Estimator of Effective Teaching*. MET Project Report. Available at: http://k12education.gatesfoundation.org/resource/a-composite-estimator-of-effective-teaching.

Miliband, D. (2003). Workforce reform: no turning back. *The Guardian* (17 June). Available at: https://www.theguardian.com/education/2003/jun/17/schools.uk7.

Misztal, B. (2013). *Trust in Modern Societies: The Search for the Bases of Social Order.* Chichester: John Wiley & Sons.

Moore, S. (2012). *Who's the Fairest of Them All? The Truth About Opportunity, Taxes, and Wealth in America.* New York and London: Encounter Books.

Morris, E. (2001). *Professionalism and Trust: The Future of Teachers and Teaching. A Speech by the Rt Hon. Estelle Morris MP, Secretary of State for Education and Skills to the Social Market Foundation* (November). Available at: https://dera.ioe.ac.uk//10112.

Morris, E. (2010). The anosognosic's dilemma: something's wrong but you'll never know what it is (part 1) [interview with David Dunning]. *New York Times* (20 June). Available at: https://opinionator.blogs.nytimes.com/2010/06/20/the-anosognosics-dilemma-1.

Muijs, D., Kyriakides, L., Van der Werf, G., Creemers, B., Timperley, H. and Earl, L. (2014). State of the art: teacher effectiveness and professional learning. *School Effectiveness and School Improvement*, 25(2), 231–256.

Muller, J. Z. (2018). *The Tyranny of Metrics.* Princeton, NJ: Princeton University Press.

NASUWT (2019). *The Big Question 2019.* Available at: https://www.nasuwt.org.uk/uploads/assets/uploaded/981c20ce-145e-400a-805969e777762b13.pdf.

Nielsen, J. S. (2011). *The Myth of Leadership: Creating Leaderless Organizations.* London: Hachette UK.

Novella, S. (2019). Misunderstanding. *Neurologica Blog* (8 January). Available at: https://theness.com/neurologicablog/index.php/misunderstanding-dunning-kruger.

Nuthall, G. (2001). The cultural myths and the realities of teaching and learning. *New Zealand Annual Review of Education*, 11, 5–30.

Nuthall, G. (2007). *The Hidden Lives of Learners.* Wellington: NZCER Press.

O'Neill, O. (2002). *A Question of Trust: The BBC Reith Lectures 2002.* Cambridge: Cambridge University Press.

Papay, J. P. and Kraft, M. A. (2015). Productivity returns to experience in the teacher labor market: methodological challenges and new evidence on long-term career improvement. *Journal of Public Economics,* 130, 105–119.

Papay, J. P. and Kraft, M. A. (2016). The myth of the performance plateau. *Educational Leadership,* 73(8), 36–42.

Peierls, R. E. (1960). Obituary: Wolfgang Ernst Pauli, 1900–1958. *Biographical Memoirs of Fellows of the Royal Society,* 5(60). Available at: https://royalsocietypublishing.org/doi/10.1098/rsbm.1960.0014.

Peña-López, I. (2016). *PISA 2015 Results (Volume II): Policies and Practices for Successful Schools.* Available at: https://www.oecd-ilibrary.org/education/pisa-2015-results-volume-ii_9789264267510-en.

Peterson, J. B. (2018). *Twelve Rules for Life: An Antidote to Chaos.* Toronto: Random House.

Peterson, K. D., Wahlquist, C. and Bone, K. (2000). Student surveys for school teacher evaluation. *Journal of Personnel Evaluation in Education,* 14(2), 135–153.

Pfeffer, J. (2015). *Leadership BS: Fixing Workplaces and Careers One Truth at a Time.* New York: Harper Business.

Pink, D. H. (2011). *Drive: The Surprising Truth About What Motivates Us.* New York: Penguin.

Poundstone, W. (1993). *Prisoner's Dilemma: John von Neumann, Game Theory and the Puzzle of the Bomb.* New York: Anchor.

Powley, R. (2018). *Powerful Pedagogy: Teach Better Quicker.* Abingdon and New York: Routledge.

Ratcliffe, S. (ed.) (2016) *Oxford Essential Quotations,* 4th edn. Oxford: Oxford University Press.

Rivkin, S. G., Hanushek, E. A. and Kain, J. F. (2005). Teachers, schools, and academic achievement. *Econometrica,* 73(2), 417–458.

Robinson, V. M. (2004). New understandings of educational leadership. *Leading & Managing*, 12(1), 62–75.

Robinson, V. M. (2006). Putting education back into educational leadership. *Leading and Managing*, 12(1), 62–75.

Robinson, V. M. (2010). From instructional leadership to leadership capabilities: empirical findings and methodological challenges. *Leadership and Policy in Schools*, 9(1), 1–26.

Rockoff, J. E. (2004). The impact of individual teachers on student achievement: evidence from panel data. *American Economic Review*, 94(2), 247–252.

Ronfeldt, M., Farmer, S. O., McQueen, K. and Grissom, J. A. (2015). Teacher collaboration in instructional teams and student achievement. *American Educational Research Journal*, 52(3), 475–514.

Rosenholtz, S. J. (1989). *Teachers' Workplace: The Social Organization of Schools.* New York: Addison-Wesley Longman.

Ross, J. and Staw, B. M. (1986). Expo 86: an escalation prototype. *Administrative Science Quarterly*, 31, 274–297.

Ross, J. and Staw, B. M. (1993). Organizational escalation and exit: lessons from the Shoreham Nuclear Power Plant. *Academy of Management Journal*, 36, 701–732.

Russell, B. (1919). *Proposed Roads to Freedom: Socialism, Anarchism and Syndicalism.* New York: Henry Holt and Co.

Schleicher, A. (2018). *Valuing Our Teachers and Raising Their Status: How Communities Can Help. International Summit on the Teaching Profession.* Available at: https://www.oecd.org/education/valuing-our-teachers-and-raising-their-status-9789264292697-en.htm.

Scott, B. and Vidakovic, I. (2018). Teacher well-being and workload survey: interim findings. *Ofsted Blog* (30 November). Available at: https://educationinspection.blog.gov.uk/2018/11/30/teacher-well-being-and-workload-survey-interim-findings.

Scruton, R. (2010). *The Uses of Pessimism: And the Danger of False Hope.* Oxford: Oxford University Press.

Secret Teacher (2018). The exodus of older teachers is draining schools of expertise. *The Guardian* (12 May). Available at: https://www.theguardian.com/teacher-network/2018/may/12/secret-teacher-the-exodus-of-older-teachers-is-draining-schools-of-expertise.

Sententiae Antiquae (2019). Fake Aristotle fakely rails against fighting inequality (23 March). Available at: https://sententiaeantiquae.com/2019/03/23/fake-aristotle-fakely-rails-against-fighting-inequality.

Shulman, L. S. and Wilson, S. M. (2004). *The Wisdom of Practice: Essays on Teaching, Learning, and Learning to Teach.* San Francisco, CA: Jossey-Bass.

Silver, N. (2012). *The Signal and the Noise: The Art and Science of Prediction.* London: Penguin.

Sims, S. and Fletcher-Wood, H. (2018). Characteristics of effective teacher professional development: what we know, what we don't, how we can find out. Available at: https://pdfs.semanticscholar.org/ce5e/ffd7f798b46c8e84311674e31f8c89f6b77c.pdf.

Smith, A. (1759). *The Theory of Moral Sentiments* (London: Andrew Millar; Edinburgh: Alexander Kincaid and J. Bell). Available at: https://oll.libertyfund.org/titles/smith-the-theory-of-moral-sentiments-and-on-the-origins-of-languages-stewart-ed.

Smith, M. L. and Fey, P. (2000). Validity and accountability in high-stakes testing. *Journal of Teacher Education*, 51(5), 334–344.

Soderstrom, N. C. and Bjork, R. A. (2015). Learning versus performance: an integrative review. *Perspectives on Psychological Science*, 10(2), 176–199.

Sowell, T. (2019). *The Vision of the Anointed: Self-Congratulation as a Basis for Social Policy.* London: Hachette UK.

Spillane, J. P. and Seashore-Louis, K. (2002). School improvement process and practices: professional learning for building instructional capacity. In J. Murphy (ed.), *The Educational Leadership Challenge: Redefining Leadership for the 21st Century.* Chicago, IL: University of Chicago Press, pp. 83–104.

Starmans, C., Sheskin, M. and Bloom, P. (2017). Why people prefer unequal societies. *Nature Human Behaviour,* 1(4), 0082.

Staw, B. M. and Cummings, L. L. (eds) (1980). *Rationality and Justification in Organizational Life, Vol. II.* Greenwich, CT: JAI Press.

Staw, B. M. and Fox, F. V. (1977). Escalation: the determinants of commitment to a chosen course of action. *Human Relations,* 30, 431–450.

Staw, B. M. and Ross, J. (1989). Understanding behavior in escalation situations. *Science,* 246, 216–220.

Stein, M. K. and Nelson, B. S. (2003). Leadership content knowledge. *Educational Evaluation and Policy Analysis,* 25, 423–448.

Steinberg, M. P. and Garrett, R. (2016). Classroom composition and measured teacher performance: what do teacher observation scores really measure? *Educational Evaluation and Policy Analysis,* 38(2), 293–317.

Strathern, M. (1997). 'Improving ratings': audit in the British University system. *European Review,* 5(3), 305–321.

Strong, M., Gargani, J. and Hacifazlioğlu, Ö. (2011). Do we know a successful teacher when we see one? Experiments in the identification of effective teachers. *Journal of Teacher Education,* 62(4), 367–382.

Surowiecki, J. (2004). *The Wisdom of Crowds: Why the Many Are Smarter Than the Few.* London: Abacus.

Syed, M. (2019). *Rebel Ideas: The Power of Diverse Thinking.* London: Hachette UK.

Taleb, N. N. (2012). *Antifragile: Things That Gain from Disorder.* New York: Random House.

Teaching Regulation Agency (2020). *Teacher Misconduct: Disciplinary Procedures for the Teaching Profession* (May). Available at: https://www.gov.uk/government/publications/teacher-misconduct-disciplinary-procedures.

Tetlock, P. E. (1983). Accountability and the perseverance of first impressions. *Social Psychology Quarterly*, 46, 285–292.

Tetlock, P. E. (1985). Accountability: a social check on the fundamental attribution error. *Social Psychology Quarterly*, 48(3), 227–236.

Tetlock, P. E. and Kim, J. I. (1987). Accountability and judgment processes in a personality prediction task. *Journal of Personality and Social Psychology*, 52, 700–709.

Thompson, E. P., Roman, R. J., Moskowitz, G. B., Chaiken, S. and Bargh, J. A. (1994). Accuracy motivation attenuates covert priming: the systematic reprocessing of social information. *Journal of Personality & Social Psychology*, 66(3), 474–489.

Tidd, M. (2016). 'Non-negotiables' drag us down, without question. *TES* (7 October). Available at: https://www.tes.com/news/non-negotiables-drag-us-down-without-question.

Tisi, J., Whitehouse, G., Maughan, S. and Burdett, N. (2013). *A Review of Literature on Marking Reliability Research*. London: Ofqual. Available at: https://www.nfer.ac.uk/publications/mark01/mark01.pdf.

Tomsett, J. (2015). *This Much I Know About Love Over Fear: Creating a Culture for Truly Great Teaching*. Carmarthen: Crown House Publishing.

U. S. Department of Defense (2002). DoD News Briefing – Secretary Rumsfeld and Gen. Myers [news transcript] (12 February). Available at: https://archive.defense.gov/Transcripts/Transcript.aspx?TranscriptID=2636.

Waley, A. (1983). *The Analects of Confucius*. London: Allen & Unwin.

Weil, S. (1997). *Gravity and Grace*, tr. A. Wills. Lincoln: Bison Books.

Whitehurst, G., Chingos, M. M. and Lindquist, K. M. (2014). *Evaluating Teachers with Classroom Observations: Lessons Learned in Four Districts.* Available at: https://www.brookings.edu/wp-content/uploads/2016/06/Evaluating-Teachers-with-Classroom-Observations.pdf.

Wiliam, D. (2016). *Leadership for Teacher Learning: Creating a Culture Where All Teachers Improve So That All Students Succeed.* West Palm Beach, FL: Learning Sciences International.

Willingham, D. (2014). Draft bill of research rights for educators. Available at: http://www.danielwillingham.com/daniel-willingham-science-and-education-blog/archives/08-2014.

Wiswall, M. (2013). The dynamics of teacher quality. *Journal of Public Economics,* 100, 61–78.

Yoon, K. S., Duncan, T., Lee, S. W. Y., Scarloss, B. and Shapley, K. L. (2007). *Reviewing the Evidence on How Teacher Professional Development Affects Student Achievement.* REL 2007 – No. 033. Available at: https://ies.ed.gov/ncee/edlabs/regions/southwest/pdf/rel_2007033_sum.pdf.

Young, M., Lambert, D., Roberts, C. and Roberts, M. (2014). *Knowledge and the Future School: Curriculum and Social Justice.* London: Bloomsbury.

INDEX

S

T

V

W

CPSIA information can be obtained
at www.ICGtesting.com
Printed in the USA
JSHW041454150822
29262JS00002B/4